STAY OUT OF THE KITCHEN COOKBOOK

BOOKS BY LYNN DALLIN

Stay Out of the Kitchen Cookbook

With Leon Dallin

Folk Songster
Christmas Caroler
Heritage Songster

STAY OUT OF THE KITCHEN COOKBOOK

Lynn Dallin

DOUBLEDAY & COMPANY, INC.
GARDEN CITY, NEW YORK
1968

Quotations from *My Country and My People* by Lin Yutang; and from *The Importance of Living* by Lin Yutang, copyright 1937 by The John Day Co., Inc., are reprinted by permission of The John Day Co., Inc., publisher.

For Leon, Judy, and Shannon
—and they know why

. . . When a man is invited to dinner, he is disappointed if he does not get something good. Everybody loves to have things which please the palate put in their way, without trouble or preparation.

SAMUEL JOHNSON

CONTENTS

[Recipes marked with an asterisk may be located by consulting
the Index.]

INTRODUCTION

I F YOU ever have been relegated to the kitchen when you would rather have been in the parlor with your guests or family, this book was written for you. It will help you work culinary wonders. Whatever your experience—or lack of it— you can be a chef par excellence with these distinctive and uncomplicated recipes. Their purpose is dual—to provide superior cuisine which does not require last minute attention, and to keep you *out of the kitchen,* cool and unruffled, until it is time to serve your festive fare.

The principal trick in the preparation of any good meal is in making everything come out even, ready at the same time and the right time. Managing this can be difficult for the experienced, and impossible for the beginner. Risks are eliminated with these recipes. There is no last minute tasting, seasoning, thickening, whipping, garnishing, and the like. You've done all that! Freed of down-to-the-wire kitchen gymnastics, you have only to set your oven, relax, and confidently sip on whatever it is that you sip on. The meal is prepared, it is superb. You know. You have sampled it. Now all that remains is to present it at the proper time to appreciative and admiring diners.

Of course, no meal prepares itself, but meals of elegance and distinction can be done with ease when they are prepared ahead at the convenience and pleasure of the cook. The recipes in STAY OUT OF THE KITCHEN COOKBOOK do not mind waiting, many of them serve in double capacities, and most of them are improved as flavors get acquainted during the delay. To double a recipe, multiply the proportions by two; to halve it, divide the proportions by two, and correct seasonings. Adjust cooking and warming times as necessary.

Foods which need to be heated should be in oven-proof

serving dishes at room temperature (all heating directions presuppose this) and placed in a cold oven before guests arrive. Set your oven if it is automatic. If it isn't, it is a simple matter to detour through the kitchen as you circulate among your guests and turn it on at the proper time. Heating temperatures and timings given are not critical. None of these recipes will be damaged by longer heating periods—within reason—than those specified. Like Griselda, they are patient. If the party is swinging and you want to put dinner off a bit, just turn the temperature down. Lay a piece of foil over any dish which might over-brown. If you have two or more dishes in the same oven, a happy compromise in heating time and temperature usually can be made without penalty. If you have two ovens, place foods which take longer to heat (main dishes, vegetables) in one, and those requiring shorter heating periods (bread, hot salads) in the other. If not, a second quick detour through the kitchen and you can pop the bread or rolls in and your guests will be none the wiser.

Sometimes a meal must be prepared without advance warning. For these emergencies, *Can Opener Quickie* recipes (indicated by "COQ"), which can be put together from the pantry shelf, are included. They are mouth-watering, can be assembled in minutes, and you are *out of the kitchen.*

The use of wine and liquor is incorporated generously in this book, and for good reason. These are the secret ingredients of flavor-conscious cooks and professional chefs. Spirits are excellent meat tenderizers, they ensure smoother frozen desserts, and they are unsurpassed in blending flavors. A touch of wine will crown a serving of any canned soup with new elegance, and turn a simple stew into something to be remembered. The alcohol (and so most of the calories) in wine and liquor, just as in extracts (lemon, 84 per cent alcohol), (vanilla, 34 per cent alcohol), evaporates well below boiling temperatures, leaving behind only subtle new flavors to transform good recipes into great ones.

The amount of salt, pepper, and spices given in each recipe is approximate, and should be corrected to suit individual preferences. Add them carefully, and taste each recipe until you are pleased before serving it with your stamp of approval. Many spices are interchangeable. Keep a light touch with the unfamiliar ones.

As in all recipes, the number of servings from any recipe is problematical. What will stuff four petite ladies on a diet will satisfy one husky man and starve one growing boy. A small pot of baked beans could serve the entire crowd with plenty to spare if everyone happens to be on the drinking man's diet. Consider your group when you eye the number of suggested servings given.

This book had its beginnings in a large Western university which was long on education, culture, good will, and hospitality. Geographically located at the "crossroads of the west," it is noted for bringing international celebrities from diverse fields of achievement to the campus. My husband, Leon Dallin, a musician (ASCAP), was appointed to the music faculty as a composer-performer. I joined the staff as public relations journalist. In these capacities we met distinguished educators, lecturers, political figures, and performing artists. During our seven years' tenure there, it was our pleasure to entertain many illustrious guests. Drudging in the kitchen was unthinkable with such fascinating personalities in the living room. I determined to *stay out of the kitchen* and started a recipe collection which would make this possible, and delectably!

Numerous recipes came from the famous guests themselves. Many of these recipes, basically common, vary widely and deliciously with minor modification. Myriad fascinating dishes can be made from a given cut of meat or a particular vegetable. These basic recipes and their variations are a distinctive feature of Stay Out of the Kitchen Cookbook.

I treasure as my finest compliment a remark confided by a friend of long standing. She said, "The first time we were invited to your home for dinner, I thought I must have misunderstood. You spent the entire evening with your guests, obviously having a wonderful time, and there was no indication we were going to dine until dinner was served."

There is no sweeter music to the ear of a host and hostess than the theme, "The food was out of this world, but how did you do it? We never once saw you go *near* the kitchen!" I invite you to share this theme and these recipes. Greet your guests at the door, enjoy your evening with them, and let memorable meals mind themselves until serving time while you *stay out of the kitchen.*

*To the many friends who shared
their favorite recipes with me . . .
thank you kindly.*

APPETIZERS

*. . . Small cheer and great welcome make
a merry feast.*

WILLIAM SHAKESPEARE

IN SOME QUARTERS appetizers are considered second in importance only to the guest list, and should be chosen with equal care. This premise has merit. Appetizers are as handy as a tight skirt on a windy corner, and there is hardly any get-together at which they are not in order. They extend a warm welcome, make excellent conversation pieces, and launch the sociabilities generally. They spark appetites, and even do double duty as an impressive first course.

Before dinner, they set the stage for the superb fare your guests were invited for in the first place. Two or three mouth-watering varieties are sufficient. A too-lavish assortment of canapés and hors d'oeuvres becomes the meal, and the resistance may be left to haunt the hostess long after over-nibbled and departed. The point is, everyone city. Appetizers are for tempting, not for filling.

The cocktail party, open house, or casual gathering is something else, and the goodies may be profuse. For these, the canapés (toppers on individual bread, cracker, or pastry bases) and hors d'oeuvres (nibbles with no base of their own) are the show. The more munificent and savory they are, the more your guests will relish them. Whatever the occasion, determine the role your appetizers will play, then choose them with an eye to color, texture, and delectability. Serve them festively—with a beverage—and enjoy the surefire compliments they will bring.

DIPPERS

Dips, dunks, and spreads are made for these crunchy nibblers. Pair them up in a likely spot and your guests will take them from there . . .

Melba toast
Toast sticks
Pumpernickel fingers
Salty rye slices
Hard roll chunks
Breadsticks
French bread cubes

Whole wheat triangles
Sourdough wedges
Crisp crackers
Potato chips
Corn crisps
Pretzel sticks
Canned French fries

Crisp, raw vegetable bites are colorful, flavorful, and compatible with a variety of dips. They also are a must for diet-conscious guests who will bless you for your thoughtfulness . . .

Broccoli buds
Carrot sticks
Green pepper wedges
Cauliflower buds
Cherry tomatoes
Radishes

Green onions
Cucumber fingers
Pickle sticks
Turnip slices
Mushroom caps
Celery sticks

If you don't have a more sophisticated dip in mind, fruit goes very well with whipped cream cheese, cream cheese thinned with pineapple juice, or equal parts of whipped cream and mayonnaise folded together. Dip fruits marked with a dagger in lemon juice to prevent discoloration . . .

Pineapple chunks
Melon balls
  watermelon . . .
  honeydew . . .
  cantaloupe . . . *casaba*
Avocado cubes†
Apple fingers†
Fresh pear wedges†

Mandarin orange slices
Fresh apricot slices†
Fresh peach chunks†
Dates
Seedless grapes
Banana chunks†
Fresh strawberries

These tasty tidbits are delicious, substantial, and mighty popular with any set. They are at their best with a spicy sauce . . .

Cooked shrimp
Lobster chunks
Tuna bites
Crab chunks
Chicken cubes
Turkey cubes
Beef cubes
Salami fingers

Ham cubes
Cocktail weiners or
weiner chunks
Vienna sausage chunks
Smoked sausage chunks
Cheese cubes
Roast pork cubes

SERVE THEM HOT . . .

STUFFED SIRLOIN BALLS

The centers vary the flavor and provide the interest . . .

1 pound lean ground
sirloin
¼ pound smoked sausage
½ cup dry bread crumbs
3 tablespoons grated onion
1 tablespoon
Worcestershire sauce
¼ teaspoon each salt and
pepper

Small stuffed olives,
cocktail onions, dill
pickle cubes, sweet
pickle cubes, sharp
cheese cubes, bleu
cheese cubes

Combine sirloin, sausage, bread crumbs, onion, Worcestershire sauce, and seasonings. Mix well. Shape 2 teaspoons of mixture around a stuffed olive, cocktail onion, pickle cube, or cheese cube. Place balls on cooky sheet and broil 4 minutes on each side. Serve hot. Makes 35–40 bite-size balls.

Note: These appetizers can be made ahead and frozen either cooked or uncooked. They can be broiled or pan fried early in the day, and reheated in a covered baking dish at 350 degrees for 20 minutes. Serve with toothpicks for spearing.

Variations

SIRLOIN BALLS FLAMBE

Place sirloin balls in a chafing dish. Cover with ⅓ cup warm cognac and ignite.

SMOKY SIRLOIN BALLS

Place broiled sirloin balls in a baking dish. Marinate overnight in 2 cups of smoky barbecue sauce. Heat in sauce before serving.

SHERRY SIRLOIN BALLS

Place sirloin balls in chafing dish. Warm ¼ cup dry sherry wine and pour over balls. Keep small amount of sherry in the bottom of the chafing dish to prevent sticking.

SIRLOIN BALLS ORIENTAL

Use whole salted almonds to stuff sirloin balls. After cooking, let them marinate overnight in this sweet-sour sauce:

¾ cup canned chicken broth
1 teaspoon soy sauce
¼ cup vinegar
¼ cup light corn syrup
3 tablespoons cornstarch

¼ cup pineapple juice from pineapple tidbits
2 green peppers chopped in bite-size chunks
1 buffet can drained pineapple tidbits

Combine chicken broth, soy sauce, vinegar, and syrup. Bring to a boil, and thicken with cornstarch mixed with pineapple juice. Simmer until clear. Before reheating with sirloin balls, add green peppers and pineapple tidbits to sauce.

COCKTAIL PIZZAS

Flavorful party favorites which may be refrigerated overnight
or frozen two weeks ahead . . .

6 sourdough French rolls
Olive oil
1 6-ounce can tomato
   paste
1 tablespoon grated onion
½ teaspoon salt
¼ teaspoon pepper
½ teaspoon ground
   oregano

¼ teaspoon sweet basil
½ pound brown-and-serve
   sausages
½ cup grated sharp
   Cheddar cheese
½ cup grated mozzarella
   cheese

Slice rolls crosswise in ¾-inch slices. Toast lightly on one side.
Brush untoasted side lightly with olive oil. Spread with a
mixture of tomato paste, onion, and seasonings. Dot with thin
slices of sausage. Sprinkle with Cheddar cheese and mozzarella
cheese. Freeze or refrigerate. Before baking, drizzle 3 or 4
drops of olive oil on each pizza. Broil 4 inches from heat
for 2 or 3 minutes or until hot and bubbly. Makes approximately
40 pizzas.

Note: Brown-and-serve rolls or English muffins cut in wedges
may be substituted for the French rolls. Variations on ingredients for these tasty bites are endless. Some are listed here:

Smoked sausage slices
Italian sausage slices
Crisp bacon crumbles
Deviled ham
Anchovy paste
Anchovy fillets
Chopped mushrooms

Salami pieces
Ripe or stuffed olive slices
Green onion pieces
Canned tuna flakes
Minced clams
Chopped dill pickle
Frankfurter slices

GOURMET COCKTAIL WIENERS   COQ

Sweet, spicy, and very quick and easy . . .

¾ cup prepared mustard   4 4-ounce jars cocktail
1½ cups red currant jelly   wieners
1 tablespoon brandy

Combine mustard, jelly, and brandy and heat gently. Add drained wieners and heat through. Serve hot from chafing dish with toothpick spears. Serves 10.

Note: Four cans of Vienna sausages, halved, or 1 pound of frankfurters, cut in chunks, may be substituted for the cocktail wieners. Spiced apple jelly may be used instead of the red currant jelly. Leftover roast is covered with glamor here.

Variations

GOURMET HAM CUBES   COQ

Substitute 3–4 cups of cubed canned or baked ham, or luncheon meat for the cocktail wieners.

GOURMET PORK CUBES   COQ

Substitute 3–4 cups of cubed pork roast for the wieners. Add:

1 teaspoon soy sauce

GOURMET TURKEY CUBES   COQ

Substitute 3–4 cups cooked turkey cubes for the wieners and 2 tablespoons dry sherry wine for the brandy.

GOURMET BEEF CUBES   COQ

Substitute 3–4 cups cooked beef cubes for the wieners. Add:

1 teaspoon prepared horseradish

CHILI CON QUESO ROSALIE   COQ

Serve this hearty dip hot . . .

1 *pound Velveeta cheese,*
chopped
1 *No. 2 can chili con*
carne without beans
1 *bunch green onions,*
chopped including tops

1 *4-ounce can chopped*
green chilis
¼ *teaspoon liquid pepper*

Mix all ingredients. Bake at 275 degrees for 1 hour. Serve hot in a chafing dish, casserole, or electric skillet. Makes approximately 4½ cups.

Note: This dip is flavorful and filling. It is an excellent cold weather item and gets the cheers after the game. Double the proportions for a large crowd. Serve it with plenty of corn chips. Use dehydrated onion to taste instead of the green if you prefer.

Variations

DIP FRIJOL   COQ

Substitute 1 No. 2 can refried beans for the chili con carne. Add:

¼ *cup dry Burgundy wine*

CALIENTE DIP   COQ

Omit canned chili con carne. Add:

3 *firm tomatoes, chopped and drained*
⅔ *cup chopped ripe olives*
1 *teaspoon chili powder*

CHEESE-BACON CRISPIES

Rich cheese crisps that are excellent served cold *or* hot . . .

½ cup butter
½ pound sharp Cheddar
  cheese, grated
¼ teaspoon salt
Dash liquid pepper
1 teaspoon Worcestershire
  sauce

¼ cup crisp bacon
  crumbles
1¼ cups sifted all-purpose
  flour
¼ teaspoon dry mustard

Soften butter. Add cheese, salt, pepper, and Worcestershire sauce, and blend. Add bacon bits, flour, and mustard. Mix well. Shape into two rolls 1 inch in diameter. Wrap in waxed paper and refrigerate overnight. Cut in ⅛-inch slices. Bake on an oiled cooky sheet in a preheated 375-degree oven for 6 minutes or until golden brown. Serve hot or cold. Makes about 6 dozen.

Note: The refrigerated rolls keep well, and may be stored for reasonably long periods before baking.

Variations

CHEESE-NUT CRISPIES

Substitute ½ cup chopped almonds or walnuts for the bacon crumbles.

HAM CRISPIES

Substitute ¼ cup slivered ham or luncheon meat for the bacon crumbles.

SPICE CRISPIES

Sprinkle any of the above roll slices with either poppy, sesame, or caraway seed before baking.

PARMESAN CRISPIES

Sprinkle any of the above roll slices with Parmesan cheese before baking.

LATIN CRISPIES

Add to cheese mixture before baking:

1 tablespoon chili powder

ALMONDS PAPRIKA

Or use any nuts you prefer—serve them hot or cold . . .

2 tablespoons each melted
   butter and cooking oil
2 tablespoons paprika
Dash liquid pepper

½ teaspoon garlic powder
2 pounds blanched
   almonds
Salt

Combine butter, oil, and seasonings. Add nuts and stir to coat. Roast in a 325-degree oven 25 minutes or until golden brown, stirring occasionally, or toast in a skillet over very low heat, stirring constantly, until golden brown. Drain on paper towels. Sprinkle with salt. When cool, store in a tightly covered container.

Note: Nuts may be reheated at 350 degrees for 10 minutes before serving.

Variations

CURRIED ALMONDS

Substitute 1 tablespoon curry powder for the paprika.

MEXICAN ALMONDS

Substitute 2 tablespoons chili powder for the paprika.

BARBECUED ALMONDS

Substitute 2 tablespoons barbecue spice for the paprika.

OREGANO ALMONDS

Substitute 1 tablespoon ground oregano for the paprika.

GARLIC ALMONDS

Omit paprika and garlic powder. Add:

2 *cloves fresh pressed garlic*

ORIENTAL ALMONDS

Omit paprika and add 1 tablespoon soy sauce. Increase liquid pepper to ⅛ teaspoon.

ONION ALMONDS

Omit paprika and salt. After removing almonds from oven, shake in brown paper bag with 1 package onion soup mix.

SPICED ALMONDS

Substitute 1 tablespoon allspice for the paprika.

BEETS MARCO

These will double as a buffet vegetable . . .

Marinate small, whole cooked beets at least 24 hours in any French salad dressing. Drain, and scoop out centers. Fill with a mixture of commercial sour cream seasoned with prepared horseradish to taste. Top with parsley flakes.

Note: Beets may be either canned or fresh.

Variations

BEETS BELASCO

Fill beets with a mixture of cream cheese, chopped pine nuts, and French dressing (from marinade) to taste.

BEETS GOLDILOCKS

Fill beets with a mixture of mashed, hard-cooked eggs, sweet pickle relish, and mayonnaise to taste.

BEETS PIQUANT

Fill beets with a mixture of chunk-style peanut butter, mayonnaise, and crisp bacon bits.

BEETS ANDALUSIA

Fill beets with a mixture of mashed avocado, lemon juice, and salt to taste.

BEETS BERMUDA

Fill beets with a mixture of commercial sour cream, grated onion, and liquid pepper to taste.

BEETS SUPERIOR

Fill beets with a mixture of cream cheese, Worcestershire sauce, and poppy seed to taste.

BEETS ORO

Fill beets with a mixture of cream cheese thinned with a few drops of orange juice and grated orange rind to taste.

BEETS SHERRY

Fill beets with a mixture of cream cheese thinned with a few crops of dry sherry wine and salt to taste.

FILLED DILLS

Perky and palatable . . .

Bore centers from dill pickles with an apple corer. Stuff cavities with a blend of equal parts of Roquefort and cream cheeses. Chill overnight. Cut in ½-inch slices. Two large pickles make 10–15 slices.

Note: A bit of finely minced celery or water chestnuts may be added for texture. These will keep for several days.

Variations

DEVILED DILLS

Stuff pickles with cream cheese flavored with chili powder to taste.

DILLY DILLS

Stuff pickles with a mixture of cream cheese and minced capers to taste.

SPICY DILLS

Stuff pickles with a mixture of cream cheese and minced chipped beef to taste.

CORNY DILLS

Stuff pickles with a mixture of garlic cream cheese and minced corned beef to taste.

ROSY DILLS

Stuff pickles with a mixture of pimiento cream cheese and minced ripe or stuffed green olives to taste.

DILLS PUEBLO

Stuff pickles with a mixture of cream cheese and deviled ham.

DILLS CON FUEGO

Stuff pickles with a mixture of cream cheese and mashed green chili peppers to taste.

DILLS ANTONIO

Stuff pickles with a mixture of chive cream cheese and finely minced salami to taste.

DILLS RAMON

Stuff pickles with a mixture of cream cheese and anchovy paste to taste.

PAT'S DILLS

Stuff pickles with a mixture of cream cheese and crisp bacon bits to taste.

OLIVES VARIANT

If you like variety, you'll love these . . .

Stuff pitted, ripe olives—the largest ones you can get—with bits or pieces of any of the following:

SALTED NUTS: *Almonds, peanuts, macadamias, filberts, cashews.*

ONIONS: *Pearl, pickled, raw slivers.*

CHEESE CUBES OR SPEARS: *Cheddar, jack, Swiss, bleu, pimiento, cream, cream chive, or any others you fancy.*

SEAFOOD: *Shrimp, crab, lobster, salmon, tuna, caviar, smoked oysters or clams, sardines, anchovies.*

VEGETABLE FINGERS: *Celery, green pepper, carrot, cucumber, radishes, watercress, pickled garbanza beans, or any others of your choosing.*

MEAT FINGERS: *Salami, smoked sausage, bologna, chicken liver, deviled ham, baked ham, dried beef, tartare beef, liverwurst, turkey, chicken, beef, smoked tongue, pork, corned beef, Vienna sausage, or any others which may have been omitted.*

OR TRY: *Capers, chutney, pimiento, peanut butter, water chestnut bits, dill pickle fingers, sweet pickle spears, herb-flavored cream cheese—curry, chili powder, oregano, marjoram, basil, celery seed, rosemary, tarragon—the list is endless.*

Note: Let your imagination go. The stuffings should be longer than the olives for eye appeal. To make garlic olives, place 4 cloves, cut, of garlic in a bowl with the olives and liquid. Marinate 48 hours in the refrigerator. Drain and stuff.

SPREADS AND DIPS . . .

FROSTED PATE BALL

This spread is easy to prepare, attractive to serve, and delicious to eat . . .

½ pound liver sausage
1 tablespoon grated onion
2 tablespoons mayonnaise
3 ounces cream cheese
¼ teaspoon garlic salt
1 tablespoon bourbon
whisky

½ cup commercial sour
cream
1 tablespoon mayonnaise
¼ teaspoon salt
Dash liquid pepper
1 teaspoon dillweed

Blend liver sausage, onion, mayonnaise, cream cheese, garlic salt, and bourbon whisky. Shape into a ball and chill, reshaping as necessary. Let stand overnight before frosting with a mixture of the sour cream, mayonnaise, salt, and liquid pepper. Sprinkle with dillweed. Makes 1⅓ cups pâté.

Note: This pâté should be prepared at least one day ahead for the flavors to "marry" as the French say. Frost early in the day, and refrigerate until serving time. The frosted ball may be decorated as elegantly as you wish with sliced stuffed olives, pieces of pimiento or dill pickle, bits of green chili, parsley, hard-cooked eggs, watercress, celery, or the like. Serve with toast wedges, toasted rye or pumpernickel rounds, or crisp assorted crackers.

Variations

DEVILED HAM PATE

Substitute three 2¼-ounce cans deviled ham for the liver sausage. Add:

½ teaspoon chili powder
¼ teaspoon dry mustard

HAM PATE

Substitute 1 cup ground ham for the liver sausage. Add:

¼ teaspoon dry mustard
1 teaspoon prepared horseradish

SALMON PATE

Substitute one 6½-ounce can smoked salmon for the liver sausage, and 1 tablespoon dry sherry wine for the whisky. Decorate frosted ball with chopped chives, celery seed, poppy seed, or dillweed.

CHILI·CHEESE LOG

Crunchy and flavorful, this may be served as a spread or as bite-size balls speared with a colored toothpick . . .

3 *ounces cream cheese*	1 *clove garlic, pressed or*
½ *pound sharp Cheddar*	*minced*
cheese, grated	*Dash liquid pepper*
1 *tablespoon lemon juice*	1 *cup minced pecans*
1 *teaspoon Worcestershire*	1 *teaspoon chili powder*
sauce	1 *teaspoon paprika*

Soften cheeses at room temperature and cream together. Add lemon juice, Worcestershire sauce, garlic, liquid pepper, and pecans. Mix thoroughly. Shape into two rolls approximately 1½ inches in diameter. Sprinkle each roll with a mixture of the chili powder and paprika (a salt shaker is excellent for this), roll in waxed paper or saran, and chill in refrigerator. Serve with toast rounds or assorted crackers. Makes approximately 130 appetizers.

Note: These logs keep well for many days. They must be made at least a day ahead. Garlic powder (¼ teaspoon) may be substituted for fresh garlic.

Variations

CURRY·CHEESE LOG

Substitute 2 teaspoons curry powder for the chili-paprika mixture to sprinkle logs.

DILL·CHEESE LOG

Substitute 3 teaspoons dillweed for the chili-paprika mixture to sprinkle logs.

BACON-CHEESE LOG

Omit chili-paprika mixture. Roll logs in 1 cup crisp bacon crumbles, well drained and cooled.

ROKA CREAM DIP

A rich, creamy, double-duty dip . . .

8 *ounces cream-style cottage cheese*	2 *tablespoons Worcestershire sauce*
8 *ounces commercial sour cream*	*Dash liquid pepper*
	Salt to taste
1 *5-ounce glass Roka cheese spread*	½ *cup minced pecans*

Whip or blend cottage cheese until smooth. Add sour cream, Roka spread, Worcestershire sauce, pepper, salt, and pecans. Chill overnight. Makes 3 cups of dip.

Note: Two packages bleu cheese dip mix may be substituted for the Roka spread. Serve with chips, crackers, or fruit dippers. This is an excellent dressing for fruit salad.

Variations

PIMIENTO CREAM DIP

Substitute a jar of pimiento cheese spread for the Roka spread. This makes a good topping for baked potatoes (omit nuts).

PIMIENTO-OLIVE CREAM DIP

Substitute a jar of pimiento-olive cheese spread for the Roka spread.

BACON-CHEESE DIP

Substitute a jar of bacon-cheese spread for the Roka spread. This is a good topping for baked potatoes (omit nuts).

GARLIC CREAM DIP

Substitute 5 ounces cream cheese for the Roka spread. Add:

1 clove garlic, pressed or minced
Monosodium glutamate

This is a fine topping for baked potatoes (omit nuts).

CHILI CREAM DIP

Substitute one 4-ounce can chopped green chilis for the Roka spread. Blend thoroughly.

CRUNCHY CREAM DIP

Substitute prepared horseradish to taste for the Roka spread. Add:

2 teaspoons chopped chives
¼ cup minced water chestnuts

PINEAPPLE CREAM DIP

Substitute 6 ounces shredded Swiss cheese for the Roka spread. Add:

½ cup crushed pineapple, well drained
½ teaspoon nutmeg

CURRY CREAM DIP

Substitute 6 ounces shredded Swiss cheese for the Roka spread. Add:

Curry powder to taste

ANCHOVY CREAM DIP

Substitute 4 tablespoons anchovy paste for the Roka spread. Add:

4 tablespoons chopped capers

Nuts may be omitted.

LEEK-CRESS DIP

Omit Roka spread and nuts. Add:

2 envelopes (1¾-ounce size) cream of leek soup mix
½ cup minced watercress leaves
2 tablespoons bourbon whisky

CRAB MEAT PIQUANT

Serve it as a cold spread—use it as a spread for hot canapés . . .

1 6½-ounce can crab meat, flaked or minced
¼ cup minced green pepper
½ cup commercial sour cream
½ cup mayonnaise
1 tablespoon lemon juice
½ teaspoon paprika
½ teaspoon salt
½ teaspoon onion powder
Dash liquid pepper
1 teaspoon Worcestershire sauce
2 tablespoons dry sherry wine

Combine all ingredients and refrigerate overnight to blend flavors. Makes 2½ cups of spread. Serve with crisp crackers.

For hot canapés slice 8–10 large refrigerator or French rolls in ¼-inch slices early in the day. Spread each slice with the crab meat mixture. Sprinkle with Parmesan cheese if desired. Place on a cooky sheet and refrigerate until serving time. Bake at

450 degrees for 5–8 minutes, or broil until delicately browned and puffy.

Note: Chopped almonds or chopped ripe olives may be substituted for the minced green pepper.

Variations

LOBSTER PIQUANT

Substitute an equal amount of chopped lobster for the crab meat.

SHRIMP PIQUANT

Substitute an equal amount of chopped shrimp for the crab meat. Add:

2 *tablespoons chili sauce*

CLAM PIQUANT

Substitute an equal amount of minced clams for the crab meat. Add:

¼ *teaspoon garlic powder*

HAM PIQUANT

Omit lemon juice. Substitute 7 ounces slivered ham for the crab meat. Add:

¼ *teaspoon dry mustard*

DEVILED HAM PIQUANT

Omit lemon juice. Substitute 5 ounces deviled ham for the crab meat. Add:

½ *teaspoon prepared horseradish*

CRAB MEAT CURRY

Substitute ¼ teaspoon curry powder for the paprika, and 2 tablespoons minced parsley for the green pepper.

CRAB MEAT TIFFIN

Substitute 3 tablespoons tomato paste for the sherry wine. Add:

½ teaspoon garlic powder

HELEN'S OYSTERS ROYALE

Omit sherry wine. Substitute two 3¼-ounce jars drained and chopped smoked oysters for the crab meat. Add:

1 clove garlic, pressed

TURKEY PAVANE

Substitute 7 ounces minced, smoked turkey for the crab meat. The green pepper is optional. Add:

¼ cup minced water chestnuts

CHICKEN CURRY LULA

Omit green pepper. Substitute 1 cup slivered chicken for the crab meat. Add:

*2 tablespoons ground or
diced almonds
2 tablespoons minced
celery*

*½ teaspoon curry powder
Pinch saffron*

GINGER DIP BOORKMAN

Ginger is the mysterious flavor; water chestnuts are the crunchy texture . . .

1 cup mayonnaise
1 cup commercial sour
   cream
¼ cup grated onion
¼ cup minced parsley
1 5-ounce can water
   chestnuts, drained and
   grated

2 tablespoons grated
   candied ginger
2 cloves garlic, pressed or
   minced
1 tablespoon soy sauce
Dash liquid pepper
Salt to taste
Monosodium glutamate

Combine all ingredients in order given and chill. Serve with potato chips, crisp crackers, or assorted dippers. Makes 3 cups.

Note: This dip should be made at least one day ahead. Garlic powder (½ teaspoon) may be substituted for fresh garlic. Fruit dippers, poultry or ham cubes, shrimp, lobster and crab chunks make excellent dippers.

Variations

CLAM DIP HULA

Add:

½ cup drained minced clams
¼ cup crushed pineapple, well drained

DOUBLE CRUNCH DIP

Add:

½ cup minced almonds
1 tablespoon prepared horseradish

LEILANI CRAB

Add:

1 6½-ounce can crab meat,   ¼ cup minced pecans
   drained and minced   ¼ teaspoon nutmeg
2 tablespoons dry sherry
   wine

DILL DIP

Omit ginger and soy sauce. Add:

½ cup minced dill pickle
½ teaspoon dillweed

SIPPERS . . . Some are for imbibers . . . some are not . . .

H.R.'S FROSTED COCKTAIL

A real sophisticate, this one . . .

½ cup sugar   2 tablespoons fresh lime
⅔ cup water   juice
⅔ cup unsweetened   2 unbeaten egg whites
   pineapple juice   4 cups finely crushed ice
⅔ cup fresh lemon juice

Simmer sugar and water together for 5 minutes. Cool. Shake all ingredients in a shaker or jar until light and frothy. Serve immediately in small, chilled cocktail glasses. Serves 6.

Note: This is a party favorite with the temperance crowd. Be prepared to serve seconds—at least.

TOMATO-CLAM VELVET   coq

Smooth and snappy . . .

3 8-ounce bottles clam
juice
2 12-ounce cans tomato
juice
3 tablespoons lemon juice
(fresh or canned)

½ teaspoon celery salt
½ teaspoon oregano
Dash liquid pepper

Mix all ingredients thoroughly. Chill overnight. Serve in small glasses. Serves 10–12.

Note: Crunchy vegetable tidbits are great go-alongs.

CRANBERRY MIST   coq

Sparkles like a ruby, sips like a dream . . .

2 1-pint bottles cranberry
juice cocktail
1 6-ounce can frozen
pineapple juice

1 quart ginger ale
25 pineapple chunks

Combine juices. Chill. Add ginger ale before serving over crushed ice in punch cups. Stick a toothpick-speared pineapple chunk in each. Serves 25.

Note: Champagne or pink champagne (⅘ quart) may be substituted for the ginger ale. Frozen lemonade or limeade may be used in place of the frozen pineapple juice for a more pointed flavor.

BLUSHING CREAM

Serve this hot or cold . . .

3 *cups tomato juice*
1½ *cups commercial sour*
cream

2 *teaspoons onion juice*
½ *teaspoon salt*
Liquid pepper

Blend tomato juice and sour cream. Add onion juice and seasonings. Serve hot with a dollop of mayonnaise or sour cream sprinkled with powdered basil. Serve cold over finely cracked ice. Serves 8.

Note: Heat slowly; do not boil. A dash of dry sherry wine may be added to each serving before the garnish.

TOMATO BOUILLON   COQ

Hot, zesty, and multiflavored . . .

1 *8½-ounce can cream of*
   tomato soup
1 *8½-ounce can cream of*
   pea soup
1 *8½-ounce can beef*
   bouillon

2½ *cups water*
¼ *cup dry sherry wine*
½ *cup commercial sour*
   cream

Combine soups and water. Heat to boiling, stirring often. Add sherry. Garnish with sour cream. Makes eight 6-ounce servings.

Note: Mayonnaise may be substituted for the sour cream garnish, or a lemon slice may be floated on the top.

SANGRITA

This is quite like a Bloody Mary . . .

2 *cups tomato juice*
2 *cups fresh orange juice*
3 *tablespoons lime juice*
3 *tablespoons*
   Worcestershire sauce

½ *pint tequila*
½ *teaspoon liquid pepper*
½ *teaspoon onion powder*
Salt
Lime slices

Combine all ingredients except lime slices. Serve in punch cups over ice, garnish with lime slices. Serves 10.

Note: This recipe doubled is fine for a crowd. Serve in a punch bowl with a block of ice.

FROSTY GOLDEN PUNCH   COQ

This can be either alcoholic or nonalcoholic . . .

1 *6-ounce can frozen*
   lemonade concentrate
1 *6-ounce can frozen*
   orange juice concentrate
1 *6-ounce can frozen*
   pineapple juice
   concentrate

1 *12-ounce can chilled*
   apricot nectar
½ *cup lemon juice*
1 *pint vodka (optional)*
2 *quart bottles chilled*
   ginger ale

Add water to frozen concentrates as directed on cans. Add chilled apricot nectar and lemon juice. Before serving over cracked ice, add vodka and ginger ale. Pour carefully to preserve carbonation. Serves 20–25.

Note: This is most attractive served with a garnish of sliced orange or lemon, pineapple chunks, green or red cherries, or a twist of citrus rind.

WYNNE'S HOT BUTTERED PUNCH

Serve it in mugs—stir with cinnamon sticks . . .

¾ cup brown sugar
1 cup water
¼ teaspoon salt
¼ teaspoon nutmeg
½ teaspoon cinnamon
½ teaspoon allspice
¾ teaspoon ground cloves

2 1-pound cans jellied
    cranberry sauce
3 cups water
1 quart pineapple juice
Butter
Cinnamon sticks

Bring sugar, 1 cup water, salt, and spices to a boil. Crush cranberry sauce with a fork and add 3 cups water. Beat with rotary beater until smooth. Add cranberry liquid and pineapple juice to hot spiced syrup. Heat to boiling. Dot with butter and add a cinnamon stick to each mug before serving. Makes 2½ quarts. Serves 20.

Note: This punch may be made well ahead, and heated just before serving.

LORRAINE'S CHAMPAGNE PUNCH

One of the best you ever tasted . . .

1 bottle (⅘ quart)
    sauterne, well chilled
½ pint brandy

1 bottle (⅘ quart)
    champagne, chilled
2 quarts ginger ale

Mix wine and brandy. Add champagne and ginger ale. Chill in punch bowl with block of ice. Serve in punch cups. Makes thirty 4-ounce servings.

Note: Each serving can be garnished with a thin slice of orange or lime, or with a whole strawberry if desired.

BILLIE'S POTENT COCKTAIL

On the order of a frozen Daiquiri—but better . . .

1 *quart cranberry juice*	1 *12-ounce can full of*
1 *12-ounce can frozen*	*bourbon whisky*
lemonade concentrate	

Freeze to slushy consistency in ice cube trays. Serve with short plastic straws in small, frosted cocktail glasses. Makes fourteen 4-ounce servings or eighteen 3-ounce servings.

Note: Serve this in *small* glasses. It's potent!

RED VELVET PUNCH

This is a crowd-pleaser . . .

8 *cups cranberry juice cocktail*	1 *6-ounce can frozen lemonade concentrate*
1 *6-ounce can frozen orange juice concentrate*	2 *cups brandy*
	2 *bottles (fifths) chilled champagne*
1 *6-ounce can frozen pineapple juice concentrate*	

Combine cranberry juice, concentrates, and brandy in a large punch bowl. Add a block of ice. Just before serving add the chilled champagne carefully. Makes 25 cups; allow 3 cups per guest.

Note: For a nonalcoholic punch substitute grape juice for the brandy, and 2 quarts of chilled ginger ale for the champagne.

SOUPS

*. . . Only the pure in heart can make a
good soup.*

LUDWIG VAN BEETHOVEN

THE THING ABOUT SOUP is that it is so versatile. Served on
the rocks, it replaces the cocktail for the otherwise empty-
handed I-never-touch-the-stuff guest. Lightly laced, it swings
for the maybe-just-a-little-one convivialist. Chilled soups are
popular starters for summer meals; hot soups make it big on the
winter scene. Serve the cold ones straight from the refrigerator.
Hold the hot ones en casserole in a 200-degree oven until
you want them. For a smart touch, have a small help-yourself
bowl of dry sherry wine nearby.

Soup can be served in glasses, mugs, pots, bowls, tureens,
or casseroles. Choose a light soup for the first course. Feature
a hearty soup at supper, after the game, or on the buffet. Make

a sophisticated soup the big thing at a luncheon for the girls.
There is a soup for almost every occasion, and it will keep you
out of the kitchen. Don't forget it.

SOUPS

GARNISHES FOR SOUPS

VEGETABLES . . . for texture, color, and flavor . . .

Avocado—diced or sliced, and sprinkled with lemon juice
Carrots—thinly sliced diagonally; grated over thick soups
*   or cream garnishes*
Celery—thinly sliced or diced including leaves
Chives—minced, or use minced green onion tops
Cucumber—unpeeled and thinly sliced
Green onions—sliced or chopped including tops
Green pepper—thinly sliced, diced, or slivered
Mushrooms—thinly sliced, diced, or minced
Onion rings—raw or French fried
Parsley—sprig or snipped
Radishes—thinly sliced
Spinach—snipped
Tomatoes—diced and well drained
Watercress—sprig or snipped

HERBS . . . for the unusual; fresh snipped or dried, or dusted
over cream garnishes . . .

Basil—bouillon, cheese, corn, green or split pea, gumbos,
*   minestrone, spinach, tomato, vegetable soups*
Chervil—good in almost all soups
Dill—bisques, borsch, cabbage, corn, cucumber, fish, mush-
*   room, vegetable soups*
Marjoram—beef, bisques, bouillon, chicken, fish, green or
*   split pea, meatball, minestrone, mushroom, onion soups*
Mint—cucumber, fish, fresh pea, Scotch broth soups
Oregano—fish, green or split pea, lentil, mushroom, spin-
*   ach, tomato, vegetable soups*
Rosemary—bisques, chicken, fish, green or split pea, mine-
*   strone, spinach soups*
Sage—bisques, bouillabaisse, cheese, chicken, fish soups

Savory—bean, beef, beet, cabbage, lentil, split pea, vegetable soups

Tarragon—asparagus, bisques, chicken, fish, green pea soups

Thyme—bean, beef, bisques, bouillabaisse, fish, green or split pea, gumbos, lentil, Scotch broth, tomato, minestrone soups

SPICES . . . just a bit for an exotic touch . . .

Allspice—bean, beef, bisques, fish, green or split pea, tomato soups

Caraway—borsch, cream soups, fish soups

Cardamom—chicken, green pea soups

Celery seed—chicken, fish, split pea, vegetable soups

Chili powder—avocado, bean, corn, split pea, tomato soups

Cloves—bean, beef, green pea, potato, tomato, vegetable soups

Cumin—bean, beef, chicken, chowders, split or green pea soups

Curry—asparagus, chicken, most cream soups, fish, mulligatawny, potato, tomato soups

Fennel—borsch, cabbage, cream soups, fish soups

Nutmeg—bean, beef, bisques, chicken, cucumber, fish, fruit, vegetable, vichyssoise soups

Poppy seed—most soups or over cream garnishes

Saffron—bouillabaisse, chicken, fish soups

Sesame seed—cream soups

MEAT OR POULTRY BITS . . . for flavor and body . . .

Chicken	*Crisp bacon crumbles*
Ham	*Frankfurters*
Salami	*Vienna sausage*

OR CONSIDER THESE . . . for interesting variety . . .

Hard-cooked egg—sliced or chopped
Toasted coconut

Chopped nuts—all kinds

Cereal bits—plain or seasoned

Croutons—made from white, whole wheat, French, rye, pumpernickel or variety breads; buttered, plain, or seasoned

Popcorn—herbed, cheesed, buttered

Cheese—all kinds, shredded or diced

Pickle—sweet or dill, thinly sliced or chopped

Olives—stuffed or ripe, sliced or minced

Water chestnuts—thinly sliced or minced

Orange, lemon, or lime—thinly sliced, or a dusting of grated rind

Commercial sour cream—plain or seasoned

Heavy whipped cream, plain, salted, or seasoned with herbs, spices, horseradish, or mustard

Mayonnaise, plain or seasoned

SOME START WITH CANS . . .

ON THE ROCKS   COQ

Double quick and very chic . . .

Pour any of the following undiluted soups or juices over ice cubes. Use lowball glasses. They make great first-course drinks. One 12-ounce can serves 3.

Beef bouillon	Vegetable juice cocktail
Chicken broth	Onion soup (strained)
Consommé	Clam broth
Tomato juice	

Note: Serve these singly or in combination. Add a dash of lemon or onion juice, Worcestershire sauce, liquid pepper, soy sauce, brandy; a touch of angostura bitters; or a pony of dry sherry wine or extra dry vermouth for interesting flavor variations.

CRAB BISQUE   COQ

These bisques are velvet-textured, and may be served piping
hot or icy cold . . .

1 10½-ounce can tomato
soup
1 10½-ounce can pea soup
2 cups light cream
½ teaspoon granulated
onion
Salt and pepper to taste

1 6-ounce can crab meat,
drained and chopped
3 tablespoons dry sherry
wine
½ cup commercial sour
cream
Grated lemon rind

Blend soups, cream, onion, and seasonings. Add crab and wine.
Heat slowly, stirring constantly. Chill thoroughly if serving
cold. Garnish with sour cream sprinkled with grated lemon
rind. Serves 6–8.

Note: In each of the variant recipes, two 10½-ounce cans of
soup are used.

Variations

SALMON BISQUE   COQ

Use 2 cans tomato soup. Substitute ¾ cup boned, mashed
salmon for the crab. Add to the soup mixture:

¼ teaspoon either oregano or thyme

Sprinkle sour cream garnish with minced green pepper.

LOBSTER BISQUE   COQ

Use pea and cream of chicken soups. Substitute an equal amount of lobster for the crab, and rum to taste for the sherry wine. Add to the soup mixture:

¼ *teaspoon* either *marjoram or curry powder*

SHRIMP BISQUE   COQ

Use cream of mushroom and frozen cream of shrimp soups. Substitute an equal amount of chopped shrimp for the crab. Add to the soup mixture:

¼ *cup chopped mushrooms*

Sprinkle the sour cream garnish with nutmeg.

OYSTER BISQUE   COQ

Use 2 cans cream of potato soup. Substitute 1 pint chopped oysters for the crab. Sprinkle the sour cream garnish with chopped chives.

SHRIMP SOUP CHAMPAGNE   COQ

Use 2 cans frozen cream of shrimp soup. Reduce the light cream to ¾ cup. Substitute ¾ cup chilled champagne for the sherry wine. Add to the soup mixture:

¼ *teaspoon saffron*

Note: Chill soup mixture thoroughly, and add champagne just before serving. If champagne isn't available, or you are serving a hot bisque, stay with the 2 cups light cream and 3 tablespoons dry sherry wine. That's good, too.

INSTANT BORSCH   COQ

Here are two of many versions of this favorite . . .

2 10½-ounce cans
consommé
3 4½-ounce jars strained
beets (baby food)
½ teaspoon sugar or to
taste
1 tablespoon lemon juice

2 tablespoons strained
onion juice
Salt to taste
½ cup commercial sour
cream
Snipped parsley

Combine soup, beets, sugar, lemon juice, onion juice, and salt.
Chill. Garnish with sour cream sprinkled with parsley. Serves
6–8.

Note: This may be served hot or cold.

Variations

EDA'S BORSCH

Substitute 2½ cups buttermilk for the 2 cans soup. Add to the
soup mixture:

½ cup cucumber juice (from grated, pressed cucumbers)
1 tablespoon Worcestershire sauce

Dot sour cream topping with caviar. Serve very cold.

CHICKEN CREAM PARMESAN COQ

This is party fare . . .

2 10½-ounce cans cream
of chicken soup
1½ cups light cream
⅓ cup grated Parmesan
cheese

½ cup sauterne wine
Salt and pepper to taste
Stiffly whipped cream,
salted
Chopped toasted almonds

Combine soup, light cream, and cheese. Heat slowly. Add wine, salt and pepper. Garnish with whipped cream sprinkled with chopped almonds. Serves 6–8.

Note: Dry sherry wine may be substituted for the sauterne.

Variations

CHICKEN PIMIENTO CREAM COQ

Substitute one 3-ounce package pimiento cream cheese for the Parmesan cheese. Blend well. Sprinkle cream garnish with chopped pimiento.

CHIVE CHICKEN CREAM COQ

Use 1 can each cream of chicken and cream of mushroom soup. Substitute one 3-ounce package chive cream cheese for the Parmesan cheese. Blend well. Blend prepared horseradish to taste into the whipped cream. Sprinkle garnish with chopped chives.

CHICKEN CURRY SOUP   COQ

Omit Parmesan cheese. Add:

1 teaspoon curry powder
1 tablespoon strained onion juice

Fold 1 tablespoon chutney into garnish. This soup may be served hot or cold.

AVOCADO FROST

Omit Parmesan cheese. Substitute 1 cup commercial sour cream for 1 cup light cream. Add:

1 tablespoon each lemon juice and onion juice
Pulp 2 large avocados, sieved

Blend until smooth. Sprinkle cream garnish with grated lemon rind.

PINK AVOCADO SOUP

Omit Parmesan cheese and cream garnish. Substitute 1 cup tomato sauce for 1 cup light cream. Add:

1 tablespoon each Worcestershire sauce, lemon juice, and onion juice
Pulp 2 large avocados, sieved

Blend until smooth. Garnish with a thin slice of lime.

ASPARAGUS SOUP HELENE   COQ

Omit Parmesan cheese. Use 1 can each cream of chicken and asparagus soup. Add:

2 teaspoons lemon juice
¼ cup mayonnaise
½ teaspoon tarragon

Sprinkle cream garnish with ham slivers. Serve hot or chilled.

MARY'S AVOCADO CREAM SOUP

Omit Parmesan cheese and wine. Use 2 cans chicken broth. Substitute 1½ cups commercial sour cream for the light cream. Add:

Pulp 2 large avocados,   2 tablespoons lime juice
  sieved   Dash liquid pepper
½ teaspoon chili powder

Blend until smooth. Sprinkle cream garnish with crisp bacon crumbles.

ALMOND CREAM SOUP

Omit Parmesan cheese. Substitute dry sherry wine for the white wine, and heavy cream for the light cream. Add:

1 cup blanched almonds   ¼ teaspoon nutmeg or
  ground to a paste   mace
1 tablespoon strained   ½ teaspoon liquid pressed
  onion juice   from grated orange rind

Sprinkle cream garnish with grated orange rind. Serve chilled.

SOUTHERN PEANUT SOUP   COQ

Omit Parmesan cheese. Substitute dry sherry wine for the white wine, and heavy cream for the light cream. Add:

½ cup cream-style peanut butter
1 teaspoon strained onion juice

Blend well. Sprinkle cream garnish with grated lemon rind. Serve hot or chilled.

ONION SOUP GASTON   COQ

A very tasty treat . . .

2 10½-ounce cans onion	2 tablespoons cognac
soup	Crisp sourdough toast
1½ cans water	cubes, well buttered

Combine soup and water. Heat. Just before serving, add cognac. Serve over toast cubes. Serves 4–6.

Note: Soup may be prepared in advance and held in a 200-degree oven until serving time.

Variations

ONION SOUP PARMESAN   COQ

Substitute 3 tablespoons dry sherry wine for the cognac. Sprinkle soup generously with grated Parmesan cheese before serving.

ONION SOUP ROQUEFORT   COQ

Sprinkle crumbled Roquefort cheese over soup before serving.

VELVET ONION SOUP   COQ

Substitute 1½ cups light cream for the water. Serve with a generous sprinkle of grated Romano cheese.

ONION SOUP FLANNEL   COQ

Use 1 can tomato soup and 1 can onion soup. Add:

¼ teaspoon garlic powder

Garnish with commercial sour cream.

BABA'S PEA SOUP   COQ

A green velvet special . . .

2 10½-ounce cans pea
  soup
1½ cups light cream
½ cup dry white wine

½ teaspoon coriander
½ cup commercial sour
  cream
Slivered ham

Blend all ingredients except ham. Heat slowly, stirring as necessary. Garnish with slivered ham. Serves 8.

Note: Dry sherry wine may be substituted for the white wine.

Variations

BABA'S BIG MEAL SOUP   COQ

Add:

1½ cups slivered ham or luncheon meat
1 tablespoon Worcestershire sauce
1 cup finely grated raw carrots

Garnish with garlic croutons or chopped hard-cooked egg.

FREEZER PEA SOUP   COQ

Omit coriander. Use 2 cans frozen pea soup. Substitute 1½ cups tomato sauce for the light cream. Garnish with French-fried onion rings.

MINTED PEA SOUP   COQ

Use 2 cans frozen pea soup. Add:

2 teaspoons snipped fresh mint

Garnish with mint sprigs.

COTTAGE PEA SOUP   COQ

Use 1 can pea soup and 1 can cream of potato soup. Add:

2 *tablespoons butter*
½ *teaspoon oregano*

Sprinkle sour cream garnish with poppy seed.

SPICY PEA SOUP   COQ

Substitute 1 teaspoon prepared horseradish for the coriander.

SEA GREEN SOUP   COQ

Omit coriander. Use dry sherry wine. Add:

2 *7-ounce cans minced clams and juice*

Garnish with chopped chives or garlic croutons. This soup is improved by standing before final heating.

VICHYSSOISE   COQ

Omit wine and coriander. Use 1 can cream of chicken soup and 1 can frozen cream of potato soup. Blend ½ cup commercial sour cream into the soup mixture. Serve chilled. Garnish with sour cream and snipped chives.

QUICK VICHYSSOISE   COQ

Omit wine and coriander. Use 1 can cream of chicken soup and 1 can frozen cream of potato soup. Substitute 2 cups heavy cream for the light cream. Serve either chilled or hot. Garnish with snipped chives.

QUICK VICHYSSOISE CREAM   COQ

Omit wine and coriander. Use 1 can cream of chicken soup and 1 can frozen cream of potato soup. Substitute 1 cup heavy cream and 1 cup commercial sour cream for the light cream. Garnish with snipped chives.

TOMATO CREAM SOUP   COQ

Spicy, creamy, and laced with sherry . . .

2 10½-ounce cans tomato
    soup
1½ cups light cream
½ cup dry sherry wine
Salt and pepper to taste
¼ teaspoon each thyme
    and marjoram

½ teaspoon each
    granulated onion and
    curry powder
½ cup commercial sour
    cream
Grated lemon rind

Combine soup, light cream, wine, and seasonings. Refrigerate overnight. Garnish with sour cream sprinkled with grated lemon rind.

Note: This soup may be served chilled or hot.

Variations

TOMATO SAVORY SOUP   COQ

Substitute 2½ cups buttermilk for the light cream and sherry, and ½ teaspoon summer savory for the curry powder. Sprinkle cream garnish with minced parsley. Serve hot or cold.

CURRY CREAM SOUP   COQ

Omit thyme and marjoram. Use 1 can each tomato soup and pea soup. Add:

1 tablespoon lemon juice

Sprinkle cream garnish with toasted coconut. Serve chilled.

SUMMER BREEZE SOUP   COQ

Omit thyme, marjoram, and curry powder. Use 1 can tomato soup and 1 can cream of mushroom soup. Sprinkle cream garnish with chopped pecans. Serve chilled.

SPICY TOMATO BROTH   COQ

Omit curry powder and sour cream garnish. Substitute 1½ cups tomato juice for the light cream. Add:

¼ teaspoon ground cloves
1 tablespoon Worcestershire sauce

Simmer soup mixture for 5 minutes. Garnish with a thin slice of lime. Serve hot or chilled.

CELERY CHEESE SOUP

This is hearty fare . . .

1 10½-ounce can celery soup
1 10½-ounce can consommé
1½ cups light cream
½ cup dry sherry wine
1 cup shredded Cheddar cheese

1 teaspoon Worcestershire sauce
1 cup commercial sour cream (reserve half for garnish)

Combine all ingredients. Heat slowly, stirring often, until cheese melts. Garnish with sour cream. Serves 8.

Note: Use low heat for all cheese soups, and serve soon after heating. Thinly sliced celery (¼ cup) may be added for texture.

Variations

GOLDEN CHEESE SOUP

Substitute 1 can Cheddar cheese soup for the celery soup. Add:

½ cup finely grated raw carrots

Sprinkle cream garnish with crisp bacon crumbles.

CHILI SOUP COMIDA

Omit sherry wine, light cream and ½ cup sour cream. Reserve ½ cup sour cream for garnish. Use 1 can chili soup and 1 can bean with bacon soup. Add:

1½ cups water
1 cup Burgundy wine
½ teaspoon each chili powder and oregano

Sprinkle sour cream garnish with chopped chives.

RED PLUSH SOPA

Use 2 cans tomato soup. Add:

½ teaspoon sweet basil

Sprinkle cream garnish with slivered salami.

SWISS CHEESE SOUP

Use 2 cans cream of chicken soup. Substitute 1 cup shredded Swiss cheese for the Cheddar. Sprinkle cream garnish with chopped parsley.

POTATO-MUSHROOM CREAM

Use 1 can cream of mushroom soup and 1 can frozen potato soup. Substitute two 3-ounce packages softened cream cheese for the Cheddar. Add:

¼ teaspoon allspice

Blend well. Sprinkle cream garnish with diced mushrooms.

SOME ARE FROM SCRATCH . . .

FROSTY CUCUMBER SOUP

All of these tasty conversation pieces are made the day before . . .

*2 medium cucumbers,
peeled, seeded, and
chopped
½ cup chopped onion
1 10½-ounce can chicken
broth*

*Salt and pepper to taste
1 tablespoon butter
3 cups mashed potatoes
2 cups heavy cream
½ cup commercial sour
cream*

Simmer cucumbers, onion, chicken broth, seasonings, and butter together gently for 25 minutes. Whirl in electric blender or blend with electric beater. Add mashed potatoes and heavy cream. Blend well. Sieve if necessary to make mixture smooth. Refrigerate overnight. Garnish with sour cream. Serves 8.

Note: One cup dry white wine or sherry may be substituted for 1 cup heavy cream. Sprinkle the garnish with dillweed, nutmeg, or chopped walnuts. This makes an attractive buffet tureen.

Variations

CARROT CREAM SOUP

Substitute 2 cups chopped carrots for the cucumbers. Add:

*1 teaspoon sugar or to taste
½ teaspoon powdered ginger
¼ cup dry sherry wine*

Sprinkle cream garnish with grated preserved ginger.

CUCUMBER SOUP PLANTATION

Add to the simmering mixture:

4 sprigs fresh mint

Sprinkle garnish with chopped mint leaves.

WATERCRESS SOUP

Substitute 2 cups chopped watercress for the cucumbers. Discard heaviest watercress stems or use only the leaves. Sprinkle cream garnish with chopped watercress leaves.

SPINACH SOUP

Substitute 2 cups chopped spinach leaves for the cucumbers. Sprinkle garnish with grated lemon rind or crisp bacon crumbles.

CREAM OF ZUCCHINI SOUP

Substitute 2 cups chopped zucchini squash for the cucumbers. Sprinkle garnish with minced pimiento.

CORN CHOWDER LOUISE

A rich and filling soup . . .

¼ cup grated onion
¼ cup butter
3 cups light cream
2 cups cooked diced
  potatoes
2 cups fresh grated corn
Salt to taste

¼ teaspoon paprika
Dash liquid pepper
1 cup commercial sour
  cream
¼ cup crisp bacon
  crumbles

Sauté onion in butter slowly until lightly browned. Combine in saucepan with cream, potatoes, corn, and seasonings. Heat slowly to boiling point. Remove from heat and fold in the sour cream. Garnish with bacon crumbles. Serves 8–10.

Note: After the corn has been grated, run the blunt edge of a knife over the cob to extract the juice. Fresh frozen corn may be substituted for the fresh corn. Mashed potatoes (1½ cups) may be blended in the cream mixture in place of the diced potatoes.

Variations

CHOWDER CHARMAINE

Add to the soup mixture before heating:

2 *cups coarsely chopped, well-drained tomato*
2 *tablespoons diced pimiento*

NEW BEDFORD CHOWDER

Add to the soup mixture before heating:

2 *10-ounce packages frozen scallops, thawed and diced*

Garnish with crisp bacon crumbles or buttered rye croutons.

JEAN'S MEATBALL SOUP

This is a worthy main dish soup . . .

3 *slices bacon, chopped*
3 *cloves garlic, pressed*
2 *large onions, chopped*
3 *tomatoes, coarsely chopped*
4 *peeled cubed potatoes*
1 *cup diagonally sliced carrots*

1 *cup sliced celery*
4 *cups meat stock or bouillon*
Salt and pepper to taste
2 *pounds ground sirloin*
1 *egg beaten*
¼ *cup flour*
Parsley

Fry bacon. Add garlic and onion and brown lightly. Combine with vegetables, meat stock, and seasonings. Simmer for 20 minutes. Mix ground sirloin with the beaten egg. Form into small balls, coat with flour, and drop carefully into hot soup mixture. Simmer 6 minutes. Garnish with parsley. Serves 8.

Note: This soup should be made the day before and heated before serving. For a more pronounced tomato flavor, substitute 1 cup tomato sauce for 1 cup meat stock.

Variations

MEAT SOUP PICADILLO

Omit beaten egg. Sauté chopped sirloin in bacon fat along with garlic and onions. Stir meat with a fork to separate chunks. Add flour. Combine with vegetables and simmer 20 minutes.

MEAT SOUP HONG KONG

Substitute fresh ground pork for the ground sirloin. Simmer 15 minutes. Add to the soup mixture:

Soy sauce to taste

BREADS

*. . . A loaf of bread, the walrus said, is
what we chiefly need.*

LEWIS CARROLL

I'VE HEARD that a hot, crusty bread is guaranteed to get even
the sketchiest meal right into orbit. If a little hot bread can
do all this for no more than *that*, think what it can do for a
meal which really got the plush treatment. Such success is
dizzying to contemplate.

It doesn't matter whether you start with a good loaf from
the bakery, or from scratch. The bread's the thing. Here are
some that are hot and tasty, and you may find them just the
thing. Besides, they *smell* good.

BREADS

HOT HERB BREAD

Crusty, flavorful, and goes with almost any meal . . .

½ pound soft butter or margarine	2 tablespoons minced fresh sweet basil leaves
¾ cup minced fresh chives	1 tablespoon minced fresh tarragon leaves
¾ cup minced fresh parsley	2 loaves unsliced sourdough French bread

Blend butter and herbs. Split loaves of bread lengthwise. Spread each cut surface with ¼ of the butter mixture. Slice each half in 2-inch wedges almost to the crust. Reassemble the loaves and wrap each in foil. To heat, place foil-wrapped loaves in a 350-degree oven for 30 minutes or until hot. Serves 12.

Note: One teaspoon dried herbs may be substituted for each tablespoon fresh herbs; French or Italian bread may be used. This bread may be refrigerated overnight, or frozen for several weeks. Fold the foil back to frame the loaf for serving.

Variations

HERB BREAD DANA

Substitute for the fresh herbs the following dried herbs:

½ teaspoon each *sweet basil, oregano, and tarragon*
¼ teaspoon each *marjoram, chervil, thyme, rosemary*

QUICK HERB BREAD

Substitute 2 tablespoons dried fines herbes for the fresh herbs.

PARMESAN BREAD

Substitute for the herbs:

½ cup mayonnaise
⅔ cup grated Parmesan
cheese
½ cup coarsely grated
and well drained onion

1 teaspoon Worcestershire
sauce

FRENCH ONION BREAD

Substitute two 1⅜-ounce packages onion soup mix for the herbs.

LEMON BREAD

Use 2 teaspoons minced parsley. Substitute for the rest of the herbs the grated rind and juice of 1 lemon.

HELENA'S BREAD

Substitute for the herbs:

⅔ cup brown sugar
2 teaspoons cinnamon
1 teaspoon nutmeg

¼ teaspoon each powdered
ginger and cloves
¼ cup dry sherry wine

Spread bread thickly. Excellent with baked beans, ham, etc.

BREAD CALEXICO

Substitute for the herbs:

2 tablespoons each paprika and chili powder
½ teaspoon each oregano and sweet basil
2 teaspoons granulated onion

DILL BREAD

Substitute 2 tablespoons dried dillweed for the herbs. This is particularly good with fish dishes.

CURRY BREAD

Substitute for the herbs:

1 tablespoon curry powder or to taste
½ teaspoon ground turmeric

BARBECUE BREAD

Substitute 2 tablespoons barbecue spice for the herbs.

CREAMY MUSTARD BREAD

Substitute for the herbs:

¼ cup prepared table mustard
2 teaspoons granulated onion
1 teaspoon dried parsley flakes

Serve this with baked ham, spareribs, or steak.

CRACKLING BREAD

Substitute 1 cup crisp bacon crumbles for the herbs.

PIMIENTO BREAD

Substitute ½ cup mashed pimientos for the herbs. Blend thoroughly with butter.

GREEN CHILI BREAD

Substitute ½ cup mashed green chilis for the herbs. Blend thoroughly with butter.

BLEU CHEESE BREAD

Substitute for the herbs:

⅔ cup softened bleu cheese
1 clove garlic, pressed (optional)
1 teaspoon granulated onion

This is excellent with steak or barbecued meat.

PEANUT BREAD

Substitute for the herbs:

1 *cup chunk-style peanut butter*
2 *tablespoons Worchestershire sauce*

ZIPPY BREAD

Substitute for the herbs:

¼ *cup prepared horseradish*
1 *teaspoon paprika*
2 *tablespoons mayonnaise*

Excellent with steak, roast, or barbecued meat.

BEER BREAD

A provocative combination of flavors . . .

½ *pound grated Swiss
cheese*
½ *teaspoon dry mustard*
1 *clove garlic, pressed*
1 *tablespoon
Worcestershire sauce*

3 *or 4 tablespoons beer
(make an easy
spreading consistency)*
1 *loaf unsliced bread—
French, Italian, or rye*

Blend or beat all ingredients (except bread) until smooth.
Split bread lengthwise and cut each half in 2-inch wedges
almost to crust. Spread all cut surfaces with the cheese mixture.
Reshape loaf and wrap in foil. Bake at 350 degrees for 25
minutes or until hot. Serves 8.

Note: A dark beer is more flavorful in this recipe.

Variations

RED BREAD

Add to the spreading mixture:

2 *tablespoons tomato paste*
1 *teaspoon paprika*
Dash *liquid pepper*

PATIO BREAD

Substitute American cheese for the Swiss cheese, and dry sherry wine for the beer.

PIZZA BREAD

A kissin' cousin of the pizza . . .

1 *6-ounce can tomato paste*
¼ *cup olive oil*
½ *teaspoon oregano*
2 *tablespoons grated onion*
1 *large loaf unsliced Italian or French bread*
1 *4-ounce can sliced olives, drained*

1 *6-ounce can sliced mushrooms, drained*
2 *2-ounce cans anchovy fillets, drained*
¼ *pound sharp Cheddar cheese, shredded*
¼ *pound mozzarella cheese, shredded*

Combine the tomato paste, olive oil, oregano, and onion. Split bread lengthwise and cut each half in 2-inch wedges almost to the crust. Spread all cut surfaces with the tomato paste mixture. On the two bread halves arrange the olives, mushrooms, and anchovy fillets. Top with the Cheddar and mozzarella cheeses. Place on a baking sheet and heat at 350 degrees until the bread is hot and the cheese bubbly. Serves 6–8.

Note: This bread should be prepared ahead and heated before serving. It is very good with most Italian food.

Variations

Any of the suggested variations for Cocktail Pizzas* can be used with Pizza Bread.

INSTANT ROQUEFORT ROLLS

Easy to fix—instantly . . .

Take the desired number of brown-and-serve butterflake rolls. Partially separate the sections and brush each lightly with your favorite Roquefort salad dressing. Bake according to package directions.

Note: These rolls may be done early in the day and baked at serving time. Any favorite salad dressing may be substituted for the Roquefort dressing.

Variations

ROLLS RAMADA

Substitute melted butter for the Roquefort dressing. Sprinkle with a mixture of minced parsley and green onion including tops.

HONEY NUT ROLLS

Substitute honey for the Roquefort dressing. Sprinkle lightly with chopped nuts of your choice.

JIFFY CINNAMON ROLLS

Sprinkle Honey Nut Rolls* with cinnamon.

MAPLE PECAN ROLLS

Substitute maple syrup for the Roquefort dressing. Sprinkle generously with chopped pecans.

PARMESAN ONION ROLLS

Try these for lively flavor . . .

⅓ cup mayonnaise	¼ cup well-drained grated
½ cup soft butter or	onion
margarine	1 tablespoon steak sauce
½ cup grated Parmesan	12 dinner rolls
cheese	

Mix mayonnaise, butter, cheese, onion, and steak sauce. Split rolls and spread cut surfaces with the mixture. Heat at 350 degrees for 10–15 minutes or until delicately browned. Makes 24 pieces.

Note: Any dinner rolls may be used. French rolls are excellent.

Variations

SPICY ROLLS

Substitute ¼ cup creamy French dressing for the mayonnaise. Add to the mixture:

½ teaspoon chili powder or paprika

TOASTED SESAME FINGERS

Serve these either hot or cold, or let them double as appetizers . . .

6 French rolls
⅔ cup butter or margarine
¾ cup sesame seed

Split each roll lengthwise, and each half lengthwise and crosswise to make eight fingers. Spread the three cut sides with butter, then dip in sesame seed. Place crust side down on foil or an unoiled cooky sheet. Bake at 375 degrees for 15 minutes or until golden brown. Makes 48 fingers.

Note: These may be made ahead and frozen or refrigerated until serving time. Sliced white bread may be substituted for the rolls—trim the crusts and cut each slice in thirds.

Variations

POPPY SEED FINGERS

Substitute ⅔ cup poppy seed for the sesame seed. Mix the seed with the soft butter, then spread.

CARAWAY FINGERS

Substitute ¼ cup caraway seed for the sesame seed. Mix the seed with the soft butter, then spread.

CARDAMOM FINGERS

Substitute ⅓ cup cardamom seed for the sesame seed. Mix the seed with the soft butter, then spread. Excellent with fruit and curry dishes.

CORIANDER FINGERS

Substitute 2 teaspoons ground coriander for the sesame seed. Mix the seed with soft butter, then spread. Excellent with Spanish or curry dishes.

PARMESAN FINGERS

Substitute ⅔ cup grated Parmesan cheese for the sesame seed. Mix the cheese with the soft butter, then spread. Dust lightly with paprika.

CARAWAY-GARLIC RYE BREAD

A bona fide man-pleaser . . .

½ cup soft butter or
margarine
1 clove garlic, pressed

2 tablespoons caraway
seed
1 loaf sliced rye bread

Mix butter, garlic, and caraway seed. Spread bread slices. Reassemble loaf and wrap in foil. Bake at 350 degrees for 30 minutes or until hot. Serves 8–10.

Note: This bread may be made ahead and frozen. It should stand at least overnight before serving.

Variations

ANCHOVY-RYE BREAD

Substitute anchovy paste to taste for the caraway seed. Garlic is optional. Excellent with steak or fish dishes.

RYE-ONION BREAD

Substitute 2 tablespoons granulated onion for the garlic.

SOME ARE YOUR VERY OWN . . .

BASIC REFRIGERATOR DOUGH

This will keep in the refrigerator one week, and many goodies can be made from it . . .

1 cake yeast
⅓ cup sugar
3 eggs, beaten
½ cup shortening

1 cup warm milk
4 cups sifted flour
¾ teaspoon salt
Melted butter

Mash yeast with 1 tablespoon sugar. Add remaining sugar to beaten eggs. Sprinkle yeast mixture gradually over egg mixture and beat. Add shortening to warm milk. Mix well. Combine with egg mixture. Add flour and salt. Mix well. Keep at room temperature for 1 hour. Cover and refrigerate overnight. Shape dough (rolls, loaves, etc.) and let rise for 3 hours. Brush with butter. Bake at 350 degrees until done—about 15 minutes for rolls, about 50–60 minutes for bread loaf. Makes about 2½ dozen rolls.

Note: Brush bread loaves again with butter 5 minutes before removing from oven for a richer crust. This dough can be used any number of ways. A few are given in the Variations.

Variations

SEEDED DINNER ROLLS

Shape dough into rolls as desired—cloverleaf, twists, crescents, dinner, or horns. For horn rolls, roll dough as for piecrust; cut in pie-wedge pieces, spread with melted butter, roll from the large end, and bend edges. Place on oiled cooky sheet, brush with beaten egg yolk. Sprinkle with poppy seed, sesame seed, or cardamom seed. Let rise for 3 hours.

DOUGHNUTS

Roll dough ⅛-inch thick. Cut with a doughnut cutter. Let rise on waxed paper for 3 hours. Drop into hot fat. Turn half way through cooking period. Remove, cool, and drain on brown paper. Frost or sprinkle with sugar.

CINNAMON ROLLS

Roll dough into oblong ¼-inch thick. Spread generously with butter, brown sugar, and cinnamon. Dot with raisins. Roll as for jelly roll, slice 1-inch thick. Lay in muffin tins which have been generously buttered and sprinkled with brown sugar. Let rise 3 hours before baking.

EGG AND CHEESE
DISHES

*. . . An egg is always an adventure; it
may be different.*

OSCAR WILDE

EGGS ARE ABOUT the neatest package of concentrated nutri-
ments around unless it's cheese, the miracle food man has
been munching almost since time began. But anyone knows
this who has been reading his encyclopedia regularly. It's also
no secret that you can do more with an egg than boil it, or
with a piece of cheese than slap it between two pieces of
bread, but when you're faced with it—what? Since both are
basic, familiar, and usually on hand, they most often are served
up boiled or between.

This section suggests some interesting ways with them for
brunch, lunch, quick meals, or parties. In some recipes eggs

and cheese are combined for the best of everything. Remember to cook them both at low temperatures over direct heat or the eggs tend to get rubbery and the cheese tough. Combined, that's the worst of everything. Both eggs and cheese are packed with protein, minerals, vitamins, and other helpful things, plus a lagniappe—economy. When you think of it, that's really quite a lot.

SOME ARE SOUFFLE TYPES . . .

CHEESE BAKE JUDY

A festive brunch or luncheon dish . . .

12 *thin slices bread,*
crusts removed
6 *thick slices sharp*
Cheddar cheese
2 *cups crisp bacon*
crumbles

3½ *cups milk*
6 *eggs, slightly beaten*
½ *teaspoon dry mustard*
Salt and pepper to taste
Paprika

Place 6 slices of bread in a buttered 9×14-inch baking dish. Cover with cheese slices, sprinkle with bacon crumbles, and top with remaining bread slices. Blend milk, eggs, dry mustard, salt, and pepper, and pour over bread layers. Dust with paprika. Mixture must stand at least 3 hours before baking, or it may be refrigerated overnight and brought to room temperature before baking. Preheat oven to 325 degrees. Bake 45 minutes or until lightly browned and puffy. Serve at once. Serves 6–8.

Note: For variety, sliced ripe or stuffed olives, chopped pickles or nuts, or sliced mushrooms may be added with the bacon crumbles.

Variations

SEAFOOD BAKE SOUFFLE

Substitute 2 cups chopped crab, lobster, shrimp, or tuna (or in combination) for the bacon crumbles. Blend ½ cup mayonnaise into the milk mixture.

CHICKEN BAKE SOUFFLE

Substitute 2 cups chopped chicken or turkey for the bacon crumbles. Sprinkle ¼ cup drained sweet pickle relish over the chicken layer. Top with ½ cup grated Parmesan cheese.

ZIPPY SOUFFLE BAKE

Substitute 2 cups shredded corned beef or salami for the bacon crumbles. Sprinkle 1 cup chopped stuffed green olives over the meat layer. Add to the milk mixture:

1 tablespoon Worcestershire sauce
3 tablespoons onion juice

HAM-CHEESE PUFF

Substitute 2 cups shredded or cubed ham for the bacon crumbles. Add to the milk mixture:

2 teaspoons prepared horseradish

INSTANT SOUFFLE   COQ

Just like it says . . .

2 10½-ounce cans cream   *4 eggs, separated*
of potato soup   *½ teaspoon dry mustard*
2 tablespoons mayonnaise   *¼ teaspoon liquid pepper*

To undiluted soup add mayonnaise, beaten egg yolks, and seasonings. Fold in stiffly beaten egg whites. Bake in six buttered individual casseroles in a preheated 375-degree oven for 15 minutes or until puffy and golden. Serves 6.

Note: This dish should be served as soon as it is baked.

Variations

PINK SOUFFLE   COQ

Add to the mixture:

2 *tablespoons tomato paste*

ONION SOUFFLE   COQ

Add to the mixture:

2 *tablespoons granulated onion*

CHEESE SOUFFLE   COQ

Substitute 1 can cheese soup for the potato soup.

MUSHROOM SOUFFLE   COQ

Substitute 1 can cream of mushroom soup for the potato soup.

CHICKEN SOUFFLE   COQ

Substitute 1 can cream of chicken soup for the potato soup.

CAROLINE'S CHEESE NUT PUFF

An unusual blend of tomato-peanut flavors . . .

6 *slices cubed buttered toast*	1 *tablespoon grated onion*
1½ *cups grated sharp Cheddar cheese*	¼ *teaspoon sugar or to taste*
½ *cup crunchy peanut butter*	½ *teaspoon oregano*
3 *eggs, slightly beaten*	1 *tablespoon steak sauce*
Salt to taste	*Dash liquid pepper*
	1 *cup tomato juice*
	1 *cup tomato sauce*

Layer toast cubes and grated cheese in a buttered baking dish. Blend the rest of the ingredients and pour over toast-cheese layers. Let stand at least 1 hour before baking in a pre-heated 350-degree oven for 40 minutes or until firm. Serves 6.

Note: One teaspoon prepared horseradish may be substituted for the steak sauce.

Variations

DOUBLE CHEESE NUT PUFF

Top with ½ cup grated Parmesan cheese before baking.

SOME ARE SAUCY . . .

MARTIN'S EGGS

The sauce makes this something special . . .

12 *hard-cooked eggs*
⅓ *cup soft butter*
2 *tablespoons* each *minced green pepper, onion, parsley, and celery*
1 *tablespoon mustard with horseradish*
Salt and pepper to taste
2 *cups commercial sour cream*

¼ *cup mayonnaise*
¼ *cup light cream*
2 *tablespoons Worcestershire sauce*
Dash liquid pepper
1 *small clove garlic, pressed*
Buttered bread crumbs

Halve eggs lengthwise. Mash yolks with butter; add vegetables and seasonings. Fill egg whites with the mixture. Place cut side down in a well-buttered 9×14-inch baking dish. Combine the sour cream, mayonnaise, light cream, Worcestershire sauce, pepper, and garlic. Pour over eggs. Sprinkle with buttered bread crumbs. Bake at 350 degrees for 20–25 minutes or until heated. Serves 8.

Note: This dish may be prepared ahead and heated before serving. Chopped nuts, canned shoestring potatoes, crushed potato chips, or cereal flakes may be substituted for the buttered crumbs. Eggs may be served on toasted English muffins, split and buttered.

Variations

EGGS MORNAY

Substitute Cream Sauce Mornay* for the sour cream mixture. Add to the stuffing mixture:

  1 cup cooked flaked crab

EGGS CHEDDAR

Substitute Cream Sauce Cheddar* for the sour cream mixture.

EGGS PARMESAN

Substitute Cream Sauce Parmesan* for the sour cream mixture.

EGGS CURRY

Substitute Cream Sauce Curry* for the sour cream mixture.

MUSHROOM EGGS

Substitute Mushroom Cream Sauce* for the sour cream mixture. Add to the stuffing mixture:

  ⅔ cup chopped mushrooms

EGGS PIMIENTO

Substitute Pimiento Cream Sauce* or Olive Pimiento Sauce* for the sour cream mixture.

EGGS ROSADO

Substitute Cream Sauce Rosado* for the sour cream mixture.

ELEGANT EGGS

Substitute Elegant Cream Sauce* for the sour cream mixture. Add to the stuffing mixture:

⅔ cup cooked minced lobster or shrimp

BACON EGGS

Substitute Bacon Cheese Sauce* for the sour cream mixture. Add to the stuffing mixture:

½ cup crisp bacon crumbles

HERBED EGGS

Substitute Cream Herb Sauce* for the sour cream mixture.

SPANISH EGGS

Substitute Wayne's Salsa* or Spanish Sauce* for the sour cream mixture.

EGGS ORIENTALE

Omit buttered crumbs. Substitute Cream Sauce Velouté* for the sour cream mixture. After eggs are placed in the baking dish sprinkle them with:

1½ cups sliced fresh mushrooms
2 tablespoons grated onion

2 tablespoons chopped pimiento
½ cup chopped toasted almonds

Cover with sauce. Top with two 3-ounce cans French-fried noodles. Serves 8–10.

SCRUMPTIOUS EGGS

Omit buttered crumbs. Substitute Cream Sauce Cheddar* for the sour cream mixture. After eggs are placed in the baking dish sprinkle them with:

1½ cups slivered ham
½ cup chopped mushrooms

Cover with sauce. Sprinkle the top with 2 cups cooked rice and 1 cup grated sharp Cheddar cheese. Serves 8–10.

BAKED EGGS   COQ

This makes a fine meal-in-a-rush . . .

Sliced bread, crusts removed
Equal portions soft butter and mayonnaise combined
Salt and pepper to taste

Spread each slice of bread with the butter-mayonnaise mixture. Place firmly in a muffin cup, spread side down. Broil or bake until bread cups are golden brown. Cool. Break 1 egg into each bread cup. Salt and pepper to taste. Bake in a preheated 350-degree oven for 15 minutes or until eggs are cooked as desired.

Note: Cups may be made several days in advance. They keep well under cover. Basic Cream Sauce* or any of the variant recipes may be served with Baked Eggs.

Variations

CHEESE BAKED EGGS   COQ

Sprinkle bread cups generously with any grated cheese of your choice before adding eggs.

BAKED DEVILED EGGS   COQ

Spread bread cups generously with deviled ham before adding eggs.

BAKED EGGS RED FLANNEL   COQ

Line bread cups with canned corned beef and sprinkle with chopped chives before adding eggs.

TOMATO EGGS   COQ

Lay 1 slice firm tomato in bread cups and sprinkle with cheese before adding eggs.

HAM 'N' EGG CUPS   COQ

Line bread cups with shredded ham or luncheon meat before adding eggs.

CHILI EGG CUPS   COQ

Line bread cups with canned chili con carne (without beans) and sprinkle with grated sharp Cheddar cheese before adding eggs.

CREAMY EGG CRUNCH   COQ

Line bread cups with chive cream cheese *or* pimiento cream cheese and sprinkle with chopped pecans before adding eggs.

AMBROSIA CUPS   COQ

Omit uncooked eggs. Sprinkle bread cups generously with grated Parmesan cheese. Fill with hot canned chicken à la king; creamed, chopped hard-cooked eggs, creamed cooked meat, creamed chipped beef, or creamed vegetables (use canned cream sauce and canned meat and vegetables); or canned shellfish of your choice in canned Newburg sauce.

EGGS CREMA

This is rich and tasty . . .

2 cups Onion Cream
   Sauce*
6 eggs

Salt and pepper to taste
⅓ cup buttered cracker
   crumbs

Pour sauce into a shallow buttered baking dish. Carefully break the eggs into the sauce, spacing them apart. Season and sprinkle with buttered cracker crumbs. Bake in a preheated 350-degree oven for 20 minutes or until eggs are cooked as desired. Serves 6.

Note: Buttered bread crumbs or crushed potato chips may be used instead of the cracker crumbs. The sauce may be made ahead. The eggs may be served on buttered toast or toasted English muffins, split and buttered. They also may be served on shallow beds of cooked rice. Most of the cream sauce variations are suitable for Eggs Crema.

Variations

SWISS EGGS CREMA

Add to the cream sauce:

½ cup shredded Swiss cheese

SHERRY EGGS CREMA

Substitute Wine Cream Sauce* (made with sherry) for the Onion Cream Sauce*.

MAIN DISHES

. . . Serenely full, the epicure would say,
"Fate cannot harm me — I have dined
today."

SYDNEY SMITH

HERE IS A SELECTION of main dishes which will rise to any occasion—dinners, buffets, luncheons, late suppers, or midnight maraudings. No run-of-the-mill dishes these, but exciting adventures in good eating. They are easy, elegant, exotic, economical, and what's more, they are ready when you need them.

MAIN DISHES

BEEF . . .

CRUSTED SWISS STEAK

A glamorous dress for an all-time favorite—and made the day
before . . .

2½-pound round steak,
   cut 1 inch thick
3 tablespoons flour
1 teaspoon salt
½ teaspoon instant coffee
½ teaspoon dillweed
3 tablespoons cooking oil
1 clove garlic, pressed or
   minced

¼ cup grated onion
½ cup bouillon
½ cup dry red wine
3 tablespoons mayonnaise
3 tablespoons prepared
   horseradish

Trim steak. Mix flour, salt, coffee, and dillweed. Pound into
both sides of steak. Brown meat in cooking oil. Drain off
excess fat; add garlic, onion, bouillon, and wine. Cover tightly
and simmer gently for 1½ hours, or until fork-tender. Remove
meat from sauce, cool, and spread with a mixture of the mayonnaise and horseradish. Before serving, place in a 375-degree
oven for 15 minutes. Turn setting to "broil" if necessary to
finish browning to a golden crusty topping. Serves 6.

Note: Meat may be cut into serving pieces before browning,
or carved at the table at serving time. It may be refrigerated
overnight after swissing. Either all bouillon or all wine may
be used for the simmering liquid.

Variations

CRUSTED SWISS STEAK MEXICO

Substitute 2 tablespoons chili powder for the horseradish.

CRUSTED SWISS STEAK PAPRIKA

Substitute 2½ tablespoons paprika for the horseradish. Add to the simmering mixture:

¼ teaspoon liquid pepper

CRUSTED SWISS STEAK PARMESAN

Substitute ½ cup grated Parmesan cheese for the horseradish.

CRUSTED SWISS STEAK CRUNCH

Substitute ½ cup chunk-style peanut butter for the horseradish. Add to the spread:

⅛ teaspoon liquid pepper
1 tablespoon Worcestershire sauce

CRUSTED SWISS STEAK ALOHA

Omit dillweed. Add 2 tablespoons soy sauce to the simmering mixture. Substitute ¼ cup toasted sesame seed for the horseradish in the spread.

CRUSTED SWISS STEAK BARBECUE

Substitute 2 tablespoons barbecue spice for the horseradish. Add to the spread:

1 tablespoon prepared mustard
½ teaspoon liquid smoke

CRUSTED SWISS STEAK ITALIAN

Substitute 2 tablespoons Italian seasoning for the horseradish. Add to the spread:

¼ cup grated Parmesan cheese
1 tablespoon olive oil

POT ROAST BAVARIAN

An elegant roast with an air of sophistication . . .

4–5-*pound beef boneless rump roast*	2 *bay leaves*
1 *teaspoon salt*	1 *teaspoon sugar*
¼ *teaspoon coarsely ground black pepper*	1 *sliced onion*
¼ *cup red wine vinegar*	1 *clove garlic, pressed or minced*
1½ *cups dry red wine*	1 *sliced orange*
1½ *cups water*	1 *sliced lemon*
2 *tablespoons brandy*	2 *tablespoons cooking oil*
	3 *tablespoons flour*

Make a marinade combining all ingredients except cooking oil and flour, and cover roast. Refrigerate from 24 to 36 hours, turning frequently. Drain roast and brown in cooking oil. Place meat and marinade in roaster or Dutch oven and simmer from 3–4 hours, or until roast is tender. Remove from pan. At this point, after the meat has cooled, it can be sliced, reshaped, and tied with string for easier serving. Strain liquid and remove fat. Reserve enough marinade for reheating roast. Thicken the remainder slightly with a flour and water paste. Serve sauce with meat.

Note: 1 cup sliced mushrooms and ½ cup dry sherry wine may be added to the strained sauce. Reheat both the sauce and roast in a 350-degree oven for approximately 25 minutes before serving. Chuck, boned 7-bone, butt, or sirloin tip cuts may be substituted for rump cut. The flavor of the meat will be improved if it is basted or turned during the simmering period. Noodles go with this.

Variations

POT ROAST SAUERBRATEN

Add to the marinade:

½ teaspoon each *whole cloves and ground ginger*
1 teaspoon *cinnamon*

Add when the sauce is reheated:

2 tablespoons *red currant jelly*
8 crumbled *gingersnaps*

½ cup *diagonally sliced (paper thin) carrots*
½ cup *diagonally sliced (paper thin) celery*

Note: Vegetables will be crisp-tender at serving time.

POT ROAST ORIENTAL

Substitute ½ cup soy sauce for the vinegar. Omit brandy and salt. Correct seasonings. Add to the strained liquid:

1 tablespoon *black sesame seed or toasted sesame seed*

Serve with rice.

POT ROAST MYSTIQUE

Omit vinegar and water from the marinade. Add to the marinade:

1½ cups *tomato sauce*
1 tablespoon *instant coffee*
2 tablespoons *brandy*

Serve with brown rice.

BEEF ROULADES

Don't even try to be modest with this triumph . . .

2 pounds round steak cut
¼ inch thick
½ teaspoon salt
½ cup flour
¼ teaspoon thyme
3 slices bacon, halved
1 large dill pickle, sliced
in sixths lengthwise
2 medium onions, thinly
sliced
3 tablespoons bacon
drippings or cooking oil

½ cup dry Burgundy wine
1 clove garlic, pressed or
minced
1 bay leaf
⅛ teaspoon liquid pepper
1 tablespoon
Worcestershire sauce
1 4-ounce can mushroom
slices, drained

Cut steak in six pieces approximately 3×5 inches. Pound with meat hammer. Dust well with a mixture of salt, flour, and thyme. On each piece, place one-half slice of bacon, one slice of dill pickle, and two slices of onion. Roll and fasten with toothpicks or small skewer, or tie with string. Wrap individually in waxed paper and refrigerate overnight. Early in the day, melt bacon drippings in a heavy pan and brown roulades on all sides. Cover with a mixture of wine, garlic, bay leaf, liquid pepper, Worcestershire sauce, and mushrooms. Cover tightly and simmer on top of the stove or bake at 350 degrees for 1½ hours or until fork-tender. Refrigerate overnight if desired. Thicken sauce with a paste of flour and water. Heat roulades and sauce in a 350-degree oven 25 minutes (remove skewers or string) before serving. Serve with rice or potatoes. Serves 6.

Note: Tomato sauce or bouillon may be substituted for the wine. Slices of cooked roast beef may be substituted for the round steak, and simmering time cut to 30 minutes.

Variations

PIQUANT ROULADES

Omit bacon and spread each serving with 1 tablespoon bulk sausage.

STUFFED ROULADES

Spread each serving with 2 tablespoons of your favorite stuffing recipe.

SPICY ROULADES

Spread each serving with a mixture of prepared mustard and prepared horseradish.

DEVILED ROULADES

Omit bacon. Spread each serving with 2 tablespoons deviled ham.

ROULADES PEPE

Omit bacon. Cover each serving with a slice of salami.

ITALIAN ROULADES

Omit dill pickle. Add to stuffing mixture:

¼ cup grated Parmesan or Romano cheese
1 teaspoon Italian seasoning

Add to simmering mixture:

1 No. 300 can tomato sauce
1 6-ounce can tomato paste

Serve with cooked spaghetti.

ROULADES ROJO

Add to each serving:

½ *teaspoon minced green chili peppers*

Sprinkle with chili powder.

BEEF CONTINENTAL

This beef boasts wonderful continental flavor . . .

3 *pounds cubed beef*
tenderloin
Salt and pepper to taste
¾ *cup flour*
½ *cup cooking oil*

1½ *cups dry red wine*
3 *cloves garlic, pressed or*
minced
2 *sliced onions*

Dredge beef cubes in seasoned flour. Brown in cooking oil. Place in baking dish with remaining ingredients. Bake at 350 degrees for 2 hours or until beef is fork-tender. Refrigerate overnight. Heat at 350 degrees for 30 minutes before serving. The sauce may be thickened and reheated. Serves 6–8.

Note: Other lean cuts of beef such as round, flank, chuck, stew, or sirloin tip may be substituted for the tenderloin. Chunk vegetables may be added for an elegant one-dish meal, but they must not be over-cooked. Brown, white, or wild rice, or noodles make an excellent accompaniment.

Variations

BEEF NERO

Add:

3 *cups canned brown gravy*
1 *cup sliced mushrooms*

GERMAN BEEF

Substitute 1½ cups beer for the red wine.

BEEF GOURMET

Substitute ¾ cup each beef bouillon and buttermilk for the red wine.

BEEF MOKA

Substitute ½ cup strong black coffee for ½ cup red wine. Add:

2 cups mushroom caps
1 tablespoon
   Worcestershire sauce
Dash liquid pepper

1 teaspoon bourbon
   whisky
1 cup commercial sour
   cream

Add sour cream before final heating.

BEEF JAVA

Substitute dry white wine for the red wine. Add:

1 cup sliced mushrooms
1 cup cubed green pepper

½ teaspoon oregano
1 No. 2 can tomatoes

Rice pilaf goes with this.

BEEF OLE

Reduce wine to ¾ cup. Add:

1 4-ounce can chopped
   green chilis
1 teaspoon chili powder

3 1-pound cans tomatoes
⅓ cup sliced stuffed
   green olives

This dish may be served with rice. If you prefer it with kidney beans, add two 1-pound cans drained kidney beans before reheating.

BEEF GINGER

Add:

1 cup diced green pepper	1 teaspoon turmeric
2 tablespoons fresh slivered ginger or 2 teaspoons powdered ginger	3 tablespoons soy sauce

BEEF FRANCAIS

Add:

¼ pound diced salt pork (brown with beef cubes)
1 crushed bay leaf to sauce mixture

TENDERLOIN PARNASSUS

This is the zenith of artistic cuisine . . .

1 4–6 pound beef tenderloin, trimmed	1 clove garlic, pressed or minced
½ pound fresh mushrooms, chopped	½ cup dry Burgundy wine
½ cup minced onion	¾ cup commercial sour cream
2 tablespoons butter	½ pound ground cooked ham
2 tablespoons bacon drippings	¼ cup seedless rye bread crumbs, fine and dry
1 pound fresh ground pork	Salt and pepper to taste

Marinade mixture:

1 cup dry Burgundy wine	Soft butter
1 teaspoon instant coffee	
1 12½-ounce can onion soup	

Split tenderloin lengthwise three-quarters of depth. Place open between sheets of waxed paper and pound until flat and symmetrical. Sauté mushrooms and onion in butter and bacon drippings for several minutes. Add pork, garlic, and ½ cup of wine. Simmer 10 minutes. Combine with sour cream, ham, bread crumbs, and seasonings. Spread mixture evenly over tenderloin. Roll and tie or skewer securely. Place in baking dish, add mixture of wine and coffee, and refrigerate overnight. Before baking add onion soup, strained if you prefer, to marinade. Spread meat with butter before serving. Bake at 350 degrees for 1 hour or at 370 degrees for 40–45 minutes for medium tenderloin. Serves 8–10.

Note: Two small tenderloins of equal weight may be substituted for one tenderloin, and cooking time adjusted to suit individual preference. Rice goes beautifully with this. Before final heating the sauce may be drained from the meat and blended with ½ cup commercial sour cream.

Variations

TENDERLOIN TREMAINE

Omit minced onion and salt to taste. Add to the stuffing mixture:

1 package dry onion soup mix
2 tablespoons Worcestershire sauce
1 teaspoon dry mustard
1 teaspoon prepared horseradish

1 6-ounce can tomato paste
2 tablespoons chopped stuffed green olives

TENDERLOIN CHATEAU

Add to the stuffing mixture:

⅓ cup crumbled Roquefort cheese
1 4-ounce can pimiento, chopped

TENDERLOIN GOLDEN GATE

Add to the stuffing mixture:

¼ cup minced pepperoni or salami

Substitute 1 cup brandy for the Burgundy in the marinade.

PORK TENDERLOIN LEVEE

Substitute:

2 large pork tenderloins
for beef tenderloin
1 pound ground fresh
veal for ground pork
1½ cups dry sherry wine
for the Burgundy wine
in the stuffing and
marinade mixtures

2 tablespoons soy sauce
for the instant coffee
1 cup ginger ale for the
onion soup

Add to the stuffing mixture:

¼ teaspoon powdered
ginger
1 teaspoon curry powder

⅓ cup tart slivered apple
2 tablespoons chopped
white raisins

PORK TENDERLOIN CONFETTI

Substitute:

2 large pork tenderloins for beef tenderloin
1 pound ground fresh veal for ground pork
1 cup tomato sauce for the onion soup

Add to the stuffing mixture:

1 tablespoon chili powder
2 ounces chopped
pimiento
2 ounces green pepper,
minced

½ cup grated sharp
Cheddar cheese

PORK TENDERLOIN GREEN VELVET

Substitute:

2 large pork tenderloins
for beef tenderloin
1 pound ground fresh
veal for ground pork
1½ cups dry white table
wine for Burgundy
wine in the stuffing
and marinade mixtures

1 tablespoon
Worcestershire sauce for
the instant coffee

Add to the stuffing mixture:

1 4-ounce can chopped
green chilis
1 teaspoon fines herbes

2 tablespoons cream-style
peanut butter
½ cup grated Swiss cheese

PORK TENDERLOIN NICOISE

Substitute:

2 large pork tenderloins
for beef tenderloin
1 pound ground fresh
veal for ground pork
1½ cups extra dry
vermouth for the
Burgundy wine in the
stuffing and marinade
mixtures

1 cup ginger ale for the
onion soup
1 teaspoon chopped fresh
parsley for the instant
coffee

Add to the stuffing mixture:

1 teaspoon grated lemon rind

TEXAS TORNADO   COQ

This whirls together in a hurry . . .

1 large package crushed
corn chips

3 No. 2 cans chili con
carne

1 bunch green onions,
chopped including tops

2 4-ounce cans sliced ripe
olives, drained

4 large firm tomatoes,
sliced

Salt and pepper to taste

1 cup grated sharp
Cheddar cheese

Place corn chips in bottom of buttered baking dish. Spoon on chili con carne. Sprinkle chopped onions over chili. Layer olives, tomatoes, and seasonings. Top with grated cheese. Bake at 350 degrees for 25 minutes or until heated through. Serves 6.

Note: Chili con carne with or without beans may be used. For a spicier flavor, combine 2 tablespoons Worcestershire sauce and liquid pepper to taste with chili con carne.

Variations

TORTILLA TORNADO   COQ

Substitute 8 corn tortillas for corn chips and layer ingredients alternately.

GREEN PABLO   COQ

Blend one 4-ounce can chopped green chilis with chili con carne. Either corn chips or tortillas may be used.

RANCHO TORNADO   COQ

Add one No. 1 can whole kernel Mexicorn, very well drained, over chili con carne layer.

Omit chili con carne. Substitute one No. 2 can refried beans blended with:

1 4-ounce can chopped green chilis
1 cup commercial sour cream
1 teaspoon chili powder

PORK . . .

SHERRIED PORK LOIN

This succulent roast doesn't mind waiting overnight to be served . . .

4–6 pound loin of pork
1 teaspoon salt
½ teaspoon coarse black pepper
1 teaspoon thyme
2 tablespoons chili powder

3 tablespoons granulated onion
1 cup tomato sauce
1 clove garlic, minced or pressed
1 cup dry sherry wine

Preheat oven to 450 degrees. Combine salt, pepper, thyme, chili powder, and onion and rub into loin. Place loin in shallow roasting pan and bake for 15 minutes. Combine tomato sauce, garlic, and sherry, and pour over loin. Reduce heat to 325 degrees and bake for 3 hours or until meat thermometer reads 185° F., basting frequently. Serves 8–10.

Note: Have the butcher loosen or remove backbone for easier carving. Fresh pork butt, picnic, or fresh ham may be used instead of the loin. After cooking is completed, the loin may be refrigerated overnight and reheated in a 350-degree oven for approximately 30 minutes before serving. Remove fat, thicken drippings with a flour-water paste, and reheat with roast for an excellent sauce.

Variations

PORK GRENADINE

Omit chili powder and tomato sauce. Substitute 1 cup dry white wine for the sherry. Add:

½ *teaspoon nutmeg*
½ *cup grenadine*

HERBED PORK LOIN

Omit chili powder. Substitute 1 cup dry white wine or 1 cup bouillon for sherry. If a tomato flavor is not desired, use both and omit tomato sauce. Add to the basting mixture:

½ *teaspoon* each *poultry seasoning, oregano, and sage*

PORK FRANCAIS D'HENRI

Omit chili powder. Substitute marjoram for the thyme. Rub raw roast with cut lemon before adding seasonings. Add to thickened sauce before final heating:

1 *cup commercial sour cream*

PORK ITALIANO

Substitute 2 teaspoons Italian seasoning for the thyme and 1 cup dry red wine for the sherry. Add to the basting mixture:

1 *6-ounce can tomato paste*

PIQUANT PORK

Substitute:

½ *teaspoon* each *cinnamon, nutmeg, and allspice for thyme and chili powder*
1 *cup sweetened canned applesauce for the tomato sauce*

BAKED HAM SUPREME

Choose your favorite glaze—make a flambé by warming ⅔ cup of rum or brandy, pouring it around the ready-to-serve ham and igniting it . . .

½ cup juice from canned spiced peaches, crab apples, or apricots
½ cup brown sugar
⅓ cup honey

1 teaspoon lemon juice
1 teaspoon dry mustard
Whole cloves (optional)
1 whole fully cooked ham

Mix spiced juice, brown sugar, honey, lemon juice, and dry mustard. Heat through, and set aside. Score ham with shallow diagonal cuts and stud with whole cloves. Pour a third of the glaze mixture over ham. Bake according to wrapper directions. During the baking period, coat the ham in two applications with the remaining glaze mixture. Do not baste. Remove ham from the oven 15 minutes before serving time for easier carving. The ham may be decorated with or surrounded by the spiced fruit.

Note: Boneless or canned hams may be sliced and tied securely before baking for higher flavor penetration and easier serving. Butchers do this on request. Uncooked hams may be cooked according to wrapper directions, removed from the oven 30–45 minutes before the cooking time is completed, then scored, glazed, and the baking completed as suggested above. Any one of the suggested glazes may be used. Fruits for decoration may include whole cherries, cranberries, pineapple, mandarin orange or fresh orange slices, peaches, or apricot halves. The choice should complement the glaze. The drippings, after the fat has been removed, make an excellent sauce.

Variations

APPLESAUCE GLAZE

Substitute 1 cup sweetened canned applesauce or apple butter for the spiced fruit juice. Add:

2 *teaspoons prepared horseradish*
2 *tablespoons tarragon vinegar*

BEER GLAZE

Substitute ½ cup beer or ale for the spiced fruit juice. Add:

1 *tablespoon prepared horseradish*
Dash liquid pepper

BRANDY GLAZE

Substitute ½ cup brandy, either regular or fruit, for the spiced fruit juice. Add:

½ *teaspoon nutmeg*

CHERRY GLAZE

Substitute 1 cup cherry jam for the spiced fruit juice. Add:

2 *drops red food coloring if desired*

CIDER GLAZE

Substitute one 8-ounce can thawed frozen apple concentrate for the spiced juice. Add:

2 *teaspoons bourbon whisky*
⅛ *teaspoon each ground cinnamon and allspice*

CRANBERRY GLAZE

Substitute 1 cup cranberry juice cocktail for the spiced juice.

GINGER GLAZE

Substitute ½ cup ginger ale for the spiced juice. Add:

½ *teaspoon powdered ginger*

HAWAIIAN GLAZE

Substitute 1 cup fruit punch concentrate for the spiced fruit juice.

LEMON GLAZE

Substitute one 8-ounce can thawed frozen lemonade concentrate for the spiced fruit juice.

MARMALADE GLAZE

Substitute ½ cup orange, grapefruit, peach, pineapple, or apricot marmalade for the spiced fruit juice. Add:

¼ *cup dry sherry wine*
Dash liquid pepper

ORANGE GLAZE

Substitute 1 cup thawed frozen orange juice concentrate for the spiced fruit juice.

PEANUT BUTTER GLAZE

Substitute ½ cup peanut butter, preferably chunk style, for the spiced fruit juice. Add:

¼ *cup dry vermouth*

PINEAPPLE GLAZE

Substitute one 8-ounce can thawed frozen pineapple concentrate *or* 1 buffet size can pineapple with juice for the spiced fruit juice.

RUBY GLAZE

Substitute 1 cup red currant or other tart jelly for the spiced fruit juice. Add:

2 tablespoons prepared horseradish

SWEET AND SOUR GLAZE

Substitute ½ cup sweet pickle juice (add ¼ cup pickle relish if desired) for the spiced fruit juice. Add:

1 tablespoon soy sauce

TOMATO GLAZE

Substitute one 6-ounce can tomato paste for the spiced fruit juice. Add:

2 tablespoons Worcestershire sauce
Dash liquid pepper
½ teaspoon pickling spice

WINE GLAZE

Substitute ½ cup cocktail sherry, champagne, muscatel, Madeira, Marsala, sauterne, sweet vermouth, port, or mulled wine for the spiced fruit juice. Add:

½ teaspoon cinnamon if desired

SPARERIBS SAVOY

A new way with an old favorite . . .

4–6 pounds lean spareribs	¼ teaspoon liquid pepper
Salt	2 tablespoons steak sauce
1 clove garlic, pressed or minced	¼ cup brown sugar
	Salt to taste
½ cup chili sauce	8 ounces beer

Cover ribs with salted water and simmer to remove excess

fat and tenderize. Simmer 50 minutes if rib bones are to be left in for serving, or until meat pulls away from the bones if they are to be removed before serving. Drain and set aside. Combine remaining ingredients, pour over ribs, and refrigerate from 24 to 36 hours, turning frequently. Bake ribs in marinade, uncovered, at 375 degrees for 45 minutes, turning and basting occasionally. Ribs may be refrigerated overnight. Before serving, warm at 350 degrees for 30 minutes or until nicely browned. Serves 6–8.

Note: An equal amount of either dry Burgundy wine or tomato juice may be substituted for the beer. Most of the glazes given for Baked Ham Supreme* are suitable variations for Spareribs Savoy. Short ribs may be used instead of spareribs. After marinating, Spareribs Savoy may be cooked on a barbecue grill or spit until golden brown. After fat has been removed, remaining sauce may be thickened either with a flour or cornstarch paste and served as a meat accompaniment or over rice.

Variations

SPARERIBS BARBECUE

Substitute ½ cup barbecue sauce, either plain, smoky, or hot, for the chili sauce. Reduce liquid pepper and add to the marinade:

  1 teaspoon chili powder
  1 tablespoon prepared mustard
  1 teaspoon onion powder

SWEET AND SOUR SPARERIBS

Omit chili sauce and beer. Add:

  1 6-ounce can frozen lemonade concentrate
  ¼ cup either pineapple juice, dry vermouth, dry sherry wine, or ginger ale
  2 tablespoons slivered candied ginger

PORK CHOPS CHANTAISSE

Rice adds the right touch here. It may be white, brown, or
wild . . .

6 *loin pork chops, 1 inch thick*	1 *2-ounce can pimiento, chopped*
Butter	1 *cup dry white wine*
6 *green onions, including tops, chopped*	¼ *teaspoon each thyme and marjoram*
½ *cup diced or slivered green pepper*	*Salt and pepper to taste*

Trim chops. Brown in butter on both sides in skillet. Remove
to baking dish and top with onions, green pepper, and pimiento.
Add wine, thyme and marjoram, and seasonings. Cover tightly
and bake at 350 degrees for 1 hour or until fork-tender.
Serves 6.

Note: Chops may be refrigerated overnight and reheated
uncovered at 350 degrees for 30 minutes. The sauce, thickened
with a flour and water paste, is excellent over the rice.

Variations

PORK CHOPS AROMATIC

Omit green pepper, thyme, marjoram, and salt. Add:

6 *sliced ripe olives*	1 *6-ounce can tomato paste*
2 *canned green chilis, seeded and chopped*	
½ *cup sliced or whole mushrooms*	

PORK CHOPS LUAU

Omit wine, pimiento, thyme, and marjoram. Add:

½ cup light molasses	1 teaspoon soy sauce
¼ cup vinegar	1 cup crushed pineapple
¼ teaspoon powdered ginger	6 chopped maraschino cherries

Mix molasses and vinegar before adding.

PORK CHOPS SAUTERNE

Omit green pepper and pimiento. Use sauterne wine. Add:

¼ cup apple jelly (combine this with the wine)
¼ teaspoon rosemary

SHERRIED PORK CHOPS

Omit green pepper, pimiento, thyme, and marjoram. Substitute dry sherry wine for the white wine. Add:

6 whole yams or sweet potatoes, peeled	1 cup white raisins
3 cooking apples, peeled and quartered	¼ teaspoon each nutmeg and allspice
	2 tablespoons honey

Place yams and apples in the bottom of baking dish. Add raisins and spices. Place chops on top. Add wine blended with honey.

KARL'S PLUM ELEGANT PORK CHOPS

Omit green pepper and pimiento. Substitute port wine for the white wine. Add:

1 5-ounce jar strained plums (baby food)	Dash liquid pepper
Juice ½ lemon	¼ teaspoon each allspice, nutmeg, savory, and sage
1 teaspoon grated lemon rind	

Blend plums and seasonings with the wine.

PORK CHOPS DIXIE

Omit green pepper, pimiento, thyme, and marjoram. Add:

3 tart apples, coarsely
  grated
⅓ cup seedless raisins

2 tablespoons brown
  sugar
½ teaspoon sage

PORK CHOPS NORMANDY

Omit green pepper, pimiento, thyme, and marjoram. Add:

1 clove garlic, pressed or
  minced
1 5-ounce jar strained
  pears (baby food)
1 tablespoon grated
  candied ginger

2 tablespoons grated
  candied citron mix
1 teaspoon grated lemon
  rind

Blend the above ingredients with the wine.

BILLIE'S SWEET AND SOUR PORK

This is a great meat-fruit-vegetable combination . . .

⅓ cup sugar
1 teaspoon salt
⅓ cup vinegar
2¼ cups water
¼ cup cornstarch
¼ cup water
3 cups cubed cooked pork
1 tablespoon soy sauce
3 small carrots, very thinly
  sliced diagonally

1 medium green pepper,
  cut into strips
3 firm tomatoes, cut into
  eighths
1 buffet can pineapple
  tidbits with juice
1 small firm cucumber,
  unpeeled and thinly
  sliced diagonally

Combine sugar, salt, vinegar, and 2¼ cups water, and heat
to boiling. Thicken with cornstarch combined with ¼ cup
water. Add pork and soy sauce and simmer 5 minutes. Refrig-

erate overnight. Before serving time, add remaining ingredients. Bake at 350 degrees for 25 minutes or until heated through. Serve with rice. Serves 6–8.

Note: Vegetables will be crisp-tender at serving time. Vinegar and sugar proportions may be altered to taste. This is an attractive dish, and an excellent choice for the buffet.

Variations

PORK TROPICALE

Omit cucumber. Add:

¼ teaspoon ginger
1 medium onion, thinly sliced
1 cup diagonally sliced (very thin) celery

1 5-ounce can water chestnuts, drained and sliced
1 cup whole toasted almonds

Add ginger and onion to the simmering mixture, and remaining ingredients with the vegetables before heating.

FAR EAST CHICKEN

Omit carrots and soy sauce. Substitute 3 cups cooked cubed chicken for the pork, and 1 cup dry white wine for 1 cup of water. Add:

1 teaspoon curry powder
1 medium onion, thinly sliced
1 tablespoon chutney
1 tablespoon slivered candied ginger

½ cup white seedless raisins
1 cup pine nuts

Add curry, onion, and chutney to the simmering mixture, and the remaining ingredients with the vegetables before heating.

TRADE WIND TURKEY

Omit cucumber. Substitute 2 cups cubed cooked turkey for the pork. Use 1 carrot only. Add:

1 clove garlic, pressed or
minced
1 cup sliced mushrooms
(canned or fresh)
6 green onions, including
tops, chopped
1 cup small cooked
shrimp

¼ cup sesame seed
2 tablespoons grated
coconut, fresh or dry
(optional)
2 tablespoons bourbon
whisky (optional)

Add garlic, mushrooms, and onions to simmering mixture, and remaining ingredients before refrigerating.

SHELLFISH PEKING

Omit cucumber and cubed pork. Add:

½ cup sliced mushrooms,
either canned or fresh
1 medium onion, chopped
1 cup diagonally sliced
(twice) fresh peapods
1 cup cooked lobster
chunks

1 cup cooked crab meat
chunks
1 cup small cooked
shrimp
1 cup whole toasted
almonds

Add mushrooms and onions to simmering mixture and remaining ingredients before refrigerating. Peapods may be purchased from specialty markets or oriental restaurants.

VEAL . . .

VEAL ROAST HUNGARIAN

Veal is succulent food fit for a feast when properly cooked . . .

*3–4 pound boneless veal
rump roast
1 teaspoon salt or to taste
¼ teaspoon crushed celery
seed
Dash liquid pepper
2 teaspoons paprika*

*1 teaspoon Worcestershire
sauce
¼ cup grated onion
1½ cups commercial sour
cream
1 cup dry white wine*

Trim roast if necessary. Combine all ingredients except the wine and spoon over the roast, coating all exposed surfaces. Refrigerate overnight. Bring to room temperature, place in covered baking dish or roaster, and surround with wine. Bake covered at 350 degrees from 2–2½ hours, or until meat thermometer reads 180° F., basting occasionally. Refrigerate overnight if desired. Bake uncovered at 350 degrees for 30 minutes or until roast is heated through and lightly browned. Serves 6–8.

Note: For easier slicing let roast stand at room temperature for 10 minutes. Thicken drippings with a flour-water paste after fat has been removed for an excellent sauce.

Variations

VIENNESE VEAL

Omit celery seed and paprika. Add:

*1 6-ounce can drained button mushrooms
½ teaspoon nutmeg*

VEAL PARMESAN

Substitute ½ cup grated Parmesan cheese for the celery seed and paprika.

VEAL NICHOLAS

Omit celery seed and paprika. Add:

¼ cup snipped fresh dill or 2 tablespoons dillweed
1 clove garlic, pressed or minced
¼ cup finely diced dill pickle

FRUITED VEAL

Substitute 2 teaspoons pickling spice for the celery seed and paprika, and dry sherry wine or champagne for the white wine. Add at the beginning of the roasting period:

1 cup dried chopped peaches, apricots, or raisins (these may be done in combination, but use only 1 cup)

VEAL BARBECUE

Substitute 1 cup barbecue sauce for the commercial sour cream, and 1 cup dry red wine for the white wine. Add 1 tablespoon dry mustard to the coating mixture.

VEAL PARMIGIANA

Sprinkle cooked rice or noodles with poppy seed to accompany this . . .

1½ pounds veal round steak, thinly sliced	*⅛ teaspoon liquid pepper*
1 egg	*½ teaspoon sugar*
1 teaspoon water	*½ teaspoon thyme*
½ cup dry bread crumbs	*1 clove garlic, pressed*
⅓ cup grated Parmesan cheese	*1 cup dry white wine*
	½ cup water
¼ cup oil	*½ pound mozzarella cheese, thinly sliced*
1 medium onion, grated or minced	*½ cup grated Parmesan cheese*
1 teaspoon salt	

Trim meat. Cut in four serving pieces and pound to ¼ inch

thickness. Dip meat pieces first in the egg beaten with 1 teaspoon water, then in a mixture of crumbs and ⅓ cup grated Parmesan cheese. Heat oil in skillet and gently brown veal pieces on both sides. Mix together the onion, seasonings, sugar, thyme, garlic, wine, and water, and set aside. Place steaks in a buttered baking dish and cover with cheese slices. Cover with seasoning mixture and sprinkle with grated Parmesan cheese. Bake covered at 350 degrees for 30 minutes or until fork-tender. Serves 4.

Note: Veal cutlets may be substituted for the veal round. Veal Parmigiana may be cooked ahead and reheated at 350 degrees for approximately 30 minutes before serving. The sauce may be thickened with a flour and water paste.

Variations

VEAL SCALLOPINI

Omit egg and bread crumbs. Dredge veal pieces in ½ cup flour seasoned with:

> *½ teaspoon each oregano, sweet basil, and marjoram or 1 teaspoon Italian seasoning*

Add to the seasoning mixture:

> *1 6-ounce can tomato paste*

VEAL MARSALA

Omit egg, crumbs, thyme, and Parmesan cheese. Dredge veal pieces in ½ cup flour mixed with ½ teaspoon powdered ginger. Substitute Marsala wine for the white wine.

VEAL SICILIAN

Top each piece of browned veal with salami slices to cover, then with a piece of sliced ham before topping with the cheese slices. Add to the seasoning mixture:

1 6-ounce can tomato paste
½ cup crisp bacon crumbles

Sharp Cheddar cheese slices may be substituted for the mozzarella slices.

VEAL VERMOUTH

Omit thyme and Parmesan cheese. Substitute 1 cup extra dry vermouth for the white wine. Add to the seasoning mixture:

1 teaspoon tarragon

DILLED VEAL

Omit thyme, Parmesan cheese, and mozzarella cheese slices. Add to the seasoning mixture:

1½ teaspoons dillweed
1 small chopped dill pickle
½ lime thinly sliced (remove before serving)

VEAL CREME

Omit mozzarella cheese slices. Add:

1 cup sliced mushrooms
½ cup sliced ripe olives
2 tablespoons chopped
fresh parsley

1 cup commercial sour
cream (add this to the
sauce before reheating)

VEAL SCALLOPINI PRONTO   COQ

This can be put together in minutes, and tastes as if it had
been worked on for hours . . .

4 frozen veal cutlets,
thawed

¼ cup bottled Italian
dressing

½ cup packaged bread
crumbs

½ cup grated Parmesan
cheese

¼ cup olive or cooking
oil

1 4-ounce can mushrooms,
drained

1 2¼-ounce package
spaghetti sauce mix

1 cup chicken bouillon

½ cup dry white wine

Dip cutlets in bottled dressing, then in a mixture of the crumbs
and Parmesan cheese. Sauté in oil until golden brown. Place
in shallow buttered baking dish. Mix drained mushrooms,
spaghetti sauce mix, bouillon, and wine; pour over cutlets and
bake covered at 350 degrees about 40 minutes or until fork-
tender. Serves 4.

Note: This jiffy scallopini may be refrigerated either before
or after baking. If there is no wine on the pantry shelf, the
mushroom liquid will substitute nicely. One 12-ounce can
cooked, white long-grain rice placed in a buttered casserole with
1 tablespoon water and covered tightly will warm along with
the cooked scallopini in a 350-degree oven for 20–25 minutes
to complete the meal.

Variations

MEAL-IN-A-DISH SCALLOPINI   COQ

Add:

Canned new potatoes, carrots, baby lima beans, and pearl
onions in the amounts which please you

Top with a package of frozen peas, defrosted, if you wish.

VEAL GARNI   COQ

Omit spaghetti sauce mix and white table wine. Add to the sauce:

½ cup extra dry vermouth
½ teaspoon each oregano and sweet basil
¼ teaspoon each rosemary and thyme

VELVET VEAL   COQ

Omit spaghetti sauce mix. Add to the sauce:

⅔ cup grated Swiss cheese

VEAL PAPRIKA

The sauce is lightly seasoned and has a delicate, provocative flavor . . .

3 pounds boneless veal
  cut in 1-inch cubes
¼ cup flour
4 teaspoons paprika
½ teaspoon salt
¼ cup cooking oil
1 large onion, chopped
1 clove garlic, pressed or
  minced
½ teaspoon sugar
2 cups mixed vegetable
  juice
Dash liquid pepper
½ cup sliced mushrooms
2 teaspoons chopped
  pimiento
1 cup commercial sour
  cream

Shake veal, flour, paprika, and salt together. Brown meat in cooking oil. Add chopped onion, garlic, sugar, vegetable juice, pepper, mushrooms, and pimiento. Bake at 350 degrees for 1 hour or until meat is fork-tender. Refrigerate overnight. Before serving, fold in sour cream and bake at 350 degrees for approximately 30 minutes. Serves 6–8.

Note: One cup of dry red wine may be substituted for 1 cup mixed vegetable juice.

Variations

MEAL-IN-A-DISH VEAL PAPRIKA

At the time the sour cream is added, ½ pound cooked, well-drained noodles *or* 3 cups cooked rice may be added. Top with 1 package frozen green peas, separated, and ½ cup chopped toasted almonds.

ALBERTO'S VEAL

Omit sour cream. Substitute 2 cups tomato sauce for the mixed vegetable juice. Add to the sauce mixture:

½ cup minced green chilis   *1 tablespoon chili powder*
1 teaspoon oregano   *½ cup sliced ripe olives*

Rice is excellent with this.

CONSUELO'S VEAL

Omit paprika, vegetable juice, and pimiento. Increase garlic to 3 cloves. Add to the sauce mixture:

2 cups dry white wine
¼ cup fresh minced parsley
1 small can anchovy fillets drained and chopped

VEAL VIVANTI

Omit cooking oil and vegetable juice. Add to the sauce mixture:

¼ pound lean salt pork, chopped and fried crisp (brown veal cubes in the pork fat)
1 cup chicken bouillon
1 cup dry white wine

LAMB . . .

GLAZED LAMB LOUISE

This is an elegant and versatile roast which may be glazed in a variety of flavors . . .

5–6 *pound lamb shoulder roast, boned and tied*
½ *teaspoon salt*
¼ *teaspoon coarsely ground pepper*
1 *teaspoon garlic powder*
3 *tablespoons flour*

1 *teaspoon dry mustard*
¼ *cup frozen orange juice concentrate*
½ *teaspoon grated orange rind*
1 *cup mint jelly*

Coat meat surface with a mixture of salt, pepper, garlic powder, flour, mustard, orange concentrate, and orange rind. Refrigerate overnight. Place roast on rack in a shallow pan and bake at 350 degrees for 1½ hours. Pour off excess fat. Spread roast with mint jelly, and return to oven for 2 hours or until meat is fork-tender. A meat thermometer reading should be 180° F. Meat may be cooked ahead, cooled, sliced, and retied for ease of serving if desired. Heat at 350 degrees for approximately 30 minutes before serving.

Note: A leg of lamb roast may be substituted for the shoulder roast. If the leg is boned, rub the cavity with the spice mixture for greater flavor penetration.

Variations

CURRANT-GLAZED LAMB

Substitute 1 cup currant jelly for the mint jelly, and 1 teaspoon prepared horseradish for the dry mustard.

APPLE-GLAZED LAMB

Omit orange concentrate and orange rind. Substitute 1 cup apple jelly for the mint jelly. Add to the coating mixture:

2 tablespoons lemon juice
1 tablespoon Worcestershire sauce
½ teaspoon crushed mint leaves

LAMB MAUI

Omit orange concentrate and orange rind. Substitute 1 cup pineapple preserves for the mint jelly. Add to the coating mixture:

½ teaspoon ginger   1 tablespoon soy sauce
1 tablespoon brown sugar
1 tablespoon
  Worcestershire sauce

SHERRIED LAMB

Omit pepper, orange concentrate, and orange rind. Substitute ½ cup dry sherry wine for the mint jelly, and use part of the wine in the coating mixture. Add to the coating mixture:

1 teaspoon paprika
Few grains cayenne pepper

HERBED LAMB

Omit mustard, orange concentrate, and orange rind. Add to the coating mixture:

2 tablespoons olive oil
1 teaspoon each marjoram, thyme, and rosemary
¼ teaspoon nutmeg

During baking period baste with 1½ cups dry white wine. Serve pan sauce, thickened with a flour-water paste if you wish, with meat or cooked rice.

PIQUANT LAMB

Omit mustard, orange juice concentrate, and orange rind. Substitute ½ cup dry red wine for the mint jelly, and use part of the wine in the coating mixture. Add:

¼ teaspoon each *tarragon, thyme, rosemary, and paprika*
¼ teaspoon *caraway seed*

FLAMING LAMB

Omit orange rind. Substitute 3 tablespoons lime juice for the orange concentrate and ¼ cup red currant jelly mixed with ½ cup dry red wine for the mint jelly. Add to the coating mixture:

½ teaspoon each *curry powder and powdered ginger*

Before serving, spoon ½ cup warm brandy over roast and set aflame. Serve pan sauce with the meat.

OVEN BARBECUED LAMB

Substitute ½ cup barbecue sauce for the mint jelly. Add to the cooking mixture:

1 tablespoon each
  Worcestershire sauce
  and lemon juice
1 tablespoon minced
  green pepper

1 tablespoon minced fresh
  celery leaves
Dash liquid pepper

MEXICAN LAMB

Omit flour and mint jelly. Combine remaining coating ingredients with the following ingredients to form a marinade:

1 cup dry red wine
¼ cup brandy
¼ cup chili sauce

1 tablespoon chili powder
1 teaspoon oregano
¼ teaspoon cumin

Note: Roast should be refrigerated in the marinade and turned frequently for at least 24 hours before cooking. Baste

meat occasionally during cooking period. Serve the pan sauce
with the meat after excess fat has been removed. Thicken it
with a flour and water paste if you prefer. It is excellent over
rice.

LAMB ARABESQUE

Lamb and eggplant, popular companions in the Far East, are
combined in this exotic dish . . .

3 tablespoons butter
1½ cups coarsely chopped
onion
3 pounds lean lamb cut
in 1-inch cubes
1 clove garlic, pressed or
minced
½ cup pine nuts
3 firm tomatoes, peeled
and diced
1 tablespoon curry powder
¼ teaspoon cayenne
pepper

1 teaspoon salt
1 teaspoon slivered
preserved ginger
½ teaspoon ground
cardamom seed
1½ cups chicken broth
or bouillon
2 cups peeled and cubed
eggplant
½ cup white raisins
2 tablespoons lime juice

Melt butter in a skillet, add onions and fry until golden.
Remove, and brown lamb cubes in remaining butter. Add
garlic, nuts, tomatoes, curry powder, cayenne, salt, ginger,
cardamom, and broth. Bring to a boil. Add eggplant, raisins,
and lime juice. Place mixture in a baking dish. Refrigerate
overnight. Bake uncovered at 325 degrees for 2½ hours or until
meat is fork-tender. This dish may be cooked ahead, and warmed
before serving at 350 degrees for approximately 30 minutes.
Serves 8.

Note: Cooked lamb may be used and baking time cut to 1
hour. Ground ginger (½ teaspoon) may be substituted for the
slivered ginger, and 1 cup dry white wine is an excellent substitute for 1 cup of the broth.

Variations

LAMB LEBANESE

Omit curry powder, raisins, and lime juice. Add:

¼ teaspoon each *nutmeg, cinnamon, and thyme*
¼ cup cracked wheat cereal or cream of wheat (add before baking)

JAVA LAMB

Omit curry powder, cardamom seed, raisins, and lime juice. Add:

2 teaspoons ground coriander
¼ teaspoon cayenne pepper
½ teaspoon each saffron and cumin

LAMB CREOLE

Omit pine nuts, curry, ginger, cardamom seed, broth, and raisins. Add:

½ cup dry red wine
1 cup tomato sauce
½ cup chopped green pepper

1 bay leaf
1 teaspoon each chili powder and paprika

LAMB JERUSALEM

Omit eggplant, raisins, and lime juice. Add:

2 No. 300 cans artichoke hearts or 3 6-ounce jars marinated artichoke hearts, drained, the last 20 minutes of cooking time

Note: If this dish is cooked ahead, add artichoke hearts before reheating.

SAVORY LAMB

The herb combination provides real character . . .

6 lamb shanks,
  approximately 1 pound
  each
⅓ cup flour
Cooking oil
1 teaspoon salt
¼ teaspoon ground pepper
¼ teaspoon each marjoram
  and rosemary

½ teaspoon each oregano
  and sweet basil
1 teaspoon chopped
  parsley flakes
¼ cup dehydrated onion
1 clove garlic, pressed or
  minced
¼ cup diced pimiento
2 cups dry white wine

Coat lamb shanks well with flour and brown on all sides in cooking oil. Place in baking dish and add remaining ingredients. Bake covered at 350 degrees for 1 hour or until meat is fork-tender. Refrigerate overnight. Reheat at 350 degrees for 30 minutes before serving. Serve sauce with meat.

Note: Sauce may be thickened with a flour and water paste. Consommé or bouillon may be substituted for the wine. Cooked rice with ½ cup seedless raisins added is an excellent accompaniment.

Variations

SAVORY LAMB ROBERTO

Substitute 2 cups tomato sauce for the wine. Add:

2 tablespoons brandy

Omit raisins from the rice accompaniment.

DILLED LAMB

Omit marjoram, rosemary, oregano, and sweet basil. Add:

1 teaspoon dillweed
½ teaspoon sage

KATE'S LAMB

Omit marjoram, rosemary, oregano, and sweet basil. Add:

1 bay leaf
1 sprig fresh mint
(optional)
½ teaspoon savory
1 cup button mushrooms

1 cup diagonally sliced
(thin) carrots
1 cup diagonally sliced
(thin) celery
½ cup extra dry vermouth

Add vegetables before reheating or the last 20 minutes of cooking time.

POULTRY . . .

MANDARIN TURKEY

This incorporates an unusual combination of companionable flavors which blend overnight . . .

1 cup barbecue sauce
1 6-ounce can frozen
orange juice concentrate
2 tablespoons lime juice
1 cup dry sauterne wine
2 tablespoons butter
½ teaspoon salt
¼ cup flour
½ cup water

8 cups cubed cooked
turkey
1 teaspoon slivered
candied ginger
1 teaspoon minced capers
2 tablespoons finely
chopped seedless raisins
½ cup whole toasted
almonds

Combine barbecue sauce, orange concentrate, lime juice, wine, butter, and salt. Bring to a boil and thicken with a paste made of the flour and water. Add turkey, ginger, capers, raisins, and almonds. Place in a buttered baking dish. Bake at 350 degrees for approximately 45 minutes. Serves 10.

Note: Cubed chicken may be substituted for the turkey. One cup pineapple chunks may be added. Buttered brown rice goes well with this.

Variations

BLUSHING MANDARIN TURKEY

Substitute 1 cup cranberry juice cocktail for the orange concentrate.

MANDARIN TURKEY SESAME

Omit capers and almonds. Add to the baking mixture:

> ½ *cup sesame seed*
> ½ *cup sliced water chestnuts*

CURRY CREAM TURKEY

Omit orange concentrate, lime juice, and capers. Substitute 1 cup light cream for the barbecue sauce. Add to the baking mixture:

> 2 *teaspoons curry powder (or to taste)*
> 1 *cup commercial sour cream*
> 1 *10½-ounce can cream of mushroom soup*

CAPITAL TURKEY

Omit orange concentrate. Add to the baking mixture:

> 1 *chopped onion*
> 1 *clove garlic, pressed or minced*
> 1 *green pepper, chopped*

Fold four firm tomatoes, peeled and diced, in with the turkey cubes.

CHICKEN INDIA

This savory dish is delightful for small dinner parties or for large buffets . . .

4 large chicken breasts, boned and split	1 cup dry sherry wine
½ teaspoon salt	1 teaspoon grated orange rind
¼ teaspoon coarse black pepper	2 tablespoons cornstarch
3 tablespoons butter or cooking oil	¼ cup water
1 teaspoon curry powder (or to taste)	1 No. 1 can chunk pineapple, drained
1 cup fruit syrup (from canned fruits)	1 No. 1 can mandarin oranges, drained
	1 No. 1 can small pearl onions, drained

Rub chicken pieces (skinned or not, as you prefer) with salt and pepper, and brown in butter or oil. Remove chicken from pan. Add curry, fruit syrup (use pineapple juice and orange juice as necessary to make 1 cup), sherry wine, and orange rind to drippings. Bring to a boil. Replace chicken breasts and cover. Simmer gently for 25 minutes or until chicken is fork-tender. Remove chicken to buttered baking dish. Thicken sauce with a mixture of the cornstarch and water. Add pineapple, mandarin oranges, and onions. Pour over chicken breasts. Serves 8.

Note: This dish may be refrigerated overnight and reheated at 350 degrees for approximately 30 minutes. Rice or noodles may be served with this.

Variations

GINGER CHICKEN

Substitute 2 tablespoons slivered candied ginger for the curry powder. Garnish with ½ cup toasted pecan halves before final heating.

WALNUT CHICKEN

Omit curry powder, orange rind, and mandarin oranges. Add to the simmering mixture:

¼ cup extra dry vermouth
1 tablespoon soy sauce
1 clove garlic, pressed or minced
½ teaspoon ground ginger

¼ cup sliced water chestnuts
1 cup toasted walnut halves (add before final heating)

HERBED HAM CHICKEN

Omit curry powder, orange rind, pineapple, and mandarin oranges. Substitute 2 cups rosé wine for the sherry and fruit syrup. Add to the simmering mixture:

½ teaspoon each thyme, oregano, and sweet basil
1 cup slivered ham
¼ cup grated Parmesan cheese

Top with 1 cup grated Monterey jack cheese before final heating.

CHICKEN ACAPULCO

This is such a piquant dish . . .

3 cups minced cooked chicken
½ teaspoon oregano
Salt and pepper to taste
1 10½-ounce can cream of chicken soup
1 pint commercial sour cream
1 cup sliced mushrooms
1 4-ounce can chopped green chilis

1 large onion, minced
½ cup toasted sliced almonds
12 corn tortillas
1 10½-ounce can cream of chicken soup
⅓ cup dry sherry wine or light cream
1 cup grated sharp Cheddar cheese

Combine chicken, oregano, seasonings, chicken soup, sour cream, mushrooms, green chilis, onion, and almonds. Divide mixture between tortillas, and roll up. Place close together in shallow baking dish. Combine 1 can chicken soup with the wine or cream, and pour over tortilla rolls. Top with cheese. Refrigerate overnight. Bake at 350 degrees for approximately 30 minutes before serving. Makes 12 rolls.

Note: Turkey may be used instead of the chicken.

Variations

QUICK CHICKEN ACAPULCO   COQ

Use canned poultry, dehydrated onion, and substitute grated Parmesan cheese for the Cheddar cheese.

PORK ACAPULCO

Substitute cooked pork for the chicken. Add to the stuffing mixture:

4 *firm tomatoes, chopped and drained*

CHICKEN GUACAMOLE

Add to stuffing mixture:

2 *large ripe avocados,*   1 *tablespoon*
peeled and mashed   *Worcestershire sauce*
1 *tablespoon lemon juice*   ½ *teaspoon dillweed*

CHICKEN ENRICO

Omit minced chilis. Substitute ½ teaspoon thyme for the oregano. Add to each roll:

2 *spears cooked asparagus*

For a more pronounced asparagus flavor, substitute 1 can asparagus soup for the chicken soup in the stuffing mixture.

CHICKEN-HAM CORTINA

Substitute 1½ cups slivered cooked ham for 1½ cups chicken. Add to the stuffing mixture:

1 cup slivered or finely diced Monterey jack cheese

CHICKEN ADOBE

Omit oregano and sliced almonds. Substitute 2 cans tomato soup for the chicken soup and ⅓ cup dry red wine for the sherry or cream. Add to stuffing mixture:

2 teaspoons chili powder
2 teaspoons paprika
1 clove garlic, pressed or minced

BEEF ADOBE

Omit sliced almonds. Substitute:

3 cups chopped cooked beef or cooked ground beef for the chicken
2½ cups tomato sauce for the chicken soup
⅓ cup dry red wine for the sherry or cream

Add to the stuffing mixture:

2 teaspoons chili powder
1 clove garlic, pressed or minced
¼ cup chopped pimientos

CHICKEN SIMONE

Omit green chilis and oregano. Substitute ⅓ cup sauterne wine for the sherry or cream and 1 cup grated Swiss cheese for the Cheddar cheese. Add to the stuffing mixture:

2 tablespoons very finely chopped chutney
½ teaspoon curry powder
¼ cup sesame seed

CHICKEN CAMERON

Reduce chicken to 2 cups. Substitute:

⅓ cup extra dry vermouth for the sherry or cream
1 can frozen cream of shrimp soup for the chicken soup in the stuffing mixture
½ teaspoon dillweed for the oregano

Add to the stuffing mixture:

1 cup cooked chopped shrimp	¼ cup chopped water chestnuts
½ cup mayonnaise	1 teaspoon minced capers

PARTY CHICKEN   COQ

An excellent dish which can be made in a jiffy . . .

1 cup commercial sour cream	1 4-ounce can water chestnuts, sliced and drained
1 10½-ounce can cream of chicken soup	1 cup cashew nuts
¼ cup dry sherry wine	½ cup sliced ripe olives
2 cups chopped cooked chicken (canned or leftover)	1 5½-ounce can French-fried noodles
¼ cup dehydrated onion	1 cup grated sharp Cheddar cheese

Mix sour cream, soup, and sherry wine. Add remaining ingredients except cheese, and combine. Place in buttered baking dish. Top with grated cheese. Set aside until serving time. Bake at 350 degrees for 30–35 minutes before serving. Serves 4.

Note: Any dry white wine may be substituted for the sherry wine. Grated Parmesan cheese may be used instead of the Cheddar. This dish may be refrigerated overnight or frozen ahead.

Variations

TURKEY CAROLINA   COQ

Omit water chestnuts. Substitute:

2 cups diced cooked turkey for the chicken
1 can cream of mushroom soup for the chicken soup
½ cup sliced mushrooms for the olives

PARTY PORK   COQ

Substitute diced canned pork tenderloin for the chicken and grated Parmesan cheese for the Cheddar. Add to the mixture:

1 teaspoon fines herbes

CHICKEN CABANA   COQ

Substitute 1 cup tomato sauce for the sour cream and 1 can tomato soup for the cream of chicken soup. Add:

½ cup minced green pepper

CHICKEN VERDI   COQ

Add to the mixture:

¼ cup diced pimiento

Layer one 10-ounce package frozen asparagus, crisp-cooked, with the mixture.

HAM AGUACATE   COQ

Substitute 2 cups diced ham for the chicken and 1 cup grated Parmesan cheese for the Cheddar cheese. Add:

1 cup diced firm ripe avocado
1 tablespoon lemon juice

SHELLFISH GULF   COQ

Substitute 1 cup small cooked shrimp and 1 cup cooked lobster chunks for the chicken, and 1 cup of mayonnaise for the sour cream.

GIRARDINI'S CRAB   COQ

Substitute 2 cups cooked crab chunks for the chicken and ½ cup mayonnaise for ½ cup sour cream. Add:

> 1 *tablespoon* each *lemon juice, prepared mustard, Worcestershire sauce, and soy sauce*
> ¼ *cup minced fresh parlsey*

OVEN CHICKEN

Cheers for this no-watch, no-spatter way to "fry" chicken . . .

4 *large chicken breasts,* *boned and split*	1 *teaspoon poultry* *seasoning*
⅔ *cup buttermilk*	*Salt and pepper to taste*
2 *cups cornflake crumbs*	

Remove skin from chicken if you prefer. Dip each piece in buttermilk. Coat with a mixture of the crumbs and seasonings. Arrange in a shallow pan or on a foil-lined cooky sheet. Bake uncovered at 350 degrees for 1 hour or until fork-tender. Serves 8.

Note: This dish may be prepared ahead and refrigerated overnight. Crushed potato chips, rice cereal crumbs, dry bread crumbs, or seasoned stuffing crumbs (omit seasonings) may be used instead of the cornflake crumbs. Melted butter or evaporated milk may be substituted for the buttermilk. Any chicken pieces of your choice may be used.

Variations

OVEN CHICKEN DEVON

Omit poultry seasoning. Blend with the buttermilk:

1 2-ounce can deviled ham
1 teaspoon each Worcestershire sauce and prepared mustard
Dash liquid pepper

OVEN CHICKEN PARMESAN

Omit poultry seasoning and 1 cup cornflakes. Blend with the buttermilk:

½ teaspoon paprika
1 cup grated Parmesan cheese

OVEN CHICKEN OREGANO

Substitute 1 tablespoon oregano for the poultry seasoning.

OVEN CHICKEN ROSEMARY

Substitute 1 tablespoon rosemary for the poultry seasoning.

OVEN CHICKEN PAPRIKA

Substitute 2 tablespoons paprika for the poultry seasoning.

OVEN CHICKEN CURRY

Substitute 1 teaspoon curry powder (or to taste) for the poultry seasoning.

OVEN CHICKEN BARBECUE

Substitute 1 tablespoon barbecue spice for the poultry seasoning.

OVEN CHICKEN HARLEQUIN

Omit poultry seasoning. Reduce buttermilk to ¼ cup; blend with:

½ cup mayonnaise
1 tablespoon grated onion
¼ teaspoon garlic powder

OVEN CHICKEN UKRAINE

Omit poultry seasoning. Reduce buttermilk to ¼ cup; blend with:

½ cup commercial sour cream
1 tablespoon lemon juice

Sprinkle chicken pieces generously with poppy seed before baking.

OVEN CHICKEN MOROCCO

Omit poultry seasoning. Add to crumb mixture:

½ teaspoon powdered turmeric
½ teaspoon each thyme and paprika

OVEN CHICKEN SAVOY

Omit poultry seasoning. Substitute ⅔ cup barbecue sauce, either regular or hot, for the buttermilk.

OVEN CHICKEN TROPICANA

Substitute one 6-ounce can frozen pineapple juice concentrate, thawed, for the buttermilk. Add to the crumb mixture:

1 3½-ounce can flaked coconut

HONEY CHICKEN

Mix ½ cup honey with 1 tablespoon soy sauce, and substitute for the buttermilk. Sprinkle chicken lightly with nutmeg before baking.

GARLIC CHICKEN

Add to the buttermilk:

2 cloves garlic, pressed

SESAME CHICKEN

Omit poultry seasoning and crumbs. Reduce buttermilk to ¼ cup and blend with ½ cup commercial sour cream. Sprinkle coated chicken generously with sesame seed.

SNAPPY CHICKEN

Omit poultry seasoning. Substitute one 7-ounce can green chili sauce for the buttermilk.

SWEET-SOUR OVEN CHICKEN

Omit poultry seasoning. Substitute one 6-ounce can frozen lemonade concentrate, thawed, for the buttermilk.

CHICKEN MORONGO

Gourmets applaud this succulent concoction . . .

¾ cup dry white table wine

2 10½-ounce cans cream of chicken soup

1 cup commercial sour cream

1 14-ounce package noodles, cooked and well drained

4 cups cubed cooked chicken

2 7-ounce cans artichoke hearts, drained and coarsely chopped

1 large can ripe pitted olives

½ cup slivered green pepper

½ cup chopped pimiento

1 large onion, minced

1 cup grated Parmesan cheese

Mix wine, soup, and sour cream. Starting with the noodles, layer all ingredients except cheese along with the wine mixture in a buttered baking dish. Top with the Parmesan cheese. Refrigerate overnight if desired. Bake at 350 degrees for approximately 45 minutes. Serves 8–10.

Note: This dish may be made ahead and frozen. Turkey cubes may be substituted for the chicken.

Variations

CHICKEN SUPREME

Omit artichoke hearts and green pepper. Substitute 2 cans cream of mushroom soup for the chicken soup. Add:

1 teaspoon curry powder (combine this with wine mixture)

1 cup toasted pecan halves

½ cup halved fresh seedless grapes

CHICKEN ASPARAGUS

Omit artichoke hearts and green pepper. Substitute 1 cup grated sharp Cheddar cheese for the Parmesan cheese. Add:

1 10-ounce package frozen asparagus spears crisp-cooked or 1 No. 303 can asparagus spears, drained or 1 pound fresh crisp-cooked asparagus (use the tender part only)

CHICKEN DIVAN

Omit artichoke hearts and green pepper. Add:

1 10-ounce package frozen broccoli spears, crisp-cooked and sliced lengthwise or coarsely chopped

CHICKEN ROCCO

Substitute 4 cups cooked rice for the noodles, and 1 cup mayonnaise for the sour cream. Add:

¾ cup toasted slivered almonds

CHICKEN GUSTAVE

Add:

1 3-ounce package dried beef shredded
½ pound bacon fried crisp and crumbled

Correct seasonings.

CHICKEN CALYPSO

Substitute 1 cup chili sauce for the sour cream. Add:

½ teaspoon angostura bitters

CHICKEN ALMOND MARIA

Omit artichoke hearts and green pepper. Add:

½ cup thinly sliced celery
½ cup thinly sliced water
chestnuts
1 cup sliced toasted
almonds

1 cup well drained bean
sprouts

CHICKEN TETRAZZINI

Substitute 1 pound thin, cooked spaghetti for the noodles.

SEAFOOD . . .

SWORDFISH MARINA

Double cooking and subtle seasonings distinguished this
dish . . .

3 pounds swordfish steak
cut ¾ inch thick
2 tablespoons melted
butter
2 tablespoons lemon juice
Salt and pepper to taste
Dillweed
½ 10-ounce can frozen
cream of shrimp soup

½ cup commercial sour
cream
¼ cup mayonnaise
2 tablespoons minced
chives
½ cup tiny shrimp
2 tablespoons minced dill
pickle

Cut fish in serving-size pieces. Butter baking dish generously.
Place fish in dish, and brush top with melted butter. Sprinkle
with lemon juice, salt, and pepper. Broil for 5 minutes, baste
with liquid, broil for 5 minutes more. Sprinkle lightly with
dillweed. Set aside. Mix defrosted soup, sour cream, mayonnaise,

chives, and shrimp. Spoon on broiled fish pieces. Garnish with dill pickle. Bake at 325 degrees for 25–30 minutes or until delicately browned. Serves 6–8.

Note: This recipe may be prepared early in the day and set aside until baking time. Halibut or tuna steaks may be substituted for the swordfish.

Variations

SWORDFISH MEDITERRANEAN

Substitute oregano for the dillweed and dill pickle garnish. Substitute one 6-ounce can tomato paste mixed with 1 clove garlic, pressed, for the sour cream.

SWORDFISH TOCINO

Omit dillweed and dill pickle. Sprinkle ½ cup toasted chopped almonds over steaks after broiling. Garnish with ½ cup crisp bacon bits.

SWORDFISH SESAME

Substitute ¾ cup sesame seed for the dillweed and the dill pickle garnish.

HALIBUT TOPANGA

Substitute halibut for the swordfish. Marinate the fish in dry white wine in the refrigerator for several hours. Drain before broiling. Add to the topping mixture:

2 *tablespoons grated Parmesan cheese*

COAST SALMON

Substitute salmon for the swordfish. Omit dillweed and dill pickle. Substitute 1 tablespoon Worcestershire sauce for 1 tablespoon lemon juice. After fish is broiled, cover each piece with a thin raw onion slice. Add to the topping mixture:

¼ cup minced green pepper

KELLY'S MAD SCREAM OF DELIGHT

This is a particularly delectable meal-in-a-dish . . . one of Kelly's most popular creations . . .

*1 10½-ounce can cream of
    mushroom soup
¼ cup milk
½ teaspoon curry powder
Salt and pepper to taste
1½ pounds rock cod fish
    fillets cut in 2-inch
    strips
1 No. 303 can peas,
    drained*

*¼ cup crisp bacon
    crumbles
1 large onion, grated
6 ripe firm tomatoes
1 cup grated sharp
    Cheddar cheese
Paprika*

Combine soup, milk, curry powder and seasonings. Butter a baking dish. Layer fish fillets, soup mixture, peas, bacon crumbles, and grated onion. Cut tomatoes almost through with 6 cross-cuts and spread to form roses. Place them on top of layered mixture, and sprinkle grated cheese over all. Dust with paprika. Bake at 350 degrees for 1 hour. Serves 6.

Note: This dish may be prepared early in the day and baked before serving. Red snapper or sea bass may be substituted for the rock cod.

Variation

KELLY'S SUPER SCREAM OF DELIGHT

Substitute ¼ cup dry sherry wine for the milk. Add to the soup mixture:

1 cup commercial sour cream

RICHARD'S SEAFOOD MEDLEY

Delicate seasonings take the bows here . . .

1 4-ounce can sliced mushrooms, drained	¼ teaspoon nutmeg
1 tablespoon butter	½ cup each cooked lobster chunks and crab chunks
1 10-ounce can frozen shrimp soup	½ cup tiny cooked shrimp
¼ cup milk	½ teaspoon paprika
¼ cup dry sherry wine	¼ cup grated Parmesan cheese
Dash liquid pepper	
Salt to taste	
2 tablespoons minced chives	

Brown mushrooms in butter. Combine soup, milk, wine, seasonings, chives and nutmeg. Add mushrooms and seafood, and heat slowly. Remove to buttered baking dish and top with paprika and Parmesan cheese. Refrigerate overnight if desired. Bake at 350 degrees for approximately 40 minutes. Serve with rice or noodles. Serves 8.

Note: Other seafoods may be used in this dish, and in any combination of your choice.

Variations

QUICK SEAFOOD MEDLEY   COQ

Substitute canned seafoods for the fresh.

SEAFOOD PIQUE

Substitute ¼ cup *each* smoked salmon and smoked albacore chunks for the lobster and crab.

SEAFOOD PACIFICA

Substitute ½ cup minced clams for the shrimp. Add:

¼ teaspoon powdered ginger
1 tablespoon lime juice
1 cup firm ripe avocado chunks

Fold avocados in mixture last to avoid mashing.

CRAB DIABLO

This tangy dish may be frozen for two weeks or refrigerated
for two days . . .

1 10½-ounce can cheese
soup
½ cup mayonnaise
2 tablespoons lemon juice
1 tablespoon
Worcestershire sauce
1 6-ounce package frozen
mushrooms, prepared
according to package
directions
1 clove garlic, pressed or
minced

¼ cup grated onion
¼ cup sliced stuffed green
olives
2 tablespoons minced
parsley
2 cups cooked crab
chunks
2 tablespoons butter
⅔ cup soda cracker
crumbs

Combine soup, mayonnaise, lemon juice, Worcestershire sauce,
mushrooms, garlic, onion, olives, and parsley. Add crab. Place
in a buttered baking dish. Melt butter, toss with cracker crumbs,
and sprinkle over crab mixture. Bake at 350 degrees for approximately 30 minutes. Serves 6.

Note: Lobster or shrimp may be substituted for the crab.
This may be baked in large shells or individual baking dishes.

Variations

DIABLO CARLOS

Substitute one 7-ounce can green chili salsa for the cheese soup.
Add:

2 *tablespoons brandy*

BAYOU CRAB

Omit Worcestershire sauce, green olives, and parsley. Add:

¼ *cup dry sherry wine*   2 *tablespoons drained*
¼ *teaspoon turmeric*   *sweet pickle relish*
1 *teaspoon curry powder*

SHELLFISH MIMETTE

This is easy—and a real compliment-grabber . . .

1 *cup cooked lobster*   ¼ *cup sliced ripe olives*
  chunks   1 *10½-ounce can Newburg*
1 *cup small cooked*   *sauce*
  shrimp   8 *slices sourdough French*
1 *cup mayonnaise*   *bread, cubed and crusts*
1 *cup commercial sour*   *removed*
  cream   2 *eggs, slightly beaten*
1 *cup diced celery*   2 *cups light cream*
1 *green pepper, diced*   1 *cup grated sharp*
1 *onion, chopped*   *Cheddar cheese*
½ *cup toasted sliced*
  almonds

Combine shellfish, mayonnaise, sour cream, vegetables, almonds,
olives, and sauce. In a buttered shallow baking dish place half
of the bread cubes. Cover with the shellfish mixture and add
the remaining bread cubes. Combine eggs and cream and pour

over baking dish mixture. Top with grated cheese. Refrigerate overnight. Bake at 350 degrees for 1 hour or until puffy and lightly browned. Serves 6–8.

Note: Milk may be used instead of light cream; white, whole wheat, or French bread may be substituted for the sourdough French.

Variations

SHELLFISH PIERRE

Substitute ½ cup dry sherry wine for ½ cup light cream. Add to the egg-cream mixture:

1 clove garlic, pressed or minced

MARCY'S SHELLFISH

Omit green pepper. Use 2 cups shellfish (crab, lobster, shrimp) either singly or in combination. Substitute ½ cup extra dry vermouth for ½ cup light cream. Add to the shellfish mixture:

½ cup sliced mushrooms

SHRIMP PROSCIUTTO

Use 2 cups shrimp. Substitute 1 can cheese soup for the Newburg sauce. Add to the shellfish mixture:

½ cup slivered prosciutto
1 tablespoon Worcestershire sauce
½ teaspoon oregano

HERBS, SPICES, AND SEASONINGS FOR BEEF

ROASTS	*Allspice, barbecue spice, basil, bay, caraway, cardamom, cayenne, cinnamon, cloves, garlic, ginger, herb seasoning, Italian seasoning, marjoram, onion, rosemary, savory, tarragon, thyme*
STEAKS, CHOPS	*Barbecue spice, cardamom, chervil, chili, dill, garlic, ginger, herb seasoning, onion, oregano, thyme*
STEWS, CASSEROLES	*Allspice, anise, barbecue spice, basil, bay, bell pepper flakes, caraway, cardamom, celery seed, chili, chives, cloves, cumin, curry, dill, fennel, garlic, ginger, herb seasoning, horseradish, Italian seasoning, mace, marjoram, mustard, onion, oregano, paprika, parsley, pickling spice, rosemary, sage, savory, tarragon, thyme*
GROUND, LOAVES	*Allspice, barbecue spice, basil, bell pepper flakes, cayenne, celery seed, chili, cumin, garlic, ginger, herb seasoning, Italian seasoning, mace, marjoram, mustard, nutmeg, onion, oregano, parsley, poultry seasoning, sage, savory, sesame seed, tarragon, thyme*
LIVER, KIDNEY, HEART	*Basil, bay, caraway, chili, garlic, herb seasoning, marjoram, mustard, paprika, parsley, rosemary, savory, tarragon, thyme*

HERBS, SPICES, AND SEASONINGS FOR PORK

ROASTS	*Caraway, cardamom, coriander, garlic, herb seasoning, marjoram, onion, oregano, pickling spice, rosemary, sage, tarragon, thyme*
STEAKS, CHOPS	*Cayenne, cinnamon, garlic, herb seasoning, marjoram, onion, oregano, rosemary, sage, thyme*
BROILED, CASSEROLES	*Bay, cayenne, caraway, coriander, garlic, ginger, herb seasoning, onion, oregano, parsley, pickling spice, sage, tarragon, thyme*
HAM	*Allspice, barbecue spice, bay, cayenne, cloves, coriander, garlic, ginger, horseradish, mustard, onion, oregano, paprika, pickling spice, sage, tarragon*

HERBS, SPICES, AND SEASONINGS FOR VEAL

ROASTS	*Basil, celery seed, coriander, garlic, herb seasoning, marjoram, mint, onion, oregano, paprika, rosemary, savory, tarragon, thyme*
STEAKS, CHOPS	*Barbecue spice, cayenne, dill, garlic, herb seasoning, mace, onion, oregano, paprika, rosemary, tarragon, thyme*
STEWS, CASSEROLES	*Anise, basil, bay, caraway, cayenne, celery seed, chili, curry, dill, garlic, ginger, marjoram, mint, mustard, onion, oregano, paprika, parsley, pickling spice, rosemary, saffron, sage, tarragon, thyme*

HERBS, SPICES, AND SEASONINGS FOR LAMB

ROASTS	*Allspice, anise, basil, caraway, garlic, herb seasoning, marjoram, mint, mustard, onion, oregano, rosemary, savory, tarragon, thyme*
STEAKS, CHOPS	*Basil, caraway, curry, dill, garlic, herb seasoning, marjoram, mint, onion, oregano, rosemary, tarragon, thyme*
STEWS, CASSEROLES	*Allspice, anise, basil, bay, caraway, cayenne, cinnamon, curry, dill, garlic, ginger, herb seasoning, marjoram, mint, onion, oregano, paprika, parsley, pickling spice, rosemary, savory, tarragon, thyme, turmeric*

HERBS, SPICES, AND SEASONINGS FOR POULTRY

BAKED	*Barbecue spice, basil, caraway, cloves, cumin, garlic, ginger, herb seasoning, Italian seasoning, marjoram, nutmeg, onion, oregano, paprika, parsley, poultry seasoning, rosemary, sage, savory, sesame seed, tarragon, thyme, turmeric*
BROILED, FRIED	*Barbecue spice, basil, coriander, cumin, garlic, ginger, herb seasoning, Italian seasoning, nutmeg, onion, oregano, paprika, parsley, poultry seasoning, rosemary, savory, tarragon, turmeric*
STEWS, FRICASSES, CASSEROLES	*Barbecue spice, basil, bay, bell pepper flakes, cayenne, chili, cinnamon, cloves, coriander, cumin, curry, dill, garlic, ginger, herb seasoning, Italian seasoning, mace, marjoram, nutmeg, onion, oregano, paprika, parsley, poultry seasoning, rosemary, saffron, sage, savory, sesame seed, tarragon, thyme, turmeric*

HERBS, SPICES, AND SEASONINGS FOR FISH

BAKED	*Barbecue spice, chives, cloves, cumin, curry, dill, garlic, marjoram, onion, oregano, paprika, parsley, pickling spice, poultry seasoning, sage, savory, sesame seed, tarragon, thyme, turmeric*
BROILED, FRIED	*Allspice, barbecue spice, bell pepper flakes, dill, garlic, marjoram, mustard, onion, oregano, paprika, parsley, pickling spice, savory, tarragon, thyme, turmeric*
BOILED, STEWS, CHOWDERS	*Allspice, basil, bay, caraway, celery seed, cinnamon, chili, cumin, curry, dill, fennel, garlic, ginger, Italian seasoning, mace, marjoram, mustard, onion, oregano, paprika, parsley, pickling spice, rosemary, saffron, sage, savory, sesame, tarragon, thyme, turmeric*
SHELLFISH	*Allspice, basil, bay, cardamom, cayenne, chili, curry, dill, garlic, ginger, mace, mustard, onion, oregano, paprika, parsley, pickling spice, saffron, sesame, tarragon, thyme, turmeric*

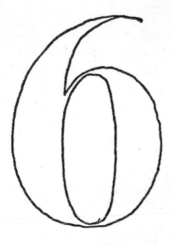

VEGETABLES

*. . . We [the Chinese] eat food for its
texture, the elastic or crisp effect it has
on our teeth, as well as for fragrance,
flavor and color.*

LIN YUTANG

IF YOU DON'T WANT to cast your vegetable dish as the star
of the dinner show, do let it play a significant supporting
role. It can help transform your meal into one worthy of an
epicure. The magic lies in the cooking, seasoning, and serving.
Vegetables are most often sinned against by drowning and
overcooking. Flavor, color, and food value go down the drain
with excess cooking liquid. As for the soggy remains—who
needs them?

Garden-fresh vegetables should be washed thoroughly, cooked
in as little liquid as possible, and rushed from the heat when
they are *barely* tender. In case of error, it is better to undercook

them a bit. This will preserve their character, texture, and appearance. If they are cooked ahead, take the warming time into account. Seasoned subtly and served dramatically, they will do you proud. They also will be eaten.

VEGETABLES

VEGETABLE PUDDING

Doubles as a starch and vegetable dish. Shines at a buffet or barbecue . . .

4 eggs, beaten	2 cups sliced ripe olives
2½ cups milk or light cream	1 cup sliced mushrooms
3 cups grated raw corn	1½ teaspoons salt
1 No. 303 can green beans, drained	¼ teaspoon liquid pepper
2 cups chopped fresh tomatoes	¾ teaspoon each paprika and chili powder
1 cup chopped onion	1⅔ cups yellow cornmeal
1½ cups chopped green pepper	1 cup melted butter
2 4-ounce cans pimiento, chopped	1 cup crisp bacon crumbles

Combine all ingredients as listed except bacon bits. Mix thoroughly and place in buttered 5-quart casserole or baking dish. Top with bacon bits. Refrigerate overnight if desired. Bake at 325 degrees about 1½ hours or until firm. Serves 12.

Note: Three cups canned golden cream-style corn may be substituted for the fresh grated corn. Mixed vegetables may be substituted for 1 cup chopped green pepper.

Variations

MEAL-IN-A-DISH VEGETABLE PUDDING

Reduce corn to 1½ cups. Add:

1½ cups cubed ham, chicken, or turkey
1 cup grated sharp Cheddar cheese

MEDLEY MARINA

Reduce corn to 1½ cups. Omit chili powder. Add:

1½ cups cooked shrimp, lobster, or crab chunks	*½ cup mayonnaise*
1 cup grated sharp Cheddar cheese	*1 teaspoon curry powder*

BARBECUED BEANS   COQ

They taste like you made them from scratch . . .

2 No. 2½ cans smoke-style barbecued beans	*Dash liquid pepper*
2 tablespoons dehydrated onion	*4 bacon slices*

Combine beans, onion, and pepper. Top with bacon slices. Bake at 350 degrees for 40 minutes. Serves 6.

Note: Drained pork and beans and ½ cup barbecue sauce may be substituted for the smoke-style beans. Serves 8.

Variations

BAKED BEANS LIZ   COQ

Substitute pork and beans for the smoke-style beans. Add:

1 medium dill pickle, minced
1 tablespoon bacon drippings or 1 slice bacon, minced

MOLOKAI BEANS   COQ

Substitute pork and beans for the smoke-style beans. Add:

1 tablespoon prepared mustard
1 cup pineapple tidbits

SHERRY BAKED BEANS   COQ

Substitute drained pork and beans for the smoke-style beans.
Add:

⅓ cup dry sherry wine   1 teaspoon dry mustard
2 tablespoons brown   1 teaspoon instant coffee
  sugar

PORKY BEANS   COQ

Add to the bean mixture:

2 cups chopped cooked or canned ham or luncheon meat

ORANGE BEANS   COQ

Substitute New England-style baked beans for the smoke-style
beans. Add:

⅓ cup orange marmalade

SPICY BAKED BEANS   COQ

Substitute New England-style baked beans for the smoke-style
beans. Add:

¾ cup catsup
¼ teaspoon each nutmeg and cinnamon
1 tablespoon slivered candied ginger

BEANS AND CHOPS

Omit bacon. Place beans in a flat baking dish. Top with 8
lean loin pork chops, fat removed. Cover each chop with a

slice of raw onion. Bake at 350 degrees 1½ hours or until chops are fork-tender. Slices of pork tenderloin may be substituted for the chops.

MARTI'S BUFFET SURPRISE

Substitute New England-style baked beans for the smoke-style beans. Add:

*1 No. 300 can whole
    kernel corn, drained*
*1½ cups grated sharp
    Cheddar cheese*

*1 6-ounce can tomato
    paste*
1 cup dry red wine

MUSHROOMS DUCHESS A LA SARA

Make this either a vegetable or a main dish . . .

16 large fresh mushrooms
2½ tablespoons butter
¼ cup minced celery
*2 tablespoons minced
    onion*
*1 teaspoon Worcestershire
    sauce*
*3 teaspoons minced
    toasted almonds*

*4 pickled walnuts, minced
    (optional)*
*1 teaspoon minced water
    chestnuts*
*2 tablespoons dry sherry
    wine*
Buttered bread crumbs
Butter

Remove stems from mushrooms. Discard tough parts, mince remaining tender parts. Melt butter in skillet, add chopped stems, celery, and onions and sauté. Mix with remaining ingredients except bread crumbs and butter. Fill caps above the edges with the mixture. Sprinkle with crumbs, dot with butter, and place cavity side up in a buttered dish. Bake at 350 degrees for 20 minutes. Makes 16 caps. Serves 4 as a main dish.

Note: Make this dish ahead and allow it to stand for flavors to blend.

Variations

MUSHROOMS GUSTO

Add to stuffing mixture:

2 *tablespoons minced parsley*

After removing from heat, add:

¼ *pound partially cooked pork sausage*
2 *tablespoons catsup*

MUSHROOMS DIABLO

Add to stuffing mixture:

¼ *cup deviled ham*

MUSHROOMS ITALIAN

Omit bread crumbs. Add to stuffing mixture:

2 *links Italian sweet sausage, minced*
2 *cloves garlic, pressed or minced*
1 *cup commercial sour cream (use to top stuffed caps)*

MUSHROOMS UNIQUE

Omit celery, Worcestershire sauce, and walnuts, and final topping of buttered bread crumbs dotted with butter. Increase sherry wine to ¼ cup. Add:

½ *cup bleu cheese*
1 *cup dry buttered bread crumbs*
½ *cup heavy cream*

Place a thin layer of cheese in each cavity. Add buttered bread crumbs, almonds, water chestnuts, and remainder of cheese to onion-mushroom skillet mixture and fill mushroom cavities. Place any leftover crumb mixture in bottom of buttered baking dish. Lay mushrooms cavity-side up on crumbs. Sprinkle wine on top. Pour cream carefully over all.

ALL AROUND THE GARDEN . . .

ASPARAGUS SUPREME

This has a mild pimiento flavor . . .

1 10½-ounce can cream of
mushroom soup
2 tablespoons chopped
onion
¼ cup milk
2 tablespoons butter
6 ounces pimiento cream
cheese spread

1 No. 2 can asparagus
spears, drained
3 hard-cooked eggs,
chopped
½ cup buttered cheese
cracker crumbs

Blend mushroom soup, onion, milk, butter, and pimiento cheese. Heat slowly until completely blended. Cover the bottom of a 1½-quart buttered casserole with half of the asparagus, eggs, and mixture. Repeat, and top with buttered cracker crumbs. Bake at 350 degrees for approximately 25 minutes. Serves 6–8.

Note: This dish may be made ahead, refrigerated overnight, and heated before serving. Crushed potato chips, buttered crushed cornflakes, or canned French-fried onions may be substituted for cracker crumb topping. Cooked fresh or frozen asparagus may be used instead of the canned asparagus.

Variations

ASPARAGUS ERNIE

Substitute one 5-ounce glass pimiento-olive cheese spread for the pimiento cream cheese. Add to soup mixture:

¼ cup sliced ripe olives

ASPARAGUS D'PAUL

Substitute one 5-ounce glass Roka cheese spread for the pimiento cream cheese. Add to soup mixture:

¼ cup chopped almonds

ASPARAGUS ADELINA

Substitute 6 ounces cream cheese for the pimiento cream cheese. Add to soup mixture:

¼ teaspoon each rosemary, thyme, and nutmeg

Sprinkle with sesame seed.

COMPANY BEETS   COQ

The sauce is sweet-tart . . .

*4 tablespoons brown
sugar
2 tablespoons cornstarch
½ teaspoon salt
1 No. 1 can pineapple
tidbits with juice*

*2 tablespoons butter
2 tablespoons lemon juice
½ teaspoon grated lemon
rind (optional)
4 cups sliced cooked beets*

Combine sugar, cornstarch, salt, and pineapple with juice. Cook until thick and clear, stirring constantly. Add butter, lemon juice, and lemon rind. Combine with beets in a baking dish. Bake at 350 degrees for 20 minutes or until hot. Serves 8.

Note: This is better if it stands a few hours or overnight. Canned or fresh beets—small whole, diced, or sliced—may be used.

Variations

ORANGE BEETS   COQ

Substitute ¾ cup frozen orange juice concentrate, thawed, for the pineapple, and grated orange rind for the lemon rind.

BEETS SAUTERNE   COQ

Substitute ¾ cup sauterne wine for the pineapple and juice.

BEETS WITH PORT   COQ

Substitute ¾ cup port wine for the pineapple and juice.

BROCCOLI PIERRE

Such elegant flavor for so little work . . .

2 10-ounce packages *frozen broccoli spears, defrosted*	1 cup commercial sour cream
¼ cup grated onion	¼ cup herb-seasoned bread crumbs
1 10½-ounce can cream of mushroom soup	

2 10-ounce packages frozen broccoli spears, defrosted
¼ cup grated onion
1 10½-ounce can cream of mushroom soup

1 cup commercial sour cream
¼ cup herb-seasoned bread crumbs

Place uncooked broccoli in baking dish. Mix onion, soup, and sour cream. Spread over broccoli. Top with bread crumbs. Bake at 350 degrees for 35 minutes, or until broccoli is just tender. Serves 6–8.

Note: This dish may be put together ahead and baked just before serving. Dehydrated onion may be used.

Variations

BROCCOLI PARMESAN

Add to the soup mixture:

⅓ cup Parmesan cheese

BROCCOLI LENA

Substitute cream of vegetable soup for the mushroom soup. Garnish with shredded raw carrots.

BROCCOLI ITALIAN

Substitute tomato soup for the mushroom soup. Add to the soup mixture:

½ cup sliced mushrooms *1 6-ounce can tomato*
½ cup sliced ripe olives   *paste*
½ teaspoon oregano

BRUSSELS SPROUTS
WITH CHESTNUTS   COQ

Easy—and aristocratic . . .

3 10½-ounce packages   *2 10½-ounce cans cream*
frozen Brussels sprouts   *of mushroom soup*
1 11-ounce can cooked   *⅓ cup dry white wine*
chestnuts, drained and
chopped

Cook sprouts until crisp-tender. Drain and place in buttered baking dish with chopped chestnuts. Cover with a mixture of the soup and wine. Bake at 350 degrees 25 minutes or until hot. Serves 8.

Note: Cream or dry sherry wine may be substituted for white wine. Chestnuts are sold in market gourmet sections or food import stores.

Variations

BRUSSELS SPROUTS NERO   COQ

Omit the cream of mushroom soup and the chestnuts. Add:

1 can cream of chicken   *1 cup canned pearl onions*
soup   *2 cups toasted whole*
1 cup commercial sour   *almonds*
cream

Sprinkle the top lightly with grated nutmeg.

CARROTS CARAMBA

Beautiful, flavorful carrots . . .

2 *pounds small carrots,* *scraped*	*¼ cup jellied cranberry* *sauce*
¼ cup butter	*½ teaspoon salt*
¼ cup brown sugar	

Boil small, whole carrots until crisp-tender. Drain. Combine other ingredients and heat until melted and blended. Place carrots in buttered baking dish. Cover with sauce. Refrigerate overnight. Turn carrots to coat with sauce. Bake at 350 degrees for approximately 20–25 minutes. Serves 4–6.

Note: Carrots may be cut diagonally in 2-inch chunks.

Variations

QUICK CARROTS CARAMBA   COQ

Substitute canned carrots for cooked, fresh carrots.

QUICK YAMS CARAMBA   COQ

Substitute canned yams for cooked, fresh carrots.

GINGER CARROTS

Substitute ¼ cup frozen orange juice concentrate, thawed, for the cranberry sauce. Add:

2 *teaspoons slivered candied ginger*

MINTED CARROTS

Substitute ¼ cup mint jelly for the cranberry sauce. Add:

1 *teaspoon lemon juice*

CRUNCHY SPICED CARROTS

Substitute apple jelly for the cranberry sauce. Add:

1 teaspoon lemon juice
½ teaspoon nutmeg
¼ teaspoon cinnamon
¼ cup toasted chopped almonds

PINEAPPLE CARROTS

Substitute ¼ cup crushed pineapple, lightly drained, for the cranberry sauce. Add:

⅛ teaspoon ground cloves

ZIPPY CARROTS

Add:

1 teaspoon prepared horseradish
½ teaspoon prepared mustard

ORANGE CARROTS

Substitute ¼ cup frozen orange juice concentrate, thawed, for the cranberry sauce. Add:

1 teaspoon grated orange rind (optional)
½ cup mandarin orange pieces

RUTH'S CABBAGE

Simple, but delicious . . .

¾ pound chopped lean
*   bacon*
2 ounces butter

1 medium head cabbage,
*   coarsely chopped*
Salt and pepper to taste

Fry bacon until crisp. Remove and set aside. Add butter, then the cabbage to bacon drippings in skillet. Add seasonings. Fry very briefly, stirring well. Remove to baking dish, sprinkle with bacon crumbles. Before serving, heat in 350-degree oven for 15 minutes or until hot. Serves 6.

Note: Do not overcook cabbage initially. It should still be crisp when it goes to the oven.

Variations

CABBAGE ROMINA

After frying cabbage add:

1 cup commercial sour cream	1 tablespoon paprika
	Salt as needed
½ teaspoon sugar	Poppy seed (sprinkle
3 tablespoons vinegar	over bacon crumbles)

COMSTOCK'S CABBAGE

After frying cabbage add:

1 cup mayonnaise
½ cup chopped onion
1 cup grated sharp Cheddar cheese (sprinkle over bacon crumbles)

CAULIFLOWER AU GRATIN

Looks spectacular—tastes spectacular . . .

1 large head cauliflower	½ cup grated Cheddar cheese
1 10½-ounce can cheese soup	Toasted whole almonds

Cook head of cauliflower whole until crisp-tender. Drain and place in shallow buttered baking dish. Combine soup and cheese. Pour over cauliflower. Stick with toasted almonds. Bake at 350 degrees for 25 minutes or until hot. Serves 8.

Note: Cauliflower should be warmed in the dish it will be served in.

Variations

CAULIFLOWER ROSY

Substitute tomato soup for the cheese soup. Sprinkle with ½ cup crisp bacon crumbles after sticking with almonds.

DEVILED CAULIFLOWER

Blend one 4-ounce can deviled ham into soup mixture. Dust with paprika.

CAULIFLOWER PIMIENTO

Add to soup mixture:

¼ *cup minced pimiento*

Dust with paprika.

CAULIFLOWER SESAME

Substitute cream of mushroom soup for the cheese soup and Swiss cheese for the Cheddar cheese. Sprinkle with ½ cup sesame seed after sticking with almonds.

GREEN BEANS ELEGANTE   COQ

Delightfully simple, and tastes simply delightful . . .

2 *1-pound cans cut
green beans, drained*
1 *10½-ounce can tomato
soup*

½ *teaspoon each oregano
and dillweed*
1 *3½-ounce can
French-fried onion rings*

Combine beans, soup, and spices. Place in baking dish and top with onion rings. Bake at 350 degrees for 25 minutes or until hot. Serves 6.

Note: This recipe may be refrigerated overnight or frozen for days. The finished product tastes nothing like canned beans.

Variations

JAN'S GREEN BEANS   COQ

Substitute cream of mushroom soup for the tomato soup. Omit dillweed.

DEVILED GREEN BEANS

Blend with the soup:

1 *5-ounce jar pimiento cheese spread*
1 *6-ounce can tomato sauce*
1 *teaspoon prepared mustard*

Add:

1 *onion, chopped*
½ *cup chopped green pepper*

GREEN BEANS SENATE   COQ

Substitute cheese soup for the tomato soup. Add:

½ cup chopped toasted almonds

GREEN BEANS SINGAPORE

Omit oregano. Substitute cream of chicken soup for the tomato soup. Add:

½ cup crisp bacon
crumbles
2 tablespoons bacon
drippings

2 tablespoons dehydrated
onion
Soy sauce to taste

GREEN BEANS SICILY

Omit tomato soup. Use Italian-style green beans. Add:

½ cup mayonnaise
¾ cup commercial
sour cream
2 tablespoons grated
Parmesan cheese

2 tablespoons minced
pimiento
½ teaspoon Italian
seasoning

GOLDEN BEANS

Use wax beans. Substitute cream of mushroom soup for the tomato soup. Add:

1 large onion, sliced
2 firm tomatoes, chopped
¾ teaspoon chili powder

DILLY LIMAS

Dillweed and sesame seed get flavor credit here . . .

3 10-ounce packages
frozen lima beans
2 tablespoons soft butter
1½ cups commercial sour
cream

Salt to taste
½ teaspoon dillweed
¼ cup sesame seed

Crisp-cook the lima beans and place in a buttered baking dish.
Combine butter, cream, salt and dillweed, and pour over beans.
Top with sesame seed. Bake at 350 degrees for 20 minutes
before serving. Serves 8–10.

Note: This may be made early in the day. For a can opener
quickie use drained canned lima beans.

Variations

LIMAS ROYALE

Omit dillweed, sesame seed, and 1 cup sour cream. Add:

1 10½-ounce can cream
of mushroom soup
1 cup sliced mushrooms
1 teaspoon Worcestershire
sauce

½ cup grated Parmesan
cheese

Top with ½ cup chopped pecans.

PARTY LIMAS

Omit dillweed and sesame seed. Add:

3 tablespoons dehydrated
onion
3 tablespoons minced
pimiento

½ cup diced water
chestnuts
¼ teaspoon sage

Top with ½ cup crisp bacon crumbles.

LIMAS LOMBARDI

Omit dillweed and sesame seed. Add:

   1 cup crumbled Roquefort cheese

Dust top with paprika.

LIMAS ROCO

Omit dillweed and sesame seed. Add:

   1 clove garlic, pressed
   ½ cup slivered salami
   ¼ teaspoon savory

Dust top with paprika.

LIMA BEAN BAKE   COQ

This is hearty . . .

   4 cups drained canned
   dry lima beans
   1 clove garlic, pressed
   ¼ cup celery flakes
   2 tablespoons dehydrated
   onion
   ½ teaspoon sweet basil

   1 tablespoon
   Worcestershire sauce
   1 8-ounce can tomato
   sauce
   6 bacon slices for
   topping (optional)

Combine ingredients in a baking dish, and top with bacon. Bake at 350 degrees for 1 hour. Serves 6–8.

Note: Canned green lima beans may be used. This dish is more flavorful when refrigerated overnight.

Variations

LIMAS LAURIE

Omit tomato sauce and sweet basil. Add:

1 8-ounce can tomato soup
1 cup commercial sour cream
½ teaspoon nutmeg

NAPOLI LIMAS

Omit celery flakes, tomato sauce, and bacon. Add:

2 cups drained canned
*   tomatoes*
Dash thyme
½ bay leaf, crushed
½ cup grated Parmesan
*   cheese*

½ pound bulk pork
*   sausage, cooked,*
*   mashed, and drained*

SCALLOPED ONIONS

These are distant relatives of French-fried onions, and more
interesting . . .

6 medium onions, peeled
*   and sliced very thin*
¼ cup butter
¼ cup flour
1¼ cups milk
½ teaspoon salt

1 teaspoon paprika
1 teaspoon Worcestershire
*   sauce*
2 cups grated sharp
*   Cheddar cheese*

Separate onions into rings, and place in a well-buttered 2-quart
casserole. Melt butter and blend in flour, milk, salt, paprika,
and Worcestershire sauce. Cook until thick. Stir in cheese and
heat until it is melted. Pour over onions. Bake uncovered at
425 degrees 15–20 minutes, or until golden. Serves 6.

Note: Onions and sauce may be prepared early in the day and combined before baking. Just before baking, onions may be sprinkled with crisp bacon crumbles or diced toasted almonds.

Variations

GOLDEN ONIONS

Add to sauce before pouring over onions:

1 cup grated raw carrots

SWISS ONIONS PATRICIA

Substitute 1 cup grated Swiss cheese for Cheddar cheese. Add to sauce mixture:

¼ teaspoon liquid pepper

Top with buttered sourdough French bread crumbs. Paprika may be omitted.

SHERRIED ONIONS

Substitute ½ cup dry sherry wine for ½ cup milk and 1½ cups grated Parmesan cheese for the Cheddar cheese.

ONIONS PIQUANT

Omit ¼ cup milk. Add:

½ cup catsup

SPANISH ONIONS

Add to sauce mixture:

2 teaspoons chili powder or to taste

ONIONS VERDE

Mash 2 ounces green chilis and cook with the sauce mixture.

WHIPPED POTATOES PIMIENTO

Rich, rosy, and flavorful . . .

6 large potatoes, peeled
and quartered
¼ cup butter or
margarine
¾ cup light cream
(or as needed to
control consistency)

3 tablespoons grated onion
1 5-ounce jar pimiento
cheese spread
Salt to taste

Boil potatoes until tender. Mash with butter and cream. Blend in remaining ingredients. Whip until smooth and fluffy. Serves 6–8.

Note: Potatoes may be prepared ahead, piled in a buttered casserole, and reheated at 350 degrees for 25 minutes or until golden on top.

Variations

INSTANT PIMIENTO POTATOES   COQ

Prepare instant mashed potatoes for 8 according to package directions. Substitute 1 tablespoon granulated onion for the grated onion.

POTATOES GARNI

Substitute 1 jar pimiento-olive spread for the pimiento cheese spread.

PRAIRIE POTATOES

Substitute 1 jar bacon-cheese spread for the pimiento cheese spread.

POTATOES DUCHESS

Omit pimiento cheese spread. Increase butter to ¾ cup. Add and whip with potato mixture:

2 egg yolks
¼ teaspoon nutmeg

Fold into the whipped potato mixture 2 egg whites beaten to a peaking consistency. May be served at once or reheated.

Note: This recipe may be used to pipe meat and vegetable casserole dishes. It also may be used for potato nests in which to serve creamed vegetable, poultry, or fish dishes. To make nests, shape potatoes on oiled or teflon-coated baking sheets, brush with lightly beaten egg white (reserve this from the beaten whites), and bake at 400 degrees until lightly browned. These may be reheated, and are lovely for the buffet.

STUFFED POTATOES

Variations in seasonings offer endless possibilities . . .

6 baking potatoes, scrubbed and oiled
¼ cup butter or margarine
½ cup commercial sour cream
¼ cup light cream (or as needed to control consistency)

2 tablespoons minced chives
Salt and pepper to taste
1 tablespoon melted butter or margarine

Bake potatoes until tender. Halve lengthwise and scoop out centers, being careful not to break the shells. Refrigerate empty shells and whip the centers with ¼ cup butter, sour and light creams, chives, and seasonings. When fluffy, pile the mixture lightly in the potato shells, brush with melted butter, and refrigerate. Heat before serving in a 350-degree oven for 20 minutes. Serves 6 or 12.

Note: Herbs of your choice, or bits of crisp bacon, cooked sausage, or cooked ham may be added to the whipped mixture.

Variations

PARMESAN POTATOES

Add to the whipping mixture:

½ *cup grated Parmesan cheese*

POTATOES ANDALUSIA

Add to the whipped mixture:

½ *cup chopped ripe olives*

Brush potato tops with olive oil instead of butter.

POTATOES AMAPOLA

Add to the whipped mixture:

¼ *cup poppy seed*

Brush potato tops with olive oil instead of butter.

ONION POTATOES

Omit salt. Add to the whipping mixture:

2 *tablespoons dry onion soup mix*

POTATOES TOPPER

Add to the whipping mixture:

2 *tablespoons prepared horseradish*
1 *teaspoon crushed dillweed*

MYSTERY POTATOES

Add to the whipping mixture:

1 cup farmer-style cottage cheese
½ teaspoon marjoram
1 teaspoon granulated onion

1 tablespoon Worcestershire sauce

POTATOES MAIZE

Add to the whipped mixture:

1 buffet can drained whole-kernel corn
1 clove pressed garlic (optional)

POTATOES CONFETTI

Increase chives to 3 tablespoons. Add to the whipped mixture:

3 tablespoons minced pimiento

POTATOES ORO

Omit chives. Add to the whipped mixture:

3 tablespoons grated onion
¾ cup grated raw carrots

POTATOES RED FLANNEL

Add to the whipped mixture:

1 cup minced corned beef
1 clove pressed garlic

POTATOES ROJO

Add to the whipping mixture:

1 6-ounce can tomato paste

Top buttered potato tops with minced salami.

POTATOES RENALDO

Add to the whipping mixture:

2 ounces chopped green chilis

POTATOES RILLO

Add to the whipped mixture:

1 cup minced canned or raw mushrooms

CRUNCHY POTATOES

Add to the whipped mixture:

½ cup chopped toasted almonds

POTATOES PARMIER

Add to the whipping mixture:

6 ounces crumbled Roquefort cheese
2 tablespoons minced parsley

Top with crisp bacon crumbles.

POTATO BOATS

Press a shallow hollow in each stuffed potato. Fill with green peas, mixed vegetables, or baby lima beans. Brush with butter before heating.

POTATOES DAVID

These are very crunchy . . .

8 medium peeled potatoes   *6 eggs, slightly beaten*
1½ cups hot water   *⅔ cup melted butter*
1 large onion, grated   *Salt and pepper to taste*

Grate potatoes coarsely and cover at once with hot water. Mix remaining ingredients. Drain potatoes well (press them a bit), and combine with egg mixture. Place in a large shallow baking dish. Bake at 350 degrees for 1½ hours or until potatoes are very crisp and brown on top. Serves 10.

Note: These are unusual, and excellent for a buffet. Chicken fat may be substituted for the melted butter.

Variations

POTATOES RAAL

Top potatoes with 1 cup crisp bacon crumbles. Substitute ¼ cup of bacon fat for ¼ cup of the butter if you wish.

GOLDEN CRUNCH POTATOES

Add to the potato mixture:

1 cup grated sharp Parmesan cheese

SHERRIED SWEET POTATOES

These are a rich golden color . . .

8 medium sweet potatoes,
  boiled and peeled
½ cup brown sugar
1 cup orange juice
1 tablespoon grated orange
  rind

⅓ cup dry sherry wine
1 cup chopped pecans
Butter

Cut potatoes in thick slices. Place half of them in a buttered baking dish. Combine the sugar, orange juice, rind, and sherry. Pour part of the mixture over the potatoes, and add half of the pecans. Add remaining potatoes and juice mixture, and top with remaining pecans. Dot generously with butter. Refrigerate overnight. Heat at 350 degrees for 30 minutes. Serves 8–10.

Note: Yams may be substituted for the sweet potatoes.

Variations

SWEET POTATOES AND PINEAPPLE

Layer 1½ cups crushed pineapple, drained, with the potatoes.

APPLE SWEET POTATOES

Add to the liquid mixture:

1 cup canned applesauce
1 teaspoon cinnamon

SWEET POTATOES ORO

For ½ cup of the orange juice substitute ½ cup apricot purée. This may be either canned or made from sieved apricots.

FRUITED SWEET POTATOES

Layer 1½ cups white raisins with the potatoes.

RUBY YAMS   COQ

Cranberries make them blush . . .

1 No. 2½ can whole   *½ cup dry sherry wine*
yams or sweet potatoes,   *⅓ cup brown sugar*
drained   *1 teaspoon grated orange*
1 1-pound can whole   *rind (optional)*
cranberry sauce   *2 tablespoons butter*

Place halved potatoes in buttered baking dish. Mix cranberries, wine, sugar, and rind. Simmer 5 minutes. Add butter. Pour over potatoes. Before serving bake at 350 degrees for 25 minutes. Serves 6–8.

Note: The potatoes will be more flavorful if they stand in the sauce before serving.

Variations

GOLDEN YAMS COQ

Substitute 1 cup apricot purée for the cranberry sauce. Add to the potato halves:

1 11-ounce can mandarin orange sections, drained

MALLOW YAMS COQ

Fold 1 cup miniature marshmallows into the warm simmering mixture before pouring over either Ruby Yams* or Golden Yams*.

PRALINE YAMS

These are spectacular on the buffet . . .

8 *medium yams, peeled* *and boiled*	½ *cup brown sugar*
¼ *cup butter*	⅔ *cup chopped pecans*
Salt and pepper to taste	8 *slices pineapple*
½ *teaspoon each nutmeg* *and cinnamon*	8 *maraschino cherries*

Mash yams with butter, seasonings, nutmeg, cinnamon, and sugar. Fold in pecans. Place pineapple slices in shallow buttered baking dish. Mound the mashed yams on the pineapple slices. Top each with a cherry. Refrigerate overnight if you wish. Bake at 350 degrees for 25 minutes before serving. Serves 8.

Note: These are delicious, and the individual servings are convenient for a small dinner or for a crowd.

Variations

WALNUT YAM PUFFS

Omit cherries. Substitute finely chopped walnuts for pecans and increase to 1½ cups—do not fold them into yams. Form 8 yam balls around 8 large marshmallows. Roll in the finely chopped nut meats. Place balls on pineapple slices.

SWEET CRUNCH BALLS

Do not mound yams, but form into 8 balls. Roll in coarsely crushed cornflakes before placing on pineapple slices.

GINGER YAMS

Add to potato mixture:

   3 *tablespoons slivered, candied ginger*

HONEY MOUNDS

Omit cherries. Heat ¼ cup mild honey with 2 tablespoons butter. After yams have been mounded on pineapple slices, make a well in the center of each mound with a spoon tip, and fill with honey-butter mixture.

MAGNOLIA YAMS

Mash 3 ripe bananas with the yams.

SWEET PYRAMIDS

Omit pecans. Cool mashed yam mixture. Add:

   1 *egg, slightly beaten*

Shape yams into pyramids, and stick with whole toasted almonds. Top with a cherry or an almond.

HOLIDAY YAMS

Reduce brown sugar to ¼ cup. Add to the mashed yams:

1 cup candied fruit mix

SPINACH SAVOY

Sumptuous is the word for this . . .

2 10-ounce packages
frozen chopped spinach,
defrosted
2 cups commercial sour
cream
½ package French onion
soup mix

½ cup buttered bread
crumbs
½ cup grated Parmesan
cheese

Drain uncooked spinach. Combine with sour cream and soup mix. Top with buttered crumbs and Parmesan cheese. Bake at 350 degrees for 20 minutes before serving. Serves 6.

Note: Make this dish early in the day—or the day before.

Variations

SPINACH ALMOND

Omit onion soup mix and Parmesan cheese. Add:

1 teaspoon Worcestershire sauce

Top with buttered crumbs and ½ cup chopped toasted almonds.

SPINACH IGOR

Omit Parmesan cheese and buttered crumbs. Add:

½ cup grated sharp Cheddar cheese
½ cup crisp bacon crumbles (for topping)

SPINACH LORAY

Add to the spinach-cream mixture:

1 3½-ounce can button mushrooms, drained
1 clove garlic, pressed
½ teaspoon dillweed

SPINACH ANNA

Omit soup mix and Parmesan cheese. Add to the spinach-cream mixture:

¼ teaspoon sweet basil
¼ teaspoon tarragon
⅛ teaspoon each mace and rosemary

SPINACH CREAM

Omit soup mix and Parmesan cheese. Add:

2 eggs, beaten
1 cup shredded Monterey jack cheese
1 cup shredded sharp Cheddar cheese
½ cup farmer-style cottage cheese
1 clove garlic, minced
½ cup melted butter

Mix thoroughly. Bake in buttered dish at 325 degrees for 45 minutes or until lightly golden. Serves 8.

STUFFED ZUCCHINI

A jewel of a recipe—freeze it for two weeks, refrigerate it for two days . . .

4 pounds zucchini squash
¼ cup melted butter
Salt and pepper to taste
1 large onion, shredded
2 cups grated sharp Cheddar cheese
8 soda crackers rolled to crumbs
1 teaspoon paprika

Boil whole squash until just tender. Cool. Split lengthwise. Scoop centers out carefully and chop fine. Add all remaining ingredients. Mix well. Place zucchini shells in shallow baking dish and fill with squash mixture. Dust with additional paprika. Bake at 350 degrees for 25 minutes before serving. Serves 8–10.

Note: Do not over-cook whole squash. The shells must be firm for filling.

Variations

ZUCCHINI SUPREME

Add:

   1 *cup commercial sour cream*
   2 *tablespoons dry sherry wine*

ZUCCHINI AND CORN

Omit chopped zucchini centers. Add to the stuffing mixture:

   ½ *cup commercial sour cream*
   1 *cup whole-kernel corn*
   ½ *cup grated Parmesan cheese*

ZUCCHINI PEDRO

Omit butter, soda crackers, and chopped zucchini centers. Add to the stuffing mixture:

   2 *cups drained mashed canned tamales*
   1 *teaspoon chili powder or to taste*

ZUCCHINI PIMIENTO

Add to the stuffing mixture:

   1 *cup commercial sour cream*
   3 *tablespoons minced pimiento*

ZUCCHINI VERDE

Omit chopped zucchini centers. Add to the stuffing mixture:

1 10-ounce package
frozen chopped spinach,
thawed and well
drained (do not cook)
1 cup commercial sour
cream

2 tablespoons dry sherry
wine
½ cup crisp bacon
crumbles for topping

HERBS, SPICES, AND SEASONINGS
FOR VEGETABLES

ARTICHOKES	*Bay, dill, garlic, lemon, olive oil, savory, tarragon*
ASPARAGUS	*Dill, lemon, mustard, nutmeg, parsley, rosemary, savory, sesame seed, tarragon, thyme*
AVOCADOS	*Coriander, dill, lemon, marjoram, olive oil, onion, sesame seed*
BEANS, BAKED	*Barbecue spice, cinnamon, cloves, garlic, ginger, mustard, onion*
GREEN OR WAX BEANS,	*Basil, bay, cumin, dill, garlic, marjoram, mustard, nutmeg, onion, oregano, paprika, rosemary, sage, savory, sesame seed, thyme*
BEANS, LIMA	*Garlic, Italian seasoning, mint, nutmeg, onion, parsley, sage, savory, sesame seed, thyme*
BEETS	*Allspice, anise, bay, caraway, cinnamon, cloves, coriander, dill, fennel, ginger, mustard, oregano, poppy seed, savory, tarragon*
BROCCOLI	*Garlic, lemon, mustard, onion, sesame seed, thyme*
BRUSSELS SPROUTS	*Celery seed, lemon, mustard, onion, paprika, rosemary, sage, sesame seed, savory, tarragon*
CABBAGE, GREEN	*Anise, caraway, celery seed, chili, cumin, curry, dill, fennel, garlic, mustard, nutmeg, onion, oregano, paprika, parsley, rosemary, savory, tarragon*
CABBAGE, RED	*Allspice, caraway, cloves, curry, dill*

CARROTS	Anise, allspice, bay, cinnamon, cloves, curry, dill, garlic, ginger, mace, marjoram, mint, nutmeg, oregano, parsley, poppy seed, rosemary, thyme
CAULIFLOWER	Basil, caraway, chili powder, dill, fennel, garlic, mace, nutmeg, paprika, parsley, rosemary, savory, sesame seed
CELERY	Caraway, chili powder, chives, garlic, onion, paprika, parsley, rosemary
CHARD	Garlic, lemon, onion, oregano, rosemary
CORN	Celery seed, chili powder, chives, garlic, onion, oregano, paprika, parsley
CUCUMBER	Caraway, chives, dill, garlic, onion, paprika, parsley
EGGPLANT	Allspice, anise, basil, bay, chili powder, dill, marjoram, olive oil, onion, oregano, rosemary, savory
ENDIVE	Basil, chives, garlic, tarragon
LEEKS	Bay, onion, oregano, parsley, rosemary, savory
OKRA	Bay, chili powder, garlic, lemon, onion, parsley, thyme
ONIONS	Basil, chili powder, cloves, ginger, marjoram, nutmeg, oregano, paprika, parsley, sage, thyme
PARSNIPS	Onion, parsley, poppy seed, rosemary, sesame seed
PEAS	Basil, cinnamon, cumin, garlic, Italian seasoning, marjoram, mint, onion, oregano, poppy seed, rosemary, sage, savory, tarragon, thyme

PEPPERS, GREEN	Basil, chili, garlic, olive oil, onion, oregano, rosemary
POTATOES, WHITE	Basil, caraway, chives, dill, garlic, nutmeg, onion, oregano, paprika, parsley, poppy seed, rosemary, saffron, sesame seed, thyme
POTATOES, SWEET	Allspice, cardamom, cinnamon, cloves, dill, ginger, nutmeg, poppy seed
RUTABAGAS	Dill, fennel, parsley, poppy seed, rosemary
SPINACH	Allspice, basil, cinnamon, dill, lemon, mace, nutmeg, oregano, rosemary, sesame seed, tarragon vinegar
SQUASH, SUMMER	Basil, dill, nutmeg, onion, paprika, savory
SQUASH, WINTER	Allspice, basil, chives, cinnamon, cloves, dill, ginger, maple, onion, oregano, parsley
SQUASH, ZUCCHINI	Caraway, chili powder, fennel, garlic, marjoram, olive oil, onion, oregano, paprika, sesame seed
TOMATOES	Allspice, basil, bay, caraway, celery seed, chili powder, dill, garlic, Italian seasoning, onion, oregano, paprika, parsley, sage, sesame seed, thyme
TURNIPS	Allspice, basil, caraway, cloves, dill, garlic, onion, paprika, parsley, poppy seed, rosemary, sesame seed
ZUCCHINI	See squash

SALADS

. . . Lettuce is like conversation: it must
be fresh and crisp, so sparkling that you
scarcely notice the bitter in it.

CHARLES DUDLEY WARNER

A READY-TO-SERVE SALAD nestling in the refrigerator is more satisfying to the hostess than mink in the closet when the cocktail hour shows signs of waning (the guests begin to refuse even a temperance-jigger refill), and the dinner hour shows signs of waxing (their glances stray toward the kitchen with increasing frequency). It doesn't matter whether the salad you whisk to the table is a crisp green or a shimmering mold. Simple or elegant, it will add a note of flavor, color, and interest to the meal.

Depending on what went into it, a salad can be the first course, the main course, an accompaniment, or it can double as a dessert. No matter which, it's ready—you can count on it. One of the nicest things that can happen to a meal is a glamorous salad. It should happen at your house.

SALADS

SOME ARE VERSATILE . . .

TOSSED GREEN SALAD

Crisp, green salads *can* be done ahead . . .

   3 *quarts assorted salad greens*
   1 *cup chopped chives (optional)*

Early in the day, wash greens and pat dry between paper towels. Tear into bite-size pieces, toss with chives, and place in the large bowl they will be served in. Purists add nothing more to this salad until it is tossed with the dressing, but there are extras which add flavor and eye appeal. These should be added at this point. Decorate the top of the greens with any combination of these: Whole cherry tomatoes (they won't wilt the greens or water the dressing), unpeeled cucumber slices, raw or cooked mushroom slices, pitted ripe or stuffed green olives, pimiento or green pepper strips, artichoke hearts, crisp-cooked green peas, beet slices, hard-cooked egg slices, citrus fruit sections, chopped salted nuts, or other additions of your choice. After the top of the salad has been decorated to your satisfaction, cover with a damp cloth or damp paper towels and refrigerate until serving time. Carry it to the table along with Guacamole Dressing* or French Parmesan Dressing* and toss it before your admiring guests. Serves 8–10.

Note: Use any of the variant dressings or your favorite salad dressing. If your decorations include any item which has been marinated in vinegar or oil, add it shortly before serving time to avoid wilted greens.

Variations

CHEF SALAD ANGELES

In decorating the torn greens, include slivers or chunks of any of the following: ham, chicken, salami, tongue; sharp Cheddar, Roquefort, Swiss, Monterey jack cheese; green beans, asparagus, carrots, celery; unsalted nuts; pineapple; avocado or apple chunks dipped in lemon juice; seedless grapes or seeded grapes of your choice.

THE SALAD TRAY

You simply can't miss with this fruit and vegetable array . . .

The salad tray is a prodigal assortment of fruit and vegetable pieces, either raw, cooked, or canned, served with complementary dips or dressings. Select these with an eye to color, flavor, texture, and contrast. For the buffet, try arranging them on a large tray—fruits at one end with a bowl of Curry Cream Dressing*, and vegetables at the other with a bowl of Roquefort Cream Dressing*, or with variant dressings of your choice. Arrange fruits and vegetables early in the day and cover with a damp cloth. Refrigerate until serving time.

Note: Any canned or marinated items should be very well drained before being arranged on the tray. The Salad Tray has many virtues. Every dieting guest can take—or leave—what he must (including the dressing) to hang in with the diet he currently is hung up on. The non-dieting guests can choose whatever pleases them. For suggested fruits and vegetables to include, see Dippers*.

MULTIBEAN SALAD

This tangy concoction doubles as a vegetable . . .

1 buffet can green lima beans, drained

1 1-pound can yellow wax beans, drained

1 1-pound can green beans, drained

1 1-pound can kidney beans, drained and rinsed

1 buffet can garbanzos, drained

1 large onion, sliced in rings

1 green pepper, sliced in rings

Combine vegetables in a bowl. Cover with a marinade of:

1 cup salad oil

1¼ cups salad vinegar

Dash liquid pepper

½ teaspoon salt or to taste

1 clove garlic, pressed

1½ teaspoons sugar or to taste (optional)

1 tablespoon onion juice

2 teaspoons salad mustard

This salad should be refrigerated at least 24 hours with occasional stirrings before serving. Serves 12–14.

Note: To serve 8, use all buffet-size cans. This salad is excellent for a buffet, barbecue, or cookout. It will keep well for several days.

Variations

MULTIBEAN HERB SALAD

Omit salad mustard. Add to marinade mixture:

⅓ teaspoon each oregano, sweet basil, thyme, and rosemary

QUICK MULTIBEAN SALAD

Omit onion and green pepper rings.

BEAN PARMESAN SALAD

Add to the marinade mixture:

⅔ *cup grated Parmesan cheese*

SWEET AND TART BEAN SALAD

Add to the marinade mixture:

¼ *cup sugar*

MAIN DISH BEAN SALAD

Add to any of the variations:

2 *cups chunks cooked ham*

BEAN MEDLEY SALAD

Omit onion and green pepper rings. Use all buffet-size cans. Add to the salad mixture ½ cup *each* of the following:

Raw carrots, thinly sliced   Stuffed green olives
* diagonally   Thinly sliced dill or*
Raw cauliflower slices   sweet pickle
Pitted ripe olives   Cocktail onions

BEAN MUSHROOM SALAD

Substitute two 6-ounce cans drained button mushrooms for the lima beans and garbanzos.

TAVERN SALAD

Add to the salad mixture:

1 *cup cubed sharp Cheddar cheese*

BEAN SALAD ROSARITA

Substitute 1 cup chopped and drained ripe firm tomatoes for the lima beans. Add to the combined mixtures:

1 teaspoon chili powder
1 cup roasted pine nuts

WESTERN BEAN SALAD

Substitute 1 buffet can drained Mexicorn for the lima beans. Add to the marinade:

1 tablespoon minced capers

CREAMY BEAN SALAD

Omit marinade. Add to the bean mixture:

4 mashed anchovies
(optional)
1 cup commercial sour
cream

1 cup mayonnaise
2 tablespoons tarragon
vinegar

AVOCADOS SIERRA

Avocados go with so many goodies . . .

4 firm ripe avocados
Filling (see variations)

Halve avocados, remove pit, and peel. Dip in lemon juice, covering all surfaces, to avoid discoloration. Place avocado halves on nests of crisp greens and fill cavities generously with any of the variant combinations. Serves 8.

Note: Fillings may be prepared in advance. Avocados should be peeled near serving time, filled, and refrigerated. Avocados left unpeeled and served in their own shell may be prepared well in advance of serving time. Brush cut surface with lemon juice. For smaller portions, quarter avocados and fill. Salad dressings of your choice may be substituted for suggested dressings. Add enough salad dressing to the filling mixtures to bind. Garnish with additional dressing.

Variations

SEAFOOD FILLING

2¼ cups chopped shrimp,   Dash liquid pepper
crab, lobster, tuna,   Salt to taste
or whitefish
¼ cup each minced
celery and minced raw
mushrooms

Serve with Russian Cream*, Chutney Cream*, Curry Cream*, or French Curry Dressing*.

MEAT FILLING

2¼ cups diced cooked   2 tablespoons chopped
beef, pork, veal, ham,   dill pickle
corned beef, or salami   2 tablespoons chopped
¼ cup shredded sharp   green onion, including
Cheddar cheese   tops

Serve with Dill Cream*, Russian Cream*, Horseradish Cream*, or Tangy French* dressing.

POULTRY FILLING

2 cups diced cooked   ¼ cup pineapple tidbits
chicken or turkey   or chopped apple
¼ cup chopped water   ¼ cup diced toasted
chestnuts   almonds

Serve with Curry Cream*, Honey-Lemon Cream*, Fruit*, Cointreau*, or Soy* dressing.

EGG FILLING

2 cups chopped
hard-cooked eggs
¼ cup chopped raw
mushrooms
¼ cup crisp bacon
crumbles, salami slivers,
or ham bits

¼ cup minced celery,
olives, pimiento, or
green pepper
1 tablespoon grated onion
1 teaspoon salad
mustard

Serve with Basic Cream*, Creamy Herb*, Russian Cream*, or
Horseradish Cream* dressing.

FRUIT FILLING

Use 2½ to 3 cups of any of the following fresh, canned, or
frozen fruits in any combination. Choose a complementary
dressing from Basic Cream Dressing* or Basic French Dressing*
or their variants.

apples
apricots
bananas
berries
cherries
grapefruit
grapes
guavas
mandarin oranges

maraschino cherries
melon
oranges
peaches
pears
persimmons
pineapple
raisins

Approximately ¼ cup celery, cucumber, coconut, nuts, slivered
candied ginger, grated cheese, or mixed candied fruit may be
used with fruit combinations.

VEGETABLE FILLING

Use 2½ to 3 cups raw, crisp-cooked, or canned vegetables in any
combination. Choose a complementary dressing from Basic
Cream* or Basic French* dressing or their variants.

SOME ARE HEARTY . . .

RICE SALAD

A main dish, a barbecue accompaniment, or the darling of the buffet . . .

1 7-ounce package precooked rice
2 cups boiling bouillon, beef or chicken
2 tablespoons butter
1 10-ounce package crisp-cooked frozen peas
1 cup chopped celery
1 cup button mushrooms
1 cup chopped green pepper

½ cup chopped green onions, including tops
2 tablespoons chopped parsley
3 tablespoons minced pimiento
¼ cup slivered raw carrots
½ cup sliced ripe olives

Add rice to bouillon and butter. Cover for 5 minutes, stir, and set aside to cool. Combine remaining ingredients, cover with a damp cloth or paper towel, and refrigerate. Make a dressing of:

1 cup mayonnaise
1 cup commercial sour cream
¼ teaspoon each sweet basil and thyme

3 tablespoons cream or dry sherry wine
1 tablespoon Worcestershire sauce
Salt and pepper to taste

Gently fold half of the dressing into the cooled rice and refrigerate for several hours. Add the remaining salad dressing to the rice, and combine carefully with the chilled vegetables. Pile lightly into serving dish and decorate as desired. Refrigerate until serving time. Serves 12.

Note: This salad may be decorated with sliced, hard-cooked egg, pimiento or green pepper strips, whole olives, slices of unpeeled cucumber, radish roses, whole toasted almonds, or whole cherry tomatoes. The rice-dressing mixture can be refrigerated overnight, and the vegetables added early in the day.

Variations

CHICKEN RICE SALAD

Reduce celery, green pepper, and peas to ½ cup each. Add:

3 cups diced cooked chicken

Add mayonnaise thinned with dry sherry wine if additional dressing is needed.

CHICKEN FRUIT SALAD

Add to Chicken Rice Salad*.

1 cup pineapple tidbits

ORIENTAL RICE SALAD

Omit carrots and pimiento from salad mixture. Substitute 1 teaspoon curry powder and ¼ teaspoon ginger for the sweet basil and thyme in the dressing mixture.

ROYAL RICE SALAD

Add to Oriental Rice Salad* recipe:

1½ cups chopped cooked crab, shrimp, or lobster

GREEN PEA AND CHEESE SALAD

It's crisp, crunchy, and can double as a vegetable . . .

4 10-ounce packages
frozen green peas
½ cup water
Salt to taste
1 teaspoon sugar
½ cup salad oil
¼ cup red wine vinegar
1 tablespoon minced
fresh mint leaves
2 tablespoons grated
onion
½ cup chopped water
chestnuts

¼ cup chopped sweet
pickle
2 cups diced sharp
Cheddar cheese
½ cup chopped toasted
almonds
½ cup mayonnaise
⅔ cup commercial sour
cream
1 cup thinly sliced
celery (optional)

Cook peas with water, salt, and sugar until peas are just heated through. Drain, reserving ¼ cup of liquid. Combine liquid with oil, vinegar, mint leaves, and grated onion. Pour over peas and marinate in refrigerator 24 hours, stirring occasionally. Shortly before serving, drain peas and combine with water chestnuts, pickle, cheese, almonds, mayonnaise, sour cream, and celery. If the dressing needs thinning, add a bit of marinade. Refrigerate until serving time. Serves 14–16.

Note: Sweet basil or rosemary may be substituted for the mint.

Variations

GREEN PEA AND MUSHROOM SALAD

Substitute 2 cups drained marinated button mushrooms for the cheese.

GREEN PEA AND ONION SALAD

Substitute 2 cups canned pearl onions for the cheese.

GREEN PEA-NUT SALAD

Omit cheese, celery, water chestnuts, and mint. Substitute ¾ cup of your favorite creamy French salad dressing for the sour cream. Reserve mayonnaise for garnish. Substitute 3 cups diced walnuts for the almonds.

SWISS GREEN PEA SALAD

Substitute 2 cups diced Swiss cheese for the Cheddar cheese. Garnish salad bowl with crisp bacon crumbles.

CORNED BEEF SALAD

A colorful meal-in-a-salad . . .

1 12-ounce can corned beef	¼ cup grated onion
1½ cups diced cooked potatoes	4 hard-cooked eggs, chopped
1½ cups diced celery	1½ cups Tangy French Dressing*
1 cup diced green pepper	Lettuce

Remove any gristle and fat from corned beef, shred, and combine with remaining ingredients. Refrigerate overnight. Serve on lettuce. Garnish with sieved hard-cooked egg if desired. Serves 8–10.

Note: The dressing is absorbed as the salad stands. Add additional dressing before serving if necessary.

Variations

CORNED BEEF SLAW

Substitute 1½ cups shredded cabbage for the potatoes and Chutney Cream* for the Tangy French Dressing*. Add:

⅓ cup sliced stuffed green olives

MURPHY'S SPECIAL SALAD

Substitute 1½ cups slivered raw carrots for the celery and Basic French Dressing* for the Tangy French Dressing*. Add:

⅓ cup chopped sweet pickle

CHOP SUEY SALAD

Substitute 2 cups cubed cooked pork for the corned beef and 1½ cups rinsed and drained kidney beans for the potatoes. Use 2 cups drained bean sprouts instead of the green pepper and Soy Dressing* for the Tangy French Dressing*. Add:

¼ cup each diced pimiento and sweet pickle

Marinate the bean sprouts in Soy Dressing* several hours before combining with remaining ingredients.

MEAL-IN-A-DISH SALAD

Substitute ½ cup chopped salami and ⅔ cup diced sharp Cheddar cheese for the corned beef and Roquefort Cream* for the Tangy French Dressing*. Add:

½ cup each shredded cabbage and slivered toasted almonds

HAM SALAD DELUXE

Substitute 2 cups chopped cooked ham for the corned beef and Horseradish Cream* for the Tangy French Dressing*. Add:

¼ cup minced dill pickle

MARJ'S SAUERKRAUT SALAD

As Marj says—it tastes much better than it looks. It's delicious . . .

2 cups sauerkraut, drained
½ cup sugar
½ cup thinly sliced celery
½ cup thinly sliced green
  pepper

1 cup shredded carrots
½ cup chopped onion

Cut sauerkraut in short pieces with scissors. Add sugar and let stand for 30 minutes. Add remaining ingredients. Cover bowl tightly and refrigerate at least 12 hours. Serves 8.

Note: This salad will keep in the refrigerator for a week.

Variations

SAUERKRAUT SALAD HELGA

Substitute ½ cup each cucumber and chopped raw apple for the carrots. Garnish with commercial sour cream.

SAUERKRAUT SALAD SURPRISE

Omit sugar and shredded carrots. Reduce sauerkraut to 1 cup. Add:

2 small cooked potatoes,
  diced
2 cooked carrots, diced
2 cooked beets, diced

2 hard-cooked eggs,
  diced
1 dill pickle, diced

Do not overcook vegetables. Chill all ingredients. Toss lightly with 1¼ cups mayonnaise. Garnish with chopped hard-cooked egg.

GERMAN POTATO SALAD

Super with corned beef or baked ham . . .

½ cup diced bacon
½ cup chopped onion
1 clove garlic, pressed
1 tablespoon flour
1 teaspoon salt or to taste
¼ teaspoon liquid pepper
1½ teaspoons sugar
½ cup white wine vinegar

½ cup bouillon
8 medium potatoes, cooked and diced
½ teaspoon celery seed
3 tablespoons minced parsley
1 egg white, slightly beaten

Fry bacon until crisp. Add onion and garlic and cook 1 minute. Add flour, salt, pepper, and sugar, then vinegar mixed with bouillon. Simmer 5 minutes, stirring constantly. Pour over sliced potatoes. Add celery seed and parsley. Toss gently. Add egg white and combine gently. Serve warm. Serves 8.

Note: Potatoes must not be overcooked. This salad may be made ahead and reheated in a covered baking dish at 300 degrees for approximately 25 minutes.

Variations

GERMAN POTATO SALAD MINCHEN

Substitute ½ cup sauterne wine for the bouillon and 2 cups commercial sour cream for the egg white. Garnish with sliced hard-cooked eggs.

GUSTY GERMAN POTATO SALAD

Substitute ½ cup beer for the bouillon. Add to the simmering mixture:

½ teaspoon dry mustard

FANCY GERMAN POTATO SALAD

Add to the simmering mixture:

⅓ *cup* each *diced green pepper and diced celery*

HOT BEAN SALAD

Omit egg white. Substitute 2 No. 2 cans rinsed and drained kidney beans for the potatoes. Add to the simmering mixture:

¼ *cup sweet pickle relish*
1 *teaspoon chili powder*

Top with 1 cup coarsely crushed corn chips. Garnish with green pepper rings.

SOME WILL DOUBLE AS DESSERTS . . .

FROZEN FRUIT SALAD

The cream cheese tempers the sweetness and highlights the flavor . . .

2 3-ounce packages
   softened cream cheese
½ cup mayonnaise
2 tablespoons lemon juice
2 tablespoons sugar
¼ teaspoon salt
½ cup chopped pecans
1½ cups miniature
   marshmallows
1 No. 2 can crushed
   pineapple, drained

½ cup quartered
   maraschino cherries
1 11-ounce can mandarin
   oranges, drained and
   chopped
1 cup heavy cream,
   whipped
1 teaspoon vanilla

Blend cream cheese, mayonnaise, lemon juice, sugar, and salt. Add nuts, marshmallows, and fruits. Fold in the whipped cream flavored with vanilla. Place in ice cube trays. Freeze until firm, preferably overnight. Serves 10.

Note: One No. 2 can drained fruit cocktail may be substituted for the pineapple. Walnuts may be used instead of pecans. During the Yule season ¼ cup each of red and green cherries will carry out the color scheme.

Variations

FROZEN EGGNOG SALAD

Substitute 3 tablespoons bourbon whisky for the lemon juice and vanilla and ½ cup candied mixed fruit for the maraschino cherries. Add:

½ teaspoon nutmeg

FROZEN STRAWBERRY SALAD

Omit maraschino cherries. Substitute 2 cups drained frozen strawberries for the mandarin oranges.

FROZEN RASPBERRY SALAD

Omit maraschino cherries. Substitute 2 cups drained canned or frozen raspberries for the mandarin oranges.

FROZEN CRANBERRY SALAD

Omit maraschino cherries. Substitute one 1-pound can whole cranberry sauce for the mandarin oranges.

HEAVENLY 24-HOUR SALAD

This must be refrigerated overnight . . .

1 cup seedless grapes
1 cup fresh or canned
pineapple tidbits
1 cup pitted cherries
1 cup chopped mandarin
orange sections
1 cup cantaloupe or
watermelon balls
¼ cup maraschino cherry
halves

½ cup chopped dates
⅔ cup pecan halves
2 cups miniature
marshmallows
2 cups commercial sour
cream
2 tablespoons sugar
2 teaspoons vanilla
1 banana, sliced
diagonally

Combine fruits (except banana), nuts, and marshmallows. Combine sour cream, sugar, and vanilla, and combine with fruit. Fold banana slices in gently to avoid breaking. Refrigerate 24 hours. Stir gently once before placing in serving dish. Refrigerate until serving time. Decorate with mint or geranium leaves if desired. Serves 10–12.

Note: For a sharper flavor, add lemon juice to taste to the sour cream mixture.

Variations

CHICO'S FRUIT SALAD

Substitute 2 cups chopped raw unpeeled apple for the melon balls and cherries.

TROPICAL FRUIT SALAD

Substitute for the cherries and watermelon balls one 9-ounce can drained chopped mangoes and 1 cup canned chopped papaya chunks. Mangoes and papayas are available in gourmet food sections.

FROZEN ISLANDS   COQ

These are easy treats . . .

Freeze a can of pears. At serving time remove contents from the can, slice, and serve with Fruit Dressing* or Sour-Sweet Cream*. Sprinkle with nuts of your choice. Serves 4–6.

Note: For a less sweet salad, choose fruit packed in light syrup. Serve on greens or garnish with watercress.

Variations

PEACH ISLANDS   COQ

Substitute canned peaches *or* canned snow peaches for the pears. Serve with Ginger Cream*. (Snow peaches are a delicate white peach from Japan. They are available in gourmet food sections.)

COT ISLANDS   COQ

Substitute canned apricots for the pears. Serve with Orange Cream*. Sprinkle with chopped pistachio nuts.

TROPICAL ISLANDS   COQ

Substitute canned fruit cocktail *or* canned fruits for salad for the pears. Serve with Sherry Cream* or Rum Cream*. Sprinkle with chopped macadamia nuts or slivered candied ginger.

PORCUPINES   COQ

Start with a can of pears . . .

Fill cavities of drained canned pear halves with a mixture of softened cream cheese and chopped nuts of your choice. Place cut side down on a nest of greens. Frost with softened cream cheese mixed with milk to a spreading consistency. Stick frosted pear half generously with toasted almond spears. Place a whole maraschino cherry at the small pear end. Allow one pear half per serving.

Note: These salads will double as desserts. Drain pears well before frosting.

Variations

GRAPE CLUSTERS

Omit almond spears. Cover frosted pear halves with halved seedless or seeded grapes. Place grape halves as close together as possible to resemble a cluster. Use a strip of candied citron rind or green pepper at the large pear end for the stem.

SNOW CHERRIES   COQ

Substitute peach halves for the pear halves. Omit almonds. Decorate frosted peach halves with whole maraschino cherries with the stems on.

JACK-O'-LANTERNS   COQ

Substitute peach halves for the pear halves. Omit almonds and cheese frosting. Make jack-o'-lantern faces with pieces of candied fruit mix.

CHRISTMAS TREES

Omit almonds. Place stuffed pear halves wide end down. Mold a small piece of cream cheese to form a tree point at the top of the small end. The shape should be triangular. Tint the cheese frosting green with food coloring, and coat the pears. Sprinkle with coconut which also has been tinted green. Decorate the pear tree with bits of candied fruit mix or gumdrop pieces.

SNOWBALLS   COQ

Omit almonds. Substitute peach halves for the pear halves. When peach cavities are filled, press two halves together to form a ball before frosting. Coat with coconut if you wish.

FROSTY BALLS

Follow Snowball* recipe. Omit cream cheese frosting. Frost with the following:

Beat 2 egg whites; gradually beat in ¼ cup powdered sugar. When glossy and firm but not dry, fold in 1 tablespoon mayonnaise, 1 tablespoon commercial sour cream, and 1 teaspoon vanilla. This will frost 6 balls.

BUTTERFLIES   COQ

Omit almonds and frosting mixture. Substitute 1 slice pineapple for each pear half. Drain pineapple well. Split each slice and reverse it so that the outer edges are placed 1 inch apart. Form the butterfly body between the halves with the cheese-nut mixture. Decorate pineapple halves with sliced stuffed green olives to resemble wings. Use candied citron slices or green pepper slices for the antennas.

CANDLES

Omit almonds and cheese-nut mixture. Substitute ½ banana for each pear half. Dip bananas in lemon juice to prevent discoloration. Stand banana cut side down in a pineapple slice holder. Dribble cheese frosting mixture over pointed end of banana to simulate melting wax. Top with a whole maraschino cherry for the flame.

BANANA SPLITS

Omit almonds. Substitute 1 small banana, split lengthwise, for the pears. Dip bananas in lemon juice to prevent discoloration. Make enough cheese-almond mixture to form 3 small mounds on the split banana. Top each mound with a different chopped drained fruit (pineapple, mandarin oranges, peaches, berries, etc.), and dribble frosting mixture over the fruit for cream. Sprinkle with chopped nuts. Top with maraschino cherries. Cottage cheese may be substituted for the cheese-almond mixture if you wish.

SOME ARE MOLDED . . .

About Getting Them in the Mold—and Out

If you don't already know them, here are some helpful scraps of information about the molding and unmolding of gelatins. Make a molded design by pouring a very thin layer of the gelatin liquid into a well-oiled metal mold and refrigerate until firm. Arrange your design on the firm gelatin, then carefully spoon enough cool liquid gelatin over it to cover. Refrigerate again until firm. The mold then may be filled with cool gelatin. If the mixture has become too firm to pour, stand it briefly in a pan of warm water and stir it a bit. Wait until the gelatin mixture has thickened slightly before adding solids or some will float, some will sink, and none will stay where they're supposed to be. Never include fresh pineapple unless you are prepared to eat the concoction with a spoon. Uncooked pineapple contains an enzyme that prevents gelatin from setting.

To unmold gelatins, dip a small pointed knife in warm water and rim the upper edge of the mold. This will break the seal and start things off auspiciously. Dip the mold almost to the top in tepid (*not* hot) water ever so briefly, then remove. Shake the mold gently. With a bit of luck, you're almost home free. Lay the serving plate over the top of the mold, grip them together firmly, and invert. The mold should lift right off. If it doesn't, cover it with a warm damp cloth for a few seconds, and try again. Repeat the warm damp cloth bit if necessary, but easy does it, or the gelatin melts and runs, the molded design slides, and need I say more? If both the surface of the gelatin and the serving plate are moistened with water, the mold will slide for easy centering. I mention this only because some molds have been known to make forced landings, in which case they promptly glue themselves to that spot forever.

CHICKEN CREAM MOLD

Keeps beautifully—is versatile, rich, and festive . . .

2 envelopes unflavored
  gelatin
2¼ cups chicken broth,
  divided
3 tablespoons grated
  onion
2 tablespoons
  Worcestershire sauce
1 tablespoon lemon juice
Dash liquid pepper
Salt to taste
¼ teaspoon paprika

2½ cups diced cooked
  chicken
½ cup toasted slivered
  almonds
¼ cup sliced ripe olives
¼ cup thinly sliced celery
½ cup mayonnaise
1½ cups commercial
  sour cream
2 tablespoons dry sherry
  wine

Sprinkle gelatin in 1 cup chicken broth to soften, then heat slowly until gelatin is dissolved. Add remaining chicken broth, onion, Worcestershire, lemon juice, pepper, salt, and paprika. Chill until slightly thickened. Fold in remaining ingredients. Pour into oiled 2-quart mold or loaf pan. Refrigerate. Early in the day, unmold on serving plate and garnish with salad greens. Refrigerate until serving time. Serves 10–12.

Note: Whole cherry tomatoes with stems placed among the garnish greens make a festive touch.

Variations

CHICKEN PINEAPPLE MOLD

Reduce chicken to 2 cups. Add:

½ *cup well-drained crushed pineapple*

HAM-CHICKEN MOLD

Substitute 1 cup chopped cooked ham for 1 cup chicken. Add:

1 *teaspoon prepared horseradish*

HAM MOLD

Omit sherry. Substitute 2½ cups chopped cooked ham for the chicken and ¼ cup sliced stuffed green olives for the ripe olives. Add:

2 *teaspoons prepared table mustard*
1 *teaspoon prepared horseradish*

SEAFOOD MOLD

Substitute 2½ cups chopped cooked seafood of your choice for the chicken and ¼ cup slivered green pepper for the olives. Add:

½ *cup hot catsup (optional)*

CHICKEN NICKI

Omit olives, Worcestershire sauce, and lemon juice. Increase sherry wine to ¼ cup. Add:

1 *teaspoon ground ginger*
1 *tablespoon soy sauce*
¼ *cup halved seedless grapes*

CHICKEN AVOCADO MOLD

Reduce chicken to 2 cups. Add:

2 *cups mashed avocado pulp*
1 *teaspoon chili powder or to taste*

Use a 2½-quart mold.

AVOCADO SHRIMP MOLD

Substitute 2 cups chopped cooked shrimp for the chicken. Add:

2 *cups mashed avocado pulp*
½ *teaspoon dillweed*

SEAFOAM CRAB

Substitute 2½ cups chopped cooked crab for the chicken, ¼ cup minced green pepper for the olives, and 1½ cups heavy cream, whipped and salted, for the sour cream (fold this in last). Use a 2½-quart mold.

WALDORF CHICKEN

Omit olives. Increase celery to ½ cup. Reduce chicken to 2 cups. Add:

3 *tart unpeeled apples, cored and chopped*

Use a 2½-quart mold.

MIDAS CHICKEN

Omit olives and celery. Reduce chicken to 2 cups. Add:

½ *cup grated raw carrots*
⅓ *cup drained crushed pineapple*
⅓ *cup chopped mandarin oranges*

CHICKEN VEGETABLE MOLD

Omit olives and almonds. Add:

1 cup cooked mixed vegetables

SHRIMP SLAW ASPIC

Omit almonds and celery. Substitute 2 cups chopped cooked shrimp for the chicken. Increase lemon juice to ¼ cup. Add:

1 cup finely chopped cabbage
1 cup grated carrots

Decorate unmolded salad with an additional ½ cup shrimp. Use half red cabbage for Christmas. Use a 2½-quart mold.

TOMATO-BASIL ASPIC

The spices make this an aristocratic aspic . . .

2 envelopes unflavored
gelatin
½ cup cold water
3 cups boiling water
¼ cup sweet basil vinegar
Generous dash liquid
pepper
2 tablespoons onion
juice

1 tablespoon
Worcestershire sauce
1 teaspoon salt or to
taste
1 teaspoon sugar or to
taste
1 6-ounce can tomato
paste

Soften gelatin in cold water. Add boiling water and other ingredients. Pour in oiled 6-cup mold or a loaf pan. Refrigerate. Serves 12.

Note: This aspic keeps well for 2 or 3 days. Early in the day it should be unmolded, frosted with the following dressing, and refrigerated until serving time. Garnish with greens.

Dressing

1 cup mayonnaise
2 teaspoons tarragon vinegar
½ teaspoon sweet basil leaves crushed to a powder

Combine and let stand overnight before using.

Variations

TOMATO-SHERRY ASPIC

Omit liquid pepper. Reduce boiling water to 2¼ cups. Substitute 1 cup dry sherry wine for the sweet basil vinegar and 1 tablespoon lemon juice for the Worcestershire sauce. In the dressing omit the tarragon vinegar and sweet basil. Add:

2 teaspoons dry sherry wine
½ teaspoon grated lemon rind

TOMATO-CLAM ASPIC

Reduce boiling water to 2 cups. Add:

1 cup clam juice

VINTAGE ASPIC

Reduce boiling water to 1 cup. Add:

⅓ cup Roka cheese spread (blend into hot water-gelatin mixture)
1½ cups canned vegetable juice cocktail
¾ cup dry white wine

HELENE'S MELON ASPIC

These salads double as desserts . . .

2 3-ounce packages
watermelon-flavored
gelatin

1½ cups boiling water

1¾ cups cold ginger ale

6 ounces softened cream
cheese

1 tablespoon slivered
candied ginger

1½ cups small watermelon
balls

½ cup halved seedless
grapes

⅔ cup chopped pecans

1 cup commercial sour
cream

1 tablespoon sugar

1 teaspoon vanilla

Dissolve gelatin in boiling water. Add ginger ale and set aside. Cream the softened cheese and blend in 1½ cups of the gelatin mixture. Refrigerate until slightly thickened. Add ginger to the remaining gelatin mixture. Set in freezer or a pan of ice cubes until slightly thickened. Add watermelon balls and grapes, and pour into an oiled 2-quart mold. Refrigerate until firm. Fold the pecans into the cheese-gelatin mixture and pour or spoon over the gelatin in the mold. Refrigerate overnight. Before serving, unmold and frost with a mixture of the sour cream, sugar, and vanilla. Serves 8.

Note: The frosted mold may be decorated with additional slivered ginger and pecan halves. Substitute ½ cup mayonnaise for ½ cup sour cream in the frosting mixture if you prefer.

Variations

VINTAGE MELON MOLD

Substitute for the ginger ale 1 cup muscatel wine, ½ cup orange juice, and ¼ cup lemon juice.

SHIMMERING PINEAPPLE

Substitute 2 packages lemon gelatin for the watermelon gelatin and 1½ cups pineapple tidbits for the melon balls.

ORANGE ASPIC MANDARIN

Substitute 2 packages lemon gelatin for the watermelon gelatin and 1½ cups mandarin orange slices for the melon balls.

GOLDEN TROPICS MOLD

Substitute 2 packages lemon gelatin for the watermelon gelatin and 1 cup unsweetened pineapple tidbits (packed in pure pineapple juice) and ½ cup chopped preserved kumquats for the melon balls. The pineapple, which tastes quite like fresh fruit, is in the market dietetic section; the kumquats are in the gourmet section.

CLEAR ASPIC JELLY

These molds are based on a jelly made with unflavored, unsweetened gelatin and flavored stock. A clear shimmering aspic is the basis for many mouth-watering food combinations . . .

Basic Recipe

2 envelopes unflavored
  gelatin
¼ cup cold water
3¼ cups seasoned meat
  or poultry stock

2 tablespoons of any one:
  lemon juice, vinegar,
  Worcestershire sauce,
  onion juice, dry sherry
  wine, dry white wine,
  extra dry vermouth, or
  brandy
Ingredients as called for in
  variant recipes

Soften gelatin in cold water. Add to 1 cup hot stock and stir until dissolved. Add remaining stock and liquid seasoning. Strain through a clean cloth. Before adding solid ingredients called for in variant recipes, refrigerate aspic until slightly thickened. Refrigerate aspics overnight before unmolding. Basic recipe serves 8.

Note: Canned stock may be used in these recipes.

Variations

CLEAR WINE ASPIC

Substitute 1 cup wines listed in basic recipe for 1 cup stock.

VEAL ASPIC

On the bottom of an oiled 9×5×3-inch pan arrange:

½ cup each sliced pimiento and sliced green pepper
3 hard-cooked eggs, sliced

Spoon on aspic to cover, refrigerate until firm, and cover with 1½ cups cool aspic. Chill. Fold 4 cups diced cooked veal into remaining partially thickened mixture. Pour into mold and refrigerate. Serve with Horseradish Cream Dressing*. Serves 10–12.

Note: Poultry, ham, beef, pork, or tongue may be substituted for the veal.

HORSERADISH MOUSSE

Use Clear Wine Aspic* made with dry white wine and onion juice. Into the slightly thickened aspic fold these combined ingredients:

1½ cups heavy cream, whipped and salted
½ cup prepared horseradish or to taste

Pour into oiled 2-quart mold. Serves 10–12.

CORNED BEEF PARTY MOLD

Use Basic Recipe* with lemon juice. Pour ½ cup aspic into an oiled 3-quart mold and refrigerate. For the first mold layer, combine the following ingredients and add to 2½ cups slightly thickened aspic:

2½ cups shredded green
  cabbage
1 cup drained crushed
  pineapple

½ cup each *mayonnaise
  and commercial sour
  cream*
½ teaspoon salt or to
  taste

Pour mixture into mold and refrigerate. When firm spread with a mixture of:

2 cups *flaked corned
  beef, gristle and fat
  removed*
1 teaspoon *prepared
  horseradish*

2 tablespoons each *grated
  onion and minced
  parsley*
2 teaspoons *prepared
  mustard*
½ cup *mayonnaise*

Spoon over enough cool aspic to cover. Refrigerate until firm. Cover with remaining aspic mixture. Garnish with mixed greens and cherry tomatoes. Serve with Tangy French Dressing* or Poppy Seed Dressing*. Serves 14–16.

BARBECUED BEAN MOLD

Use Clear Wine Aspic* made with dry white wine and Worcestershire sauce. Pour 1 cup aspic into an oiled 2-quart mold and refrigerate until firm. To the remaining partially thickened aspic add these combined ingredients:

2 1-pound cans
  barbecued beans, very
  well drained
Dash liquid pepper

2 tablespoons brown
  sugar or to taste
1 6-ounce can tomato
  paste

HAM SUPPER SALAD

Use Clear Wine Aspic* made with extra dry vermouth and onion juice. Make a design of sliced stuffed green olives in the bottom of an oiled 2-quart mold. Spoon over aspic to cover and refrigerate. When firm cover with 1 cup cool aspic and refrigerate. To the remaining partially thickened aspic add:

3 cups diced cooked ham
¼ cup each minced celery and minced green pepper

Pour into mold. Serves 10–12.

VEGETABLE PATCH ASPIC

Use Basic Recipe* made with onion juice or extra dry vermouth. Pour ⅔ cup aspic into an oiled 2-quart mold and refrigerate until firm. Into the remainder of the slightly thickened aspic fold 3 cups cooked or raw vegetable pieces (shredded carrots, beets, green peppers; cooked frozen mixed vegetables; chopped red or green cabbage, etc.). For additional flavor add chopped cheese, olives, pimiento, or green onion. Pour mixture into mold. Serves 10–12.

ARTICHOKE-PIMIENTO ASPIC

Use Basic Recipe* made with onion juice. Pour 1 cup aspic in an oiled 2-quart mold and refrigerate until set. To the remaining partially thickened aspic add:

2 cups well-drained and coarsely chopped marinated artichoke hearts
1 4-ounce jar pimientos, chopped

1 clove garlic, pressed
3 green onions, including tops, chopped

Pour into mold. Serves 10–12.

FLAVORED GELATIN MOLDS

These molds are based on a jelly made with sweetened, flavored gelatin . . .

Basic Recipe

2 3-ounce packages   2¼ cups cold liquid
  flavored gelatin   Salt to taste
1½ cups boiling water

Dissolve gelatin in boiling water. Add cold liquid. Chill until slightly thickened before adding ingredients called for in variant recipes. Pour into oiled mold, and refrigerate overnight. Unmold, decorate, and refrigerate until serving time.

Note: Some of these salads double as desserts.

Variations

ELLIE'S CRANBERRY MOLD

Use 2 packages raspberry gelatin. Use 1¼ cups port wine and 1 cup ginger ale for the cold liquid. To the slightly thickened mixture add these combined ingredients:

1 1-pound can whole cranberry sauce, mashed with a fork
2 cups well-drained crushed pineapple
1 cup each chopped celery and chopped walnuts

Pour into oiled 2½-quart mold. Frost the unmolded salad with a mixture of:

1 cup commercial sour cream
1 tablespoon sugar
1 teaspoon grated orange rind

Sprinkle with chopped nuts. Serves 12–14.

GOLDEN MEDLEY CREAM

Use 2 packages lemon gelatin. Use 1¼ cups ginger ale and 1 cup dry sherry wine for the cold liquid. Blend two 3-ounce packages softened cream cheese into the warm gelatin mixture. When the gelatin has slightly thickened, add:

1 cup candied fruit mix	½ cup chopped dates
¼ cup chopped preserved kumquats	⅔ cup chopped pecans

Pour into oiled 2-quart mold. Serve with Ginger Cream*. Serves 10–12.

BETH'S GOOSEBERRY SALAD

Use 2 packages lime gelatin. Use 1 cup cold water, 1 tablespoon lemon juice, and syrup from the gooseberries for the cold liquid. To the slightly thickened mixture add:

1 1-pound can gooseberries	⅔ cup chopped pecans
½ cup minced celery	
½ cup grated mild Cheddar cheese	

Use an oiled 2-quart mold or 9×13-inch pan. Serves 10–12.

BLAINE'S LIME MOLD

Use 2 packages lime gelatin. Use ½ cup cold water and syrup from the pineapple for the cold liquid. When the gelatin mixture starts to thicken, whip until frothy. Add the following ingredients:

1 No. 2 can crushed pineapple	1 cup mayonnaise
2 cups farmer-style cottage cheese	½ cup chopped pecans
1 tablespoon prepared horseradish	Juice from 1 lemon

Use an oiled 2½-quart mold. Serves 12–14.

FAR WEST SALAD

Use 2 packages lemon gelatin. Substitute 2¾ cups hot tomato juice for the boiling water. Use 1 cup extra dry vermouth for the cold liquid. Add these combined ingredients to the slightly thickened mixture:

1 cup sliced stuffed green olives *½ teaspoon each liquid pepper and chili powder*	*2 tablespoons lemon juice* *2 large avocados, chopped*

Use an oiled 2-quart mold. Serves 10–12.

AVOCADO CREAM MOLD

Use 2 packages lime gelatin. Increase boiling water to 3 cups. Use ¾ cup dry sherry wine for the cold liquid. Add the following ingredients:

2 3-ounce packages softened cream cheese *1 cup mayonnaise* *2 tablespoons grated onion*	*2 tablespoons lemon juice* *2 large avocados, mashed*

Whip the slightly thickened gelatin mixture until frothy. Cream the cheese and mayonnaise together and add along with the other ingredients. Use an oiled 2-quart mold. Serves 10–12.

STRAWBERRY-PINEAPPLE CREST

Use 1 package each strawberry and pineapple gelatin. Dissolve each separately in 1 cup boiling water. Add to the cooled but unthickened strawberry gelatin mixture:

½ cup rosé wine
1 10-ounce package thawed frozen sliced strawberries

Place in an oiled 2-quart mold and chill. Add to the pineapple gelatin the juice from 1 No. 2 can crushed pineapple. When cooled fold in 1 cup commercial sour cream. When slightly thickened add:

1 No. 2 can drained crushed pineapple
1 cup chopped pecans

Pour over strawberry layer. Garnish with whipped cream and chopped pecans before serving. Serves 10–12.

MARGARET'S APRICOT CHEESE SALAD

Use 2 packages orange gelatin. Use 1½ cups fruit juice (from canned fruit) for the cold liquid. Add to the thickened mixture:

1 No. 2½ can apricots, drained and chopped
1 No. 2 can crushed pineapple, drained
½ cup sliced maraschino cherries

1 cup miniature marshmallows
½ cup grated mild Cheddar cheese

Place in an oiled 3-quart mold or 9×13-inch pan. Frost before serving with this topping:

3 tablespoons flour
⅓ cup sugar
1 egg, slightly beaten
1 cup cream sherry wine

2 tablespoons butter
1 cup heavy cream, whipped
¼ cup grated Parmesan cheese

Combine flour and sugar in a saucepan. Blend in egg, then wine, and cook over low heat, stirring constantly, until thick. Add butter. Chill. Fold in whipped cream. Spread over salad and sprinkle with Parmesan cheese. Refrigerate until topping is set before serving. Serves 14–16.

GOURMET SALAD BETH

Use 2 packages lemon gelatin. Blend one 3-ounce package softened cream cheese into the warm gelatin. Use 2 cups grapefruit juice for the cold liquid. Add to the slightly thickened mixture:

2 cups mashed or finely chopped persimmons
¼ cup slivered candied ginger
1 cup chopped walnuts

Use an oiled 2-quart mold. Serve with Sherry Cream*. Serves 10–12.

BING SPECIAL SALAD

Use 2 packages cherry gelatin. Blend two 3-ounce packages softened cream cheese into the warm gelatin. Use cherry juice (from canned cherries) and 1 cup port wine for the cold liquid. Add to the thickened gelatin:

1 No. 2½ can pitted bing cherries
1 cup chopped walnuts

Use an oiled 2-quart mold. Serve with Brandy Cream*. Serves 10–12.

JEWELED GRAPEFRUIT MOLD

Use 2 packages lemon gelatin. Use 1¼ cups ginger ale and 1 cup sauterne wine for the cold liquid. Add to the slightly thickened mixture:

2 cups canned grapefruit sections, cut in pieces
1 cup quartered maraschino cherries

Use an oiled 2-quart mold. Serve with Ginger Cream*. Serves 10–12.

PERSIAN PEACH SALAD

Use 2 packages orange gelatin. Use peach juice (from canned peaches), 2 tablespoons wine vinegar, and cold water to make 2¼ cups for the cold liquid. Add to the slightly thickened mixture:

1 No. 2½ can spiced peaches, drained
1 cup pecan halves

Peaches may be used halved, chopped, or sliced to form a molded design. Serves 10–12.

PEACH CHABLIS MOLD

Use 2 packages orange-pineapple gelatin. Use 1 cup lemon-flavored sparkling water and 1¼ cups Chablis wine for the cold liquid. Add to the slightly thickened mixture:

1½ cups peach slices
1½ cups halved seedless grapes

Use some of the peach slices and grapes to make a molded design if you wish. Garnish with cream cheese whipped to the consistency of whipped cream and seasoned with ½ teaspoon of allspice. Use an oiled 2-quart mold. Serves 10–12.

CARDINAL CREAM

Use 2 packages lemon gelatin. Use 1¾ cups beet juice and ¼ cup salad vinegar for the cold liquid. Add to the slightly thickened mixture:

2 tablespoons each grated onion, minced green pepper, and prepared horseradish
1 cup diced celery

2 cups diced cooked beets
½ cup chopped pecans
1½ cups commercial sour cream

Canned beets may be used. Use an oiled 2½-quart mold. Serves 12–14.

PASTAS, RICE, AND CEREALS

. . . If a man will be sensible and one fine morning, while he is lying in bed, count at the tips of his fingers how many things in life truly give him enjoyment, invariably he will find food is the first one.

LIN YUTANG

I SHOULD STATE RIGHT OFF that I am a potato fan, but there are times when a pasta, rice, or cereal dish will serve the cause better, and for several reasons. They keep well, and as regulars on the pantry shelf are johnny-on-the-spot when you need them. Generally speaking, they can be prepared more quickly than uncooked potatoes, they offer interesting variety, and they have toothsome identities of their own. They can be a main dish as well as an accompaniment, and they are great go-alongs with meats from the barbecue. So when you have to come up with something more substantial than tea and fortune cookies in a hurry, or you decide it's time for a change, check these recipes. They will help you to cope.

SOME ARE PASTAS . . .

NOODLES ROMANOFF

The interest comes from the cottage cheese and sour cream . . .

1 8-ounce package egg
noodles
1 cup farmer-style cottage
cheese
1½ cups commercial sour
cream
2 garlic cloves, pressed
¼ cup grated onion

1 tablespoon
Worcestershire sauce
¼ teaspoon liquid pepper
½ teaspoon salt or to
taste
2 tablespoons butter
1 cup grated sharp
Cheddar cheese

Boil noodles in salted water until just tender. Drain and combine gently with remaining ingredients except Cheddar cheese. Place in a buttered baking dish and top with the cheese. Bake uncovered at 350 degrees for 30 minutes. Serves 8.

Note: This dish improves with overnight refrigeration. Grated Parmesan cheese may be substituted for the Cheddar.

Variations

NOODLES WITH CABBAGE

Chop 1 small head green cabbage in 1-inch pieces. Fry until wilted in 4 tablespoons bacon drippings or butter. Combine with noodle mixture. Sprinkle generously with poppy seed before adding cheese topping.

HELEN'S NOODLES

Combine 1 cup crisp bacon crumbles with the noodle mixture.

KRAUT AND NOODLES

Omit salt from cooking water and noodle mixture. Add to the noodle mixture:

2 cups drained chopped sauerkraut

FIDEOS

Omit sour cream. Add to the noodle mixture:

1 tablespoon chili powder   *½ cup minced green*
1 cup sliced ripe olives   *pepper*
1½ cups tomato sauce

NOODLES WITH ALMONDS

Add to the noodle mixture:

1 cup chopped toasted almonds

ROSY NOODLES

Add to the noodle mixture:

1 6-ounce can tomato paste
1 cup sliced mushrooms
½ teaspoon sweet basil

OLD MISS NOODLES

Add to the noodle mixture:

¼ cup chopped pimiento
1½ cups chili sauce
1 pound ground sirloin, simmered and drained

FULL MEAL NOODLES

Add to the noodle mixture:

2 cups chopped cooked ham

ORIENTAL PORK AND NOODLES

Omit cottage cheese, sour cream, Worcestershire sauce, and Cheddar cheese. Use fine noodles. Add to the noodle mixture:

3 cups cooked cubed pork
½ cup sliced (paper thin) celery

½ cup sliced water chestnuts
Soy sauce to taste

BELASCO NOODLES

This is creamy and very rich . . .

1 8-ounce package broad noodles
1 cup Cream Celery Sauce*
1 cup mayonnaise (not salad dressing)
2 tablespoons minced pimiento

2 teaspoons chopped fresh dill
¼ cup grated onion
2 cups coarse garlic-flavored bread crumbs

Boil noodles in salted water until just tender. Combine with remaining ingredients, reserving bread crumbs for topping. Bake at 350 degrees approximately 30 minutes. Serves 8–10.

Note: A shallow baking dish is best for this recipe.

Variations

CREAMY RICH NOODLES

Omit pimiento and dill. Substitute Cream Sauce Mornay* for the Cream Celery Sauce*. Add to the noodle mixture:

1 cup grated Monterey jack cheese (or Swiss cheese)

Toss ¼ cup grated Parmesan cheese with the bread crumbs before topping the noodle mixture.

NOODLES VERDE

Omit pimiento and dill. Use green noodles. Add to the noodle mixture:

2 *tablespoons poppy seed*

HERBED NOODLES

Omit pimiento and dill. Use green or white noodles. Substitute Basic Cream Sauce* for the Cream Celery Sauce*. Add to the noodle mixture:

¼ *teaspoon* each *sweet basil, thyme, savory, and tarragon*

NOODLES FIESTA

Increase pimiento to ¼ cup. Add to the noodle mixture:

½ *cup slivered green pepper*

LASAGNA MIA

The sauce is the main feature here . . .

1 *pound lasagna noodles*
*Del's Spaghetti Sauce**
1 *pound mozzarella*
   cheese, thinly sliced
1 *pound ricotta cheese*

1 *pint commercial sour*
   cream
½ *cup grated Romano*
   or Parmesan cheese

Cook noodles according to package directions. Drain well. Pour a layer of sauce in a shallow 5-quart baking dish. Cover with a layer each of noodles, mozzarella, ricotta, sour cream, and a sprinkle of Romano or Parmesan; continue layering, ending with a top layer of sauce sprinkled with Romano or Parmesan. Bake at 350 degrees for 40 minutes or until hot and bubbly. Serves 10–12.

Note: This dish is much better after an overnight wait in the refrigerator. Cottage cheese may be substituted for the ricotta.

Variations

LASAGNA PROSCIUTTO

Sprinkle each layer of sauce with chopped prosciutto ham, using approximately ⅓ pound ham.

LASAGNA WITH MUSHROOMS

Sprinkle each layer of sauce with chopped or sliced raw mushrooms, using approximately ½ pound mushrooms.

MACARONI AND CHEESE SUPREME   COQ

Macaroni in a hurry . . .

3 1-pound cans macaroni and cheese	½ cup chopped toasted almonds
1 4-ounce can drained ripe olives, sliced	½ cup commercial sour cream
1 cup grated sharp Cheddar cheese	½ cup mayonnaise
	Salt and pepper to taste

Combine all ingredients and pour in buttered baking dish. Bake at 350 degrees 30 minutes. Serves 8.

Note: Part of the cheese may be reserved for topping if you wish.

Variations

MAIN DISH MACARONI   COQ

Layer a 1-pound can of ham or cooked beef, chopped, in the baking dish with the macaroni mixture.

MEAL-IN-A-DISH MACARONI   COQ

Add either in the center or on top of the cheese mixture:

16 precooked sausages or 16 Vienna sausages

MACARONI MARQUITA   COQ

Add to the macaroni mixture:

1 6-ounce can tomato paste
½ teaspoon each sweet basil and oregano

Top with 2 cups crushed corn chips.

MACARONI SACRAMENTO   COQ

Pour half of the macaroni mixture into the baking dish. Add:

2 cups chopped canned chicken

Cover chicken layer with 2 cups chopped avocado pulp mixed with 1 tablespoon lemon juice or 1 buffet can drained asparagus spears. Top with remaining macaroni mixture.

SPAGHETTI MILANO   COQ

Omit almonds, sour cream, and mayonnaise. Substitute 3 1-pounds cans spaghetti in tomato-cheese sauce for the macaroni. Combine the following and simmer 5 minutes:

½ teaspoon each oregano,   *¼ cup each tomato paste*
sweet basil, tarragon,   *and chili sauce*
and garlic powder   *½ cup dry sherry wine*
¼ teaspoon each anise
and rosemary

Combine with the spaghetti mixture. This dish is better if it is refrigerated overnight. Top with Parmesan cheese.

SPAGHETTI SUPPER   COQ

Layer Spaghetti Milano* with 3 cups canned or cooked cubed beef, pork, or ham. Top with a generous layer of grated Parmesan cheese.

SOME ARE RICE . . .

ORIENTAL RICE   COQ

Used canned or precooked rice . . .

¼ cup butter
½ teaspoon curry powder
4 cups cooked rice
⅓ cup chopped parsley

Salt to taste
⅓ cup slivered peanuts
or toasted almonds

Melt butter. Add curry powder. Combine with remaining ingredients. Cover and bake at 350 degrees for approximately 25 minutes. Serves 6–8.

Note: 1 clove pressed garlic may be added to the butter mixture.

Variations

GREEN RICE

Omit curry powder and nuts. Increase parsley to 1 cup. Add:

¼ cup minced onion
1 clove garlic, pressed
2 cups grated pimiento cheese

1½ cups milk
2 eggs, well beaten

Mix well. Bake at 350 degrees for approximately 1 hour or until set.

ALMOND RICE

Omit parsley and curry powder. Increase almonds to 1 cup. Add:

½ cup each *chopped onion, green pepper, and water chestnuts*
1 *clove garlic, pressed*
1 *tablespoon minced pimiento*

Dash liquid pepper
¼ *cup soy sauce or to taste*

Sauté onion, green pepper, water chestnuts, garlic, and pimiento in butter. Combine with remaining ingredients.

RICE MARGRETTA

Omit parsley and nuts. Add:

1 *4-ounce can chopped green chilis*
1 *cup grated Monterey jack cheese*
½ *cup grated sharp Cheddar cheese*

3 *cups commercial sour cream*
Salt to taste

Mix all ingredients well.

CHEESE-PINEAPPLE RICE   COQ

Omit parsley. Add:

2 *packages dry cheese-sauce mix*
1 *No. 2½ can crushed pineapple with juice*

1 *cup grated Cheddar cheese*
2 *tablespoons grated candied ginger*

Mix all ingredients well.

RICE SAUTE

White wine makes this unusual . . .

¼ cup butter or olive oil	1 cup minced celery
1 bunch green onions, chopped, including tops	3 cups chicken bouillon
2 cups uncooked long-grain rice	1 cup dry white wine
1 cup minced green pepper	Salt and pepper to taste

Heat butter or oil in frying pan. Add onion and sauté until crisp-tender. Add rice and stir until rice is brown. Add green pepper and celery and cook 1 minute. Put rice mixture, bouillon, wine, and seasonings in a buttered baking dish. Bake at 350 degrees for 45 minutes or until liquid is absorbed. Serves 8–10.

Note: Rice mixture may be prepared in advance and combined with liquid before baking. Beef stock may replace the chicken stock. Toss rice halfway through the cooking period if you wish.

Variations

RICE ITALIANO

Use olive oil. Substitute 2 cups tomato juice for 2 cups bouillon and 1 cup chopped fresh mushrooms for the celery. Add to the baking mixture:

1 teaspoon Italian seasoning
1 cup grated Parmesan cheese

PARISIAN RICE

Substitute 2 cups chopped fresh mushrooms for the green pepper and celery. Increase chopped green onions to 2 bunches.

RICE CURRY

Use butter. Substitute ¼ cup chopped parsley for the green pepper. Celery optional. Add to the baking mixture:

2 teaspoons curry powder or to taste
1 cup white raisins (optional)

BRAZIL NUT PILAF

Omit green pepper and celery. Use butter. Add to the baking mixture:

1 cup sliced toasted Brazil nuts
1 cup sliced mushrooms

Brazil nuts may be sautéed with rice until lightly golden.

RICE AMANDINE

Add:

1 cup slivered almonds

These may be sautéed with the rice to a golden brown.

ORANGE RICE

Use butter. Substitute 2 cups thinly sliced carrots for the green pepper and celery. Add to the baking mixture:

½ teaspoon powdered ginger
1 teaspoon grated orange rind
1 tablespoon chopped parsley

YELLOW RICE

Add to the baking mixture:

2 teaspoons ground turmeric

SOME ARE CEREALS . . .

MILDRED'S BAKED HOMINY GRITS

A fine potato substitute or barbecue accompaniment . . .

4 cups milk
½ cup butter broken into chunks
1 cup hominy grits (not quick-cooking)
1 teaspoon salt

Pepper to taste
¼ cup melted butter
1 cup grated Gruyère cheese
⅓ cup grated Parmesan cheese

Bring milk to a boil. Add butter chunks. When butter is melted gradually stir in grits. Continue cooking, stirring constantly, until mixture takes on the appearance of cooked farina. Remove from heat; add seasonings. Beat with an electric beater set at high speed for 5 minutes or until the grits become creamy in appearance. Pour into shallow buttered baking dish, and top with melted butter and cheeses. Bake at 350 degrees for 45 minutes. Serves 8.

Note: This dish may be made ahead and heated before serving.

Variations

GRITS GOLDEN

Omit Gruyère and Parmesan cheeses. Add to beaten mixture:

1 teaspoon garlic powder
1 tablespoon Worcestershire sauce
Liquid pepper to taste

2 eggs, well-beaten
3 cups diced sharp Cheddar cheese

Use paprika for topping over melted butter.

GRITS LUIS

Substitute 1 cup grated Swiss cheese for the Gruyère and Parmesan cheeses for topping. Add to the beaten mixture:

1 egg, beaten
½ cup grated Parmesan cheese

Combine the following and spoon over Swiss cheese topping:

¼ cup grated onion   *1 clove garlic, minced*
¼ cup slivered green   *1 cup tomato sauce*
pepper

GINA'S POLENTA

Omit ¼ cup melted butter, Gruyère and Parmesan cheeses. Mix 1½ cups tomato sauce with 1 teaspoon Italian seasoning. Pour 1 cup of the sauce over the grits after they are in the baking dish. Top the sauce layer with a layer of thinly sliced mozzarella cheese (½ pound). Dribble the remainder of the sauce over the sliced cheese, and top with 1 cup grated sharp Cheddar cheese.

DONNA'S OLE SPECIAL   COQ

This is a tasty dish for after-the-game, or any time . . .

1 No. 2½ can golden   *1 No. 2½ can tamales,*
hominy, drained   *drained*
2 8½-ounce cans cream   *2 cups grated sharp*
of mushroom soup   *Cheddar cheese*

Combine hominy and soup. Cut tamales in 1-inch chunks and add carefully to the hominy mixture. Top with cheese. Bake at 350 degrees for 30 minutes. Serves 6–8.

Note: Tamales should not be mashed, but remain in chunks.

Variations

VIVA EL TORO   COQ

Substitute one 1-pound can chili con carne for the mushroom soup. Add to the hominy mixture:

> ¼ *cup grated onion*
> 2 *tablespoons minced green chilis*
> ⅓ *cup dry red wine*

Fold cheese into the above mixture before adding tamales. Top with crushed corn chips.

RIO GRANDE PRONTO   COQ

Substitute 1 can each chili beef soup and tomato soup for the cream of mushroom soup. Add to the hominy mixture:

> 2 *bunches green onions, chopped, including tops*
> 2 *cups chopped and drained firm tomatoes (fresh or canned)*
> 1 *teaspoon chili powder*

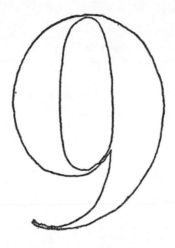

DESSERTS

*. . . I toast the feast for which I came,
and you who did prepare it; and if there
is a good dessert I'll toast you twice—and
share it.*

EARL HARDY NICHOLES

IF YOU'RE LOOKING for a sweet way to wind up a meal, here's how! There are 227 sweet things in this section, and they are something to carry on about. The wide assortment of recipes is on purpose. Dessert should be the climax of the meal, not the anti. Even your dieting friends won't appreciate that water-pack fruit under the blob of yogurt. They had that at home *last* night. If you served the Salad Tray* earlier, they saved enough calories to make them gung-ho to tackle your best efforts, which had better be several cuts above that water-pack you-know-what. They may hate themselves in the morning, but they'll know you cared enough to serve the very best.

DESSERTS

SOME HAVE A GELATIN BASE† . . .

ANGEL FOOD CREAM ENID

A delicate dessert which should be made the day before, and will keep well three or four days . . .

2 egg yolks, beaten
2 cups sugar
¼ teaspoon salt
2 cups light cream
2 envelopes unflavored
  gelatin
½ cup cold water
2 egg whites, stiffly
  beaten

1½ cups heavy cream,
  whipped
1 10-inch unfrosted angel
  food cake
2 10-ounce packages
  frozen raspberries,
  thawed

Cook egg yolks, sugar, salt, and light cream in a double boiler until mixture coats a spoon. Dissolve gelatin in cold water and add to hot custard mixture. Cool. When beginning to set, fold in stiffly beaten egg whites and whipped cream. Break angel food cake into small chunks and cover the bottom of a 9×13-inch pan. Cover cake pieces with part of the custard, and continue layering, ending with a custard layer on the top. Refrigerate until set, preferably overnight. Cut in squares. Before serving top with raspberries including juice. Serves 14–16.

Note: Any berries of your choice may be substituted for the raspberries.

---

† For molds, see About Getting Them in the Mold—and Out

Variations

CHERRY ANGEL

Omit raspberries. Add to the cooled custard mixture:

1 cup chopped maraschino cherries

Garnish with whipped cream and maraschino cherries.

LEMON ANGEL

Substitute two 3-ounce packages lemon gelatin for the un-flavored gelatin. Dissolve in ½ cup boiling water before adding to the hot custard mixture. Raspberries optional, or garnish with whipped cream and crushed lemon drops.

CHOCOLATE ANGEL

Shave 1 cake German sweet chocolate into the hot custard mixture. Raspberries optional, or garnish with whipped cream and semisweet chocolate shavings.

ANGEL IMPERIAL

Add to the cooled custard mixture:

1 cup minced dates
1 cup chopped pecans

Raspberries optional, or garnish with whipped cream and date pieces.

TUTTI FRUTTI ANGEL

Add to the cooled custard mixture:

1 cup chopped candied fruit mix
1 cup chopped walnuts

Raspberries optional, or garnish with whipped cream and walnut halves.

SHERRY ANGEL

Substitute ½ cup dry sherry wine for ½ cup light cream. This recipe may be used with most of the variations.

PINEAPPLE ANGEL

Omit raspberries. Add to the cooled custard mixture:

2 *cups well-drained pineapple*
1 *cup chopped pecans*

Garnish with whipped cream and pecan halves or candied pineapple pieces.

SPIFLICATED ANGEL

Use 1 cup whisky, rum, or brandy, *or* 1 cup sherry, port, muscatel, or Madeira wine to sprinkle the broken cake layers before adding the custard layers. This is done easily with a clothes-sprinkling cork. If a sweet wine is used, the sugar in the custard mixture may be reduced to taste.

MOLD MODERNE

Light and luscious . . .

2 3-*ounce packages*
  raspberry gelatin
1½ *cups boiling water*
1 *pint raspberry ice*
  cream
1 10-*ounce package*
  frozen raspberries,
  defrosted

¼ *cup dry sherry wine*
1½ *cups commercial*
  sour cream

Dissolve gelatin in boiling water. Cool slightly. Blend with remaining ingredients. Refrigerate until starting to thicken.

Blend thoroughly, and place in an oiled 2-quart mold. Refrigerate overnight. Garnish with Sour-Sweet Cream* or a variation of your choice. Serves 8–10.

Note: For a molded design, reserve enough clear gelatin to cover bottom of mold and fruit decorations of your choice.

Variations

BLACK BEAUTY FROST

Omit raspberries. Substitute black cherry gelatin and ice cream (or cherry ice cream) for the raspberry gelatin and ice cream. Add to the slightly thickened mixture:

> 2 *cups chopped dark sweet cherries*

STRAWBERRY RIKKI

Substitute strawberry gelatin and ice cream for the raspberry gelatin and ice cream, and strawberries for the raspberries.

GRAPE FROST

Omit raspberries. Substitute lemon gelatin and vanilla ice cream for the raspberry gelatin and ice cream. Add to the slightly thickened mixture:

> 1 *cup halved seedless grapes*

ROYAL PURPLE

Substitute black raspberry gelatin and ice cream (or raspberry ice cream) for the raspberry gelatin and ice cream, and 2 cups black raspberries for the red raspberries.

PINK CHERRY ANNIE

Substitute cherry gelatin and ice cream for the raspberry gelatin and ice cream. Add to the slightly thickened mixture:

> 2 *cups well-drained light sweet cherry halves*

ORANGE FLIP

Omit raspberries. Substitute orange gelatin and vanilla ice cream for the raspberry gelatin and ice cream. Add to the slightly thickened mixture:

2 cups chopped mandarin oranges

TOP BANANA MOLD

Omit raspberries. Substitute orange-banana gelatin and banana-nut ice cream for the raspberry gelatin and ice cream. Add to the slightly thickened mixture:

2 cups chopped or sliced bananas

PINEAPPLE DREAM

Omit raspberries. Substitute pineapple gelatin and ice cream for the raspberry gelatin and ice cream. Add to the slightly thickened mixture:

2 cups pineapple tidbits

DREAMY PEACH MOLD

Omit raspberries. Substitute peach gelatin and ice cream for the raspberry gelatin and ice cream. Add to the slightly thickened mixture:

2 cups well-drained peach slices or chunks

BAVARIAN CREAM

Light . . . and smooth as satin . . .

*1 envelope unflavored
    gelatin
⅓ cup sugar
Salt to taste
2 eggs, separated*

*1 cup light cream
2 teaspoons vanilla
1 cup heavy cream,
    whipped*

Combine gelatin, half of the sugar, salt, and egg yolks in a double boiler top. Blend in the light cream. Cook over boiling water, stirring constantly, until mixture coats a spoon. Chill until slightly thickened. Beat egg whites until glossy, gradually adding the rest of the sugar. Fold into the custard mixture along with the vanilla and whipped cream. Place in a lightly oiled 1½-quart mold. Cover and refrigerate for several hours or overnight. Serves 8.

Note: This dessert if worthy of your fanciest mold. Decorate it with assorted fruits of your choice before serving. Individual molds may be used.

Variations

CHARLOTTE RUSSE

Line mold with split ladyfingers. Sprinkle them lightly with rum before filling the mold with Bavarian Cream*.

SHERRY BAVARIAN

Substitute ⅓ cup dry sherry wine for ⅓ cup light cream.

RUM BAVARIAN

Reduce light cream ¼ cup. Add to cooked mixture:

¼ *cup rum*

GRENADINE BAVARIAN

Add to the cooked mixture:

1 *teaspoon rum extract*

Serve with a topping of Grenadine syrup instead of fruit.

MOCHA BAVARIAN

Add to the cooking mixture:

1½ *tablespoons instant coffee*

BAVARIAN MEXICO

Add to the cooking mixture:

2 *teaspoons instant coffee*
½ *teaspoon cinnamon*

CHOCOLATE BAVARIAN

Add to the cooking mixture:

3 *ounces shaved dark sweet chocolate*

ALMOND BAVARIAN

Add to the cooked mixture:

1 *teaspoon almond extract*

Use ¾ cup minced toasted almonds for a molded topping if desired.

PINEAPPLE MOUSSE

Add to the cooking mixture:

2 *cups well-drained crushed pineapple*

GOOSEBERRY MOUSSE

Substitute rum extract for the vanilla. Add to the cooking mixture:

Sieved pulp of 1 cup canned gooseberries

SPANISH CREAM

Omit whipped cream. Fold beaten egg whites in gently and pour into mold. This dessert will separate to form a layer of custard on the top and jelly on the bottom. Serve with whipped cream, berries, or fruit of your choice. For a very special effect serve with canned chestnut spread.

ALMENDRADO

Mexico takes the bows for this triple-threat dessert. It is as beautiful as a rainbow, light as a cloud, and as delectable as it looks . . .

1 envelope unflavored
  gelatin
1¼ cups sugar
1¼ cups water
6 egg whites, beaten
Dash salt

¼ teaspoon almond extract
1 cup finely chopped
  blanched almonds
Red and green food
  coloring

Combine gelatin, sugar, and water in a saucepan. Cook until gelatin is dissolved. Chill until mixture is slightly thickened. Beat egg whites and salt until stiff. Add almond extract. Beat gelatin mixture until frothy. Carefully fold in beaten egg whites and almonds. Divide into three bowls. Color one either red or pink, one green, and leave the other white. Pour into an oiled loaf pan or 1½-quart mold of your choice. The first layer should be pink, the center layer white, and the third layer green. Refrigerate overnight. Unmold and serve with cold Custard Sauce*. Serves 8.

Note: The second and third layers should be spooned into the mold very carefully to avoid mixing the colors.

Variations

ALMENDRADO VINO DE JEREZ

Substitute ⅓ cup dry sherry wine for ⅓ cup water. Add the sherry to the whipped gelatin mixture. Serve with Sherry Custard Sauce*.

SOME ARE ELEGANT AND EASY . . .

CREME BRULEE

This is worthy of any epicure . . .

8 *egg yolks, well beaten*	1 *teaspoon vanilla*
¼ *teaspoon salt*	1 *cup sifted light brown*
½ *cup sugar*	*sugar*
4 *cups heavy cream,*	*Assorted fruits*
scalded	

Blend egg yolks, salt, and sugar in top of double boiler. Slowly add scalded cream, stirring constantly. Cook over simmering water until mixture coats a spoon. Do not over-cook. Remove from heat. Add vanilla. Pour into a 2-quart shallow baking dish and refrigerate overnight. Several hours before serving sift the brown sugar evenly over the top of the mixture and place under the broiler until the sugar melts to a shiny carmel topping. Turn pan if necessary and watch carefully. Return to refrigerator immediately for several hours. Serve with assorted fruits or with cold heavy cream. Serves 8–10.

Note: Some of the crusty glaze should be included with each serving.

Variations

CREME BRULEE AMANDINE

Substitute almond extract for the vanilla.

CREME BRULEE AU RHUM

Substitute 2 tablespoons dark rum for the vanilla.

ZABAGLIONE

Omit vanilla and brown sugar. Increase sugar to 2 cups. Substitute 1 cup Marsala wine for the 4 cups cream.

Note: Add the wine to the egg-sugar mixture very slowly while beating constantly with a rotary beater. Remove from simmering water when the mixture is like whipped cream. Do not over-cook. Serve hot or chilled in glasses or as a topping for fruit. To serve chilled place cooked mixture in a bowl of cracked ice and whip until chilled. Dry sherry, port, or Tokay wine may be substituted for the Marsala, but Marsala is traditional for this lovely Italian dessert.

POTS DE CREME

Omit brown sugar and fruits. Reduce cream to 3 cups. Remove from simmering water when mixture thickens and coats a spoon. Do not over-cook. Serve in *petits pots* (small covered pots) or custard cups, chilled, with heavy cream. The secret of this famous French dessert is the slow cooking.

POTS DE CREME AU CHOCOLAT

Melt 3 ounces bittersweet chocolate with a bit of cream over hot water. Stir into Pots de Crème* cooking mixture.

POTS DE CREME AU CAFE

Add to the Pots de Crème* cooking mixture:

2 tablespoons instant coffee

INSTANT LEMON LOVELY   COQ

For the coolest kitchen ever . . .

1 9-inch baked angel food cake	2 cups heavy cream, whipped
1 No. 2 can lemon pie filling	⅓ cup crushed lemon drops

Line a loaf pan with waxed paper. Tear cake into bite-size pieces. Reserve enough whipped cream and candy to garnish; fold remainder into the lemon filling. Layer filling and cake, beginning and ending with the filling mixture. Refrigerate overnight. Unmold. Remove paper and garnish with whipped cream and candy. Serves 10–12.

Note: A 9-inch tube pan may be used in place of the loaf pan.

Variations

INSTANT CHOCOLATE LOVELY   COQ

Substitute canned chocolate pudding for the lemon filling, ⅔ cup chopped toasted almonds for the lemon drops and shaved chocolate for the candy garnish.

INSTANT COFFEE-DATE LOVELY   COQ

Substitute canned vanilla pudding for the lemon filling. Add to the pudding mixture:

2 teaspoons instant coffee
1 cup chopped dates

Garnish with dates and pecan halves instead of the lemon drops.

INSTANT BUTTERSCOTCH LOVELY   COQ

Substitute canned butterscotch pudding for the lemon filling and 1 cup crushed peanut brittle for the lemon drops.

INSTANT NESSELRODE LOVELY   COQ

Substitute canned vanilla pudding for the lemon filling. Add to the pudding mixture:

2 *tablespoons bourbon or brandy*
1 *cup chopped candied fruit mix*

Garnish with candied fruit pieces and shaved dark chocolate instead of the lemon drops.

FRIED CREAM

This is a specialty in San Francisco . . .

3 *cups heavy cream*	2 *tablespoons flour*
¼ *teaspoon soda*	1 *cup heavy cream*
½ *teaspoon salt*	2 *teaspoons vanilla*
1½-inch *stick cinnamon*	1 *tablespoon butter*
8 *egg yolks, well beaten*	*Egg white*
1 *cup sugar*	*Very fine crumbs*
¼ *cup cornstarch*	*Cooking oil*

Combine 3 cups cream, soda, salt, and cinnamon in a double boiler top and scald over boiling water. Combine egg yolks with sugar, cornstarch, flour, and 1 cup heavy cream. Add slowly to hot cream mixture, stirring constantly. When thick, remove from stove, and discard cinnamon stick. Add vanilla and butter, and beat well. Pour into a buttered 8-inch square pan and refrigerate overnight. Early in the day, cut into squares, dip in egg white, then in crumbs. Deep fry at 360 degrees or pan fry in 2 inches cooking oil until very lightly browned. Drain on brown paper. Serve hot with hot Brandy Cream Sauce* or hot Rum Cream Sauce*. Serves 8.

Note: Fried custard squares may be reheated in a 200-degree oven for 10 minutes before serving time.

Variations

FRIED CREAM FLAMBE

Add to the cooked custard mixture:

1 *jigger rum*

Substitute ground almonds for the fine crumbs. Dust coated squares with cinnamon before frying. Before serving arrange heated fried squares on the dish they are to be served in. Pour 2 jiggers warm rum or brandy over them and ignite.

PERSIMMON PUDDING LOUISE

A treat for the holiday season . . .

2 *cups chopped persimmon pulp*	3 *teaspoons soda*
	1 *cup milk*
2 *cups sugar*	3 *cups flour*
1 *egg*	1 *teaspoon each*
3 *tablespoons melted butter*	*cinnamon and nutmeg*
	2 *cups chopped walnuts*
1 *teaspoon salt*	
3 *teaspoons baking powder*	

Combine ingredients in order given. Mix well. Fill two large well-buttered and floured loaf pans three-quarters full. Bake at 350 degrees for 1½ hours or until firm in the center. Serve warm or cold with Lemon Custard Sauce*, Brandy Custard Sauce*, or Hard Sauce*. Makes 2 loaves.

Note: Nut halves, cherries, and other glazed fruit pieces may be arranged in the bottom of the pans for decorative toppings. Puddings may be steamed for 2½ hours if preferred.

Variations

PERSIMMON-DATE PUDDING

Substitute ¼ cup brandy or rum for ¼ cup milk. Add:

1 cup chopped dates

PERSIMMON FRUIT CAKE

Omit egg. Increase sugar to 3 cups. Add:

*⅓ cup brandy, rum, or
   bourbon whisky
¾ cup chopped dates
¾ cup white or seedless
   raisins*

*½ cup currants
2 cups mixed glazed fruit
1 cup glazed whole
   cherries
1 cup pecan halves*

Bake at 350 degrees for 1½ hours or until cake shrinks from sides of pan. Cover cake with foil for the first hour of baking. Cool in pan. This is a moist cake, and slices of it make an excellent pudding served with Hard Sauce* or Drinkin' Cousin Sauce*.

SNOWBALLS MINA

These do-aheads freeze well, and are just right for any number of occasions . . .

*1 15-ounce can sweetened
   condensed milk (not
   evaporated)
2½ cups graham cracker
   crumbs
2 squares melted
   unsweetened chocolate*

*½ cup chopped walnuts
   or pecans
1 teaspoon vanilla
Shredded coconut*

Mix all ingredients except coconut. Roll into balls, then in coconut to coat. Keep mix cool—it will be easier to work with. Makes 12 medium size balls. The size of the snowballs determines the number of servings.

Note: Drizzle Snowballs with Chocolate Sauce* or Eggnog Sauce*. A tray of bite-size balls is excellent for the buffet. Use colored coconut for a rainbow effect, for Easter eggs, or to carry out a color sheme.

Variations

CRUNCH BALLS

Substitute chopped nuts for the coconut coating.

SNOW LOGS

Roll mixture into a 3-inch log and refrigerate. Cut in 1-inch slices and serve with Vanilla Sauce* or an appropriate variation.

COCONUT CHERRY CREAMS

Omit chocolate. Substitute 3 cups shredded coconut for the cracker crumbs. Add:

½ *cup chopped candied cherries*

Roll balls in chopped pecans.

HOLIDAY BALLS

Omit chocolate and coconut. Substitute 2½ cups macaroon cooky crumbs for the cracker crumbs. Add:

⅔ *cup candied fruit mix*
1 *teaspoon brandy extract*

Roll balls in powdered sugar.

RUM BALLS

Chocolate optional. Substitute 3 cups vanilla wafer crumbs for the cracker crumbs. Add:

¼ cup dark rum

Roll in either coconut or powdered sugar.

BOURBON BALLS

Substitute ¼ cup bourbon whisky for the rum in Rum Balls* recipe.

PEANUT CRUNCH

Omit chocolate and coconut. Substitute 2 cups cornflake crumbs for the cracker crumbs. Increase nuts to 1 cup chopped peanuts. Roll in powdered sugar.

VERY CHOCOLATE SNOWBALLS

Substitute 2½ cups chocolate cooky crumbs for the cracker crumbs. Add:

½ teaspoon almond extract

GINGER-DATE BALLS

Omit chocolate. Substitute 2 cups gingersnap crumbs for the cracker crumbs. Add:

1 cup diced dates
1 teaspoon brandy extract or 1 teaspoon instant coffee

ORANGE-APRICOT BALLS

Omit chocolate. Substitute 2 cups vanilla wafer crumbs or gingersnap crumbs for cracker crumbs. Add:

⅔ cup ground dried apricots
2 tablespoons grated orange rind

FROZEN DESSERT BALLS

Substitute ice cream for the condensed milk-crumb mixture. Roll ice cream balls of any flavor in white or colored coconut or chopped nuts or cooky crumbs of your choice. Freeze until serving time. Serve plain or with a complementary sauce.

CHERRIES JUBILEE COQ

What a climax for any meal . . .

2 *cups canned pitted*
  black bing cherries
¾ *cup cherry juice from*
  can

1 *cup white corn syrup*
½ *cup warm cognac*
Vanilla ice cream

Heat cherries, juice, and syrup in a chafing dish. Add warm cognac. Ignite. When the flames die down, ladle over individual servings of vanilla ice cream. Serves 6–8.

Note: Cherries Jubilee also may be served over slices of sponge or pound cake.

Variations

CHERRIES JUBILEE DIXIE COQ

Substitute ½ cup Southern Comfort for the cognac.

CHERRIES JUBILEE ANDRE COQ

Add to the chafing dish mixture:

¼ *cup rum*

CHERRIES JUBILEE MARTI COQ

Substitute ½ cup bourbon whisky for the cognac.

CHERRIES JUBILEE MARISSA   COQ

Add to the chafing dish mixture:

2 *thin slices lemon*
½ *teaspoon cinnamon*

CHERRIES JUBILEE GRAND MARNIER COQ

Add to the chafing dish mixture:

2 *ounces Grand Marnier liqueur*

CROWN CHERRIES JUBILEE   COQ

Add to the chafing dish mixture:

2 *ounces Cointreau liqueur*

INSTANT CHERRIES JUBILEE   COQ

For the cherries, juice, and syrup, substitute one 1-pound jar brandied cherries jubilee (from the gourmet section).

STRAWBERRIES ROMANOFF

This lovely dessert requires last minute combination, so make that part of the festivities . . .

2 *quarts fresh strawberries,*   1 *cup heavy cream,*
   cleaned and hulled   *whipped*
¼ *cup sugar*   1 *pint vanilla ice cream*
¼ *cup Cointreau or*
   curaçao

Sprinkle berries with sugar and refrigerate for 2 or 3 hours. Two hours before serving, combine the berries with the Cointreau. Stir gently a time or two to marinate berries well. Shortly before serving whip the cream stiff, and the ice cream until it is soft. Combine the two in a serving bowl that will also accommodate the berries. Carry both the berries and the cream mixture to the table, and combine before your guests.

Note: In combining the two mixtures, be careful to leave the berries whole.

Variations

STRAWBERRIES ROYALE

Substitute ½ cup Kirsch for the Cointreau.

STRAWBERRIES ALEX

Substitute ½ cup rum for the Cointreau.

LISA'S STRAWBERRIES

Substitute ½ cup Galliano for the Cointreau.

STRAWBERRIES ROLLO

Substitute ½ cup Triple Sec for the Cointreau.

CHERRY SOPHISTICATE

Cream cheese does it for this . . .

20 graham cracker squares
  rolled to crumbs
¼ cup melted butter
¼ cup sugar
1 8-ounce package
  softened cream cheese
½ cup powdered sugar

1 cup heavy cream,
  whipped
¾ cup chopped pecans
2 No. 2 cans cherry pie
  filling
1 teaspoon cherry extract
Salt to taste

Combine cracker crumbs, butter, and ¼ cup sugar. Spread over a 9×13-inch pan and bake at 375 degrees for 8 minutes. Cool. Beat cheese and powdered sugar until fluffy. Fold in whipped cream and pecans. Spread over crust mixture. Combine filling, flavoring, and salt. Spread over cream cheese mixture. Refrigerate overnight. Serves 12.

Note: A teaspoon of red food coloring may be added to the filling mixture for additional color. Servings may be garnished with whipped cream or Sour-Sweet Cream* or suitable variations.

Variations

BLUEBERRY CHEESE DESSERT

Omit cherry extract. Substitute two No. 2 cans blueberry pie filling mixed with 2 tablespoons lemon juice for the cherry filling.

STRAWBERRY SOPHISTICATE

Substitute 1 teaspoon strawberry flavoring for the cherry extract and 2 No. 2 cans strawberry pie filling for the cherry filling.

PEACHY KEEN DESSERT

Substitute 2 tablespoons lemon juice for the cherry extract and 2 No. 2 cans peach pie filling for the cherry filling.

LEMON SOPHISTICATE

Substitute 2 tablespoons lemon juice for the cherry extract and 2 No. 2 cans lemon pie filling for the cherry filling.

ORANGE BAKED BANANAS

Serve these either as a dessert or a main dish accompaniment . . .

6 large green-tipped bananas	⅓ cup brown sugar
1 cup fresh orange juice	¼ teaspoon allspice
2 tablespoons lime juice	Butter

Place peeled bananas, halved lengthwise, in a shallow baking dish. Add remaining ingredients (except butter). Dot with butter. Bake at 350 degrees for 20–25 minutes or until bananas are golden. Serves 6 or 12.

Note: Bananas should be slightly underripe. Serve them as a meat accompaniment with pork, ham, or chicken, either hot or cold, or serve them as a dessert.

Variations

SHERRIED BANANAS

Substitute 1 cup dry sherry wine for the orange juice.

MANDARIN BANANAS

Add to the baking mixture:

> *1 11-ounce can mandarin orange pieces, drained*

PINEAPPLE BANANAS

Substitute 1 cup unsweetened pineapple juice for the orange juice. Add to the baking mixture:

> *1 cup pineapple tidbits*

GINGER-PINEAPPLE BANANAS

Add to Pineapple Bananas* recipe:

> *¼ cup grated candied ginger*

CHERRY BANANAS

Add to the baking mixture:

> *2 cups pitted cherries or 1 cup maraschino cherries*

HONEY-ORANGE BANANAS

Substitute ¼ cup honey for the brown sugar. Add to the baking mixture:

1 teaspoon grated orange rind

FRUITED BANANAS

Add to the baking mixture:

2 cups drained fruit cocktail

BANANAS FLAMBE

Substitute 1 cup dry sherry wine for the orange juice. Just before serving, warm ¼ cup brandy or rum, pour over bananas, and ignite. Serve warm.

BANANA CRUNCH

Add to the baking mixture:

1 cup any one of the following: whole almonds, macadamia or filbert nuts, walnut or pecan halves, or sliced Brazil nuts

BANANAS AMBROSIA

Add to the baking mixture:

½ cup grated coconut

Substitute 1 cup canned coconut milk for the orange juice if you wish.

PRINCESS PEARS

Omit allspice. Substitute 12 canned pear halves for the bananas. Reduce orange juice to ½ cup. Add to the baking mixture:

½ cup Kirsch

BRANDY PEACHES

Substitute 12 canned peach halves for the bananas and ⅓ cup brandy for ⅓ cup orange juice.

PEACHES FLAMBE

Heat ¼ cup brandy, pour over warm Brandy Peaches*, and ignite.

STUFFED BRANDY PEACHES

Place 1 tablespoon brandied mincemeat in each peach half cavity. Follow recipe for Brandy Peaches*.

CRANBERRY PEACHES

Fill each peach half cavity with 1 tablespoon canned whole cranberry sauce.

BLUSHING PEACHES

Reduce sugar to ¼ cup. Melt ½ cup red currant jelly and add to the baking mixture.

CAKES

SOME ARE MADE FROM SCRATCH . . .

BD'S OATMEAL CAKE

You can serve this hot or cold . . .

1½ cups boiling water	1 teaspoon soda
1 cup quick oats	½ teaspoon salt
1 cup granulated sugar	1 teaspoon cinnamon
1 cup brown sugar	½ teaspoon nutmeg
½ cup softened butter	1 teaspoon vanilla
2 eggs, beaten	1 cup chopped walnuts
1½ cups cake flour	

Pour boiling water over oats. Let stand for 20 minutes. Cream sugars and butter; add eggs; beat 5 minutes. Add oats, flour, soda, and the remaining ingredients. Mix well. Pour batter into well-oiled 9×13-inch pan. Bake in a preheated 350-degree oven 45 minutes or until done. Leave cake in pan, and top with:

⅓ cup butter	1 tablespoon flour
1 cup brown sugar	¼ cup condensed milk
1 cup chopped walnuts	1 teaspoon vanilla

Combine all ingredients and spread over warm cake. Slip under the broiler until bubbly. Serves 16.

Note: This is a moist cake which keeps very well. The topping may be omitted and the cake served with a sauce of your choice.

Variations

ALMOND OATMEAL CAKE

Substitute chopped toasted almonds for the chopped walnuts in both the cake and the topping mixtures. For a more pronounced almond flavor, substitute almond extract for the vanilla in both mixtures.

COCONUT OATMEAL CAKE

Substitute 1 cup coconut for the walnuts in both the cake and topping mixtures.

CHOCOLATE CROWN OATMEAL CAKE

Add to the topping mixture:

1 cup chocolate chips

OATMEAL CAKE COGNAC

Substitute ½ cup cognac for the condensed milk in the topping.

$100 CAKE

One hundred dollars is said to be the price paid to a famous New York chef for this recipe. The appreciative diner declared it worth every cent . . .

2 cups sifted cake flour	*1 cup mayonnaise (not*
1 cup sugar	*salad dressing)*
2 teaspoons baking soda	*1 cup cold water*
½ cup cocoa	*1 teaspoon vanilla*
¼ teaspoon salt	

Sift together flour, sugar, soda, cocoa, and salt. Add mayonnaise, cold water, and vanilla. Blend thoroughly. Pour into two 8-inch oiled, floured cake pans. Bake in a preheated oven at 350 degrees about 30 minutes or until cake shrinks from sides of pan. Remove from pans, cool, and frost with Rich Mocha Frosting*. Serves 8.

Note: This cake crumbles rather easily and should be handled with a bit of care. There is no error in the listed ingredients— it calls for no eggs, milk, or shortening.

Variations

FUDGE NUT CAKE

Substitute Minute Fudge Frosting Hendry* for the Rich Mocha Frosting*. Sprinkle each frosted layer with chopped pecans.

CHOCOLATE LEMON CAKE

Substitute Lemon Frosting* for the Rich Mocha Frosting*. Sprinkle layers lightly with slivered candied ginger.

BB'S FRUIT PUDDING CAKE

It's moist, and it keeps, or it freezes for unexpected company . . .

1 cup sugar	1 teaspoon baking soda
1 egg	¼ teaspoon salt
1 No. 2 can fruit cocktail with syrup	1¼ cups sifted cake flour

Combine all ingredients. Pour into an unbuttered 9×13-inch pan. Top with a mixture of:

1 cup brown sugar
1 cup chopped nuts

Bake in a preheated oven for 45 minutes. Serve warm with whipped cream, Sherry Cream*, or Apple Fluff*. Serves 8.

Note: This cake can be rewarmed—about 10 minutes at 200 degrees—before serving.

Variations

SPICY FRUIT PUDDING CAKE

Add:

½ teaspoon each *cinnamon, nutmeg, and allspice*

Serve with Hard Sauce*, Lemon Custard Sauce*, or Brandy Custard Sauce*. Serve sauces warm over warm cake.

CHEESECAKE SUPREME HEADLEY

Magnificent . . . that's what it is . . .

Crust

6 graham cracker squares rolled to crumbs
¼ cup melted butter
2 tablespoons sugar

Combine and press firmly against bottom and sides of a deep 9-inch pie plate. Refrigerate.

Filling

3 3-ounce packages
softened cream cheese
1 cup commercial sour
cream
2 eggs, beaten

½ cup sugar
½ teaspoon grated lemon
rind (optional)
½ teaspoon vanilla

Cream the cheese in a bowl. Add sour cream and mix well. Combine the eggs, sugar, lemon rind, and vanilla, and blend with the cheese mixture. Pour into crust. Bake in preheated oven at 375 degrees for 20 minutes. Cool.

Topping

1 cup commercial sour cream
2 tablespoons sugar
½ teaspoon vanilla

Combine and spread on cooled cheesecake. Bake in preheated oven at 475 degrees for 5 minutes. Chill thoroughly, even overnight, before serving. Serves 10–12.

Note: You may use a square pan for this if you prefer.

Variations

FRUIT-GLAZED CHEESECAKE

Omit topping and glaze with any of the glaze recipes given for Cheese Pie*.

FORGOTTEN TORTE

Simple to make, bakes while you sleep, and looks and tastes scrumptious . . .

Set oven at 450 degrees.

*6 egg whites, room
   temperature*
¼ teaspoon salt
*½ teaspoon cream of
   tartar*
1½ cups sugar

1 teaspoon vanilla
*½ pint heavy cream,
   whipped*
*Candied fruit pieces for
   garnish*
Pecan halves for garnish

Butter a 9-inch angel food cake pan. Beat egg whites with salt and cream of tartar until almost stiff. Add sugar slowly, 1 tablespoon at a time, and continue beating until meringue is very stiff. Beat in vanilla and spread evenly in the pan.

Put it in the oven, turn the heat off immediately, and leave overnight or until oven is absolutely cold. Do not open the oven door until it is time to take the torte out. Loosen the edges and turn out on the serving plate. Before serving frost the top and sides with the whipped cream. Decorate with the candied fruit pieces and pecan halves. Serves 10–12.

Note: Fresh or canned fruit, well drained, may be substituted for the candied fruit. The torte may be decorated shortly before guests arrive and refrigerated until serving time.

Variations

CREAM TORTE

Substitute Sour-Sweet Cream* or any of the variations for the whipped cream.

CHOCOLATE ALMOND TORTE

Omit whipped cream, fruit pieces, and nuts. Melt one 6-ounce package semisweet chocolate pieces over hot water. Stir into ¾ cup commercial sour cream. Fold in 1 cup chopped toasted almonds. Frost torte with this mixture and decorate with whole toasted almonds and miniature marshmallows.

ORANGE TORTE

Omit whipped cream, fruit pieces, and nuts. Fold ¼ cup orange marmalade into ¾ cup commercial sour cream. Frost torte with mixture and decorate with candied orange strips.

CHERRY TORTE

Omit whipped cream, fruit pieces, and nuts. Fold 1 cup chopped maraschino cherries into ¾ cup commercial sour cream. Add 2 tablespoons Kirsch. Frost torte with this mixture and decorate with whole maraschino cherry flowers. These are made with 5 diagonal cuts made lengthwise almost to the bottom of each cherry.

PINEAPPLE TORTE

Fold 1 cup very well-drained pineapple into the whipped cream (or ¾ cup commercial sour cream). Decorate torte with candied pineapple pieces and nut halves.

TOFFEE MOCHA TORTE

Omit fruit pieces and pecan halves. Fold 1 tablespoon instant coffee into the whipped cream. Decorate torte with crushed English toffee candy.

TORTE VIENNA

Omit fruit pieces and pecan halves. Spread torte with a thin layer of apricot or raspberry jam; frost with the whipped cream, and sprinkle the top with shaved unsweetened chocolate.

DATE NUT TORTE

Fold 1 cup each chopped dates and chopped pecans into whipped cream. Dust frosted torte lightly with cinnamon. Decorate with date pieces and pecans.

MERINGUE MARASCHINO

Fill these meringues with ice cream, fruit, custard, or what pleases you . . .

*1⅛ cups egg whites, room
temperature
½ teaspoon salt
2 teaspoons vinegar*

*1½ teaspoons vanilla
2 cups sifted powdered
sugar*

Beat egg whites, salt, and vinegar until mixture forms peaks. Add vanilla. Add sugar 1 tablespoon at a time. Beat at medium speed until sugar is dissolved and mixture is fine-textured, shiny, and stiff. Do not underbeat. A pinch of the meringue should be smooth to the fingertips. Spread mixture carefully into two

9-inch round cake pans with blade scrapers (or line pans with oiled brown paper). Bake in a preheated 250-degree oven for 1½ hours. Open the oven door and leave the meringues in the oven to cool completely before removing from pans.

Filling

½ cup drained crushed pineapple	½ cup chopped dates
¾ cup drained quartered maraschino cherries	1 cup chopped pecans
	2 cups heavy cream, whipped

Combine all filling ingredients. Spread half of the mixture on one meringue, top with second meringue, and add remaining filling mixture. Refrigerate. Serves 14.

Note: This recipe will make approximately 14–16 individual meringues formed in well-oiled muffin cups. These may be baked overnight. Follow baking directions for Forgotten Torte*. For special occasions form meringues in appropriate shapes (hearts, shamrocks, etc.) and fill with suitable mixtures.

Variations

BERRY MERINGUE

Substitute 2 cups sweetened berries of your choice, fresh, canned, or frozen, for the pineapple, cherries, and dates.

RAINBOW MERINGUE

Substitute 2 cups of well-drained fruit cocktail for the pineapple, cherries, and dates. Add to the filling mixture:

2 tablespoons dry sherry wine

ORANGE MERINGUE

Substitute 2 cups chopped mandarin oranges for the pineapple, cherries, and dates. Add to the filling mixture:

2 tablespoons Cointreau

HOLIDAY MERINGUE

Substitute 1½ cups candied fruit mix for the pineapple and cherries. Add to the filling mixture:

2 tablespoons rum
Dash allspice

MERINGUE ORIENTALE

Substitute 1 cup shredded coconut for the nuts. Add to the filling mixture:

2 tablespoons grated candied ginger

PEPPERMINT PINK MERINGUE

Substitute 1⅔ cups crushed peppermint candy for the pineapple, cherries, and dates.

TOFFEE MOCHA MERINGUE

Substitute 1⅔ cups crushed English toffee candy and 1 teaspoon instant coffee for the pineapple and cherries.

SOME HAVE A HEAD START . . .

CREAM CAKE FRANCAIS

This rich, rich cake *must* be refrigerated 24 hours before serving . . . what could be sweeter . . .

2 cups vanilla wafer crumbs
½ cup soft butter
1 cup confectioners' sugar
2 eggs, room temperature, beaten

1 cup heavy cream, whipped
1 cup chopped pecans
1 cup well-drained crushed pineapple

Place 1 cup crumbs in an unbuttered 8-inch square pan. Cream butter and sugar, add eggs, and beat mixture *well.* Spoon or pour carefully over crumbs. Combine cream, nuts, and pineapple, and spread over egg mixture. Sprinkle with remaining crumbs. Refrigerate 24 hours. Serves 8.

Note: Garnish with whipped cream if you wish.

Variations

FRENCH RUM CAKE

Add to the cream mixture:

1 ounce rum

RASPBERRY CREAM CAKE

Substitute 1 cup well-drained frozen raspberries for the pineapple.

APRICOT CREAM CAKE

Substitute 1 cup chopped canned apricots for the pineapple and ½ cup chopped almonds for the pecans. Add to the cream mixture:

½ teaspoon almond extract

BLUEBERRY CREAM CAKE

Substitute 1 cup canned blueberry pie filling for the pineapple.

ORANGE-PINEAPPLE CAKE

Blend ½ cup orange marmalade with the pineapple before combining with the cream and nuts.

CHERRY CHOCOLATE CAKE

Substitute 2 cups chocolate wafer crumbs for the vanilla crumbs and 1 cup chopped maraschino cherries for the pineapple.

LADY KATHERYN'S LEMON CAKE

A delicious cake from a regal lady . . .

1 *package lemon chiffon*	4 *whole eggs*
cake mix	¾ *cup water*
1 *package lemon gelatin*	¾ *cup cooking oil*

Combine all ingredients. Beat for 5 minutes. Pour in a 10×14-inch oiled, floured pan. Bake in a preheated 350-degree oven for approximately 50 minutes or until cake shrinks from the sides of the pan. Remove from oven and stick hot cake full of holes with a toothpick. Glaze immediately with a mixture of:

> 3 *cups powdered sugar*
> 1 *teaspoon grated lemon rind*
> *Juice 4 lemons*

Serve warm or cold. Serves 12–16.

Note: Do not test this cake before it starts to shrink from the sides of the pan.

Variations

ORANGE CAKE

Substitute orange gelatin for the lemon gelatin in the cake mixture, and ⅓ cup defrosted frozen orange juice concentrate for the lemon juice in the glaze.

STRAWBERRY DELIGHT CAKE

Substitute strawberry gelatin for the lemon gelatin in the cake mixture. Glaze with a well-beaten mixture of:

> *Juice 1 lemon plus enough fruit syrup to make ⅓ cup*
> ½ *cup drained frozen or canned strawberries*

ST. PATRICK CAKE

Substitute lime gelatin for the lemon gelatin in the cake mix, and add green food coloring if desired. Substitute grated lime rind and lime juice for the lemon in the glaze.

LECADRE QUEEN CAKE FRANCAIS

A very rich and unusual recipe from France . . .

Choose a mold of the desired size and butter lightly. Split ladyfingers and line mold. Spread thinly with apricot jam and sprinkle lightly with watered rum. Press layers gently, ladyfingers, jam, and rum. Cake should be moist but not soggy. Refrigerate overnight. Serve with chilled Custard Sauce*.

Note: Make the portions of this dessert very small.

Variations

ALMOND QUEEN CAKE FRANCAIS

Mix 2 tablespoons almond paste (or to taste) with the jam before spreading.

FRENCH SHERRY CAKE

Substitute dry sherry wine for the watered rum.

CHERRY QUEEN CAKE

Substitute cherry jam for the apricot jam, and port wine for the watered rum.

QUEEN CAKE EXTRAORDINAIRE

Substitute apricot-pineapple jam for the apricot jam.

FROZEN CREAM CAKE

Add a 1-inch layer of vanilla ice cream over each layer which has been rum-sprinkled. Freeze overnight.

FROZEN RASPBERRY CREAM CAKE

Substitute raspberry jam for the apricot jam in Frozen Cream Cake*.

PARTY ANGEL CAKE

The baker starts you off . . .

1 10-inch angel food cake
1 envelope unflavored
    gelatin
¼ cup cold water
Dash salt
½ cup powdered sugar or
    to taste
2 cups heavy cream,
    whipped

2 teaspoons brandy extract
½ pound crushed English
    toffee candy
½ cup toasted slivered
    almonds
Whole toasted almonds

Slice cake crosswise into 4 layers. Soften gelatin in water and dissolve over low heat. Refrigerate until slightly thickened and whip until smooth. Fold salt, sugar, and brandy extract into the whipped cream, and combine with the gelatin mixture. Reassemble cake. Spread each layer generously with the cream, and sprinkle with crushed toffee. Frost the top and sides of cake. Rim the edge with slivered almonds. Define rim with whole almonds. Sprinkle center portion of cake with crushed toffee. Refrigerate until serving time. Serves 12–14.

Note: For a spicier flavor, add ½ teaspoon each nutmeg and cinnamon to the whipped cream. This frosting holds up well.

Variations

PARTY PEANUT ANGEL

Substitute bourbon whisky for the brandy, peanut brittle for the English toffee, and peanuts for the almonds.

MAPLE NUT ANGEL PINOCHE

Substitute rum for the brandy, chopped pecan pralines for the English toffee, and pecans for the almonds.

CRUNCHY PEPPERMINT ANGEL

Substitute dry sherry wine for the brandy and crushed peppermint candy for the English toffee.

HEAVENLY HASH ANGEL

Substitute 1½ cups candied fruit mix for the English toffee and walnuts for the almonds.

DATE NUT ANGEL

Substitute chopped brandied dates, drained, for the English toffee.

CHERRY NUT ANGEL

Substitute 1½ cups chopped maraschino cherries for the English toffee.

CHERRY BRANDY CAKE

Moisten each cake section with cherry brandy before adding the filling. Follow the recipe for Cherry Nut Angel*.

TIPSY ANGEL

Moisten each cake section with rum, bourbon whisky, or brandy before adding the filling mixture. This may be done with any liquor called for in any variation for a stronger liquor flavor.

*. . . A meal my hunger to appease—A
handsome pie to crown it, please!*
               EARL HARDY NICHOLES

PIES

A PIECRUST FOR EVERY OCCASION . . .

FOOLPROOF PIECRUST LIZ

This makes a double crust . . .

⅓ cup sifted flour   *1 teaspoon salt*
¼ cup water   *⅔ cup shortening*
1⅔ cups sifted flour

Stir ⅓ cup flour and water to a smooth paste. Mix 1⅔ cups
flour with salt; cut shortening in until mixture is a mealy
texture. Add paste mixture to shortening mixture and blend
well. Divide and roll on a well-floured board. Makes 2 crusts.

Note: Do not over-blend the shortening mixture—it should
be a coarse-meal consistency.

KARLA'S CRUNCHY CRUST

This will make a 9-inch pie . . .

½ cup butter or margarine   *1 cup sifted flour*
¼ cup packed light brown   *½ cup chopped of any*
    sugar   *one: almonds, pecans,*
½ teaspoon salt   *walnuts, Brazil nuts,*
½ teaspoon nutmeg   *peanuts, or coconut*
    (optional)

Mix well and press into a 9- or 10-inch pie plate, bottom and sides. Bake at 375 degrees 10 minutes or until well browned. Refrigerate for 1 hour before filling, and for at least 1 hour after filling before serving.

Variations

PECAN COCONUT CRUST

Use ½ cup *each* minced pecans and chopped shredded coconut.

SHORT CRUST

Substitute 1 tablespoon granulated sugar for the brown sugar. Nutmeg may be omitted. After all ingredients are combined, mix in 1 egg. Press into ungreased pie plate, bottom and sides. Bake at 375 degrees for 20 minutes. Cool before filling.

CORNFLAKE CRUST

This makes a 9- or 10-inch pie . . .

1½ cups crushed cornflakes
¼ cup powdered sugar
⅓ cup melted butter

Mix all ingredients and press into a 9-inch pie plate. Bake at 325 degrees for 10 minutes. Refrigerate for 1 hour before filling.

Note: After filling is added, chill thoroughly before serving. In crumb crusts, whole or half wafers may be placed around sides of pan for the side crust.

Variations

GINGER CRUMB CRUST

Substitute 1¼ cups gingersnap crumbs for the cornflakes.

CHOCOLATE CRUMB SHELL

Substitute 1¼ cups chocolate wafer crumbs for the cornflakes.

LEMON CRUMB CRUST

Substitute 1¼ cups lemon wafer crumbs for the cornflakes.

VANILLA CRUMB CRUST

Substitute 1½ cups vanilla wafer crumbs for the cornflakes.

GRAHAM CRACKER CRUST

Substitute 1½ cups graham cracker crumbs for the cornflakes.

COCONUT PIE SHELL

Reduce butter to ¼ cup and powdered sugar to 2 tablespoons. Substitute 2½ cups flaked coconut for the cornflakes.

LADYFINGER CRUST

Omit crumb mixture. Split 1½ dozen ladyfingers and arrange them flat side down over the bottom and sides of a buttered 9-inch pie plate.

MERINGUE CRUST

See Meringue Maraschino*.

SOME ARE CREAM, CHIFFON, OR FROZEN . . .

FUDGE CRUNCH PIE

Peanut brittle is the sweet surprise . . .

1 6-ounce package semisweet chocolate chips	3 egg whites, stiffly beaten
½ cup sugar	1¼ cups heavy cream, whipped
⅓ cup cream	9-inch Graham Cracker
2 tablespoons butter	Crust*
3 egg yolks, beaten	1 cup crushed peanut
1 teaspoon vanilla	brittle

In the top of a double boiler stir chocolate pieces, sugar, cream, and butter until smooth. Beat egg yolks in very slowly. Cook 5 minutes and remove from heat. Add vanilla and set aside to cool. Fold in beaten egg whites and whipped cream. Pour into chilled crust and sprinkle with peanut brittle. Refrigerate overnight or for several hours before serving. Serves 10.

Note: A Chocolate Crumb Shell* or baked pastry crust (see Foolproof Piecrust Liz* or Short Crust*) may be used.

Variations

BUTTERSCOTCH BRITTLE PIE

Substitute one 6-ounce package butterscotch chips for the chocolate chips and ¼ cup brown sugar for the white sugar.

ORANGE FUDGE PIE

Substitute 1 teaspoon orange extract for the vanilla. Add to the cooking mixture:

2 teaspoons grated orange rind

YUM YUM PIE

Omit sugar and peanut brittle. Substitute 6 small chocolate almond candy bars for the chocolate chips. Use Karla's Crunchy Crust* made with almonds.

BROWN MOCHA PIE

Substitute ⅓ cup chopped toasted almonds for the peanut brittle and 1 teaspoon almond extract for the vanilla. Add to the hot mixture:

2 teaspoons instant coffee

FUDGE NESSELRODE PIE

Substitute ½ cup chopped pecans for the peanut brittle. Add to the cooked filling mixture:

⅔ cup mixed candied fruit, which has been soaked in brandy and drained
1 teaspoon brandy extract

RUMMY FUDGE PIE

Substitute 1½ teaspoons rum extract for the vanilla. Use a Chocolate Crumb Shell*.

CHOCOLATE PEPPERMINT PIE

Substitute ⅔ cup crushed peppermint candy for the peanut brittle. Add to the cooked filling mixture:

½ teaspoon peppermint extract

Use a Chocolate Crumb Shell*.

CHOCOLATE BOURBON PIE

Add to the cooked filling mixture:

2 tablespoons bourbon whisky

Use a Vanilla Crumb Crust*.

CHOCOLATE CHEESE PIE

Substitute ¾ cup light brown sugar for the granulated sugar. Blend one 3-ounce package softened cream cheese into the cool cooked mixture.

FUDGE CHERRY PIE

Omit peanut brittle. Add:

1 1-pound can pitted dark cherries, very well drained

Arange cherries evenly in the piecrust before adding the filling. Use a Vanilla Crumb Crust*.

PARTY PUMPKIN PIE BETH

This is a perfect do-ahead—it's refrigerated overnight . . .

1 envelope unflavored gelatin	*3 egg yolks, beaten*
¼ cup cold water	*½ cup light cream*
⅔ cup packed brown sugar	*1½ cups canned pumpkin*
½ teaspoon salt	*3 egg whites, stiffly beaten*
½ teaspoon nutmeg	*¼ cup sugar*
1 teaspoon cinnamon	*1 teaspoon grated orange rind*
⅛ teaspoon ground cloves	*1 9-inch Ginger Crumb Crust**
¼ teaspoon ginger	

Soften gelatin in cold water. In the top of a double boiler combine the brown sugar, salt, nutmeg, cinnamon, cloves, ginger, egg yolks, cream, and pumpkin. Cook over boiling water until mixture is hot, stirring constantly. Add the gelatin and remove from heat. Chill until mixture begins to thicken, then fold in egg whites which have been beaten with the sugar, and the grated orange rind. Pour into pie shell and refrigerate overnight or for several hours. Serves 8.

Note: This pie may be garnished with sweetened whipped cream, Ginger Cream*, Apple Fluff*, or Orange Cream*.

Variations

BUTTERSCOTCH PUMPKIN PIE

Add to the pumpkin mixture:

1 6-ounce package butterscotch chips which have been melted over hot water

ORANGE PUMPKIN PIE

Increase grated orange rind to 1 tablespoon. Add to the pumpkin mixture:

1 teaspoon orange extract

PUMPKIN PEANUT PIE

Blend ½ cup smooth peanut butter into the pumpkin mixture. Top pie with crushed peanut brittle if you wish. Use Karla's Crunchy Crust* made with peanuts for the shell.

PINK LADY PIE

This pie may be refrigerated overnight . . .

⅔ cup orange juice
48 large marshmallows
1 10-ounce package frozen raspberries, thawed and drained

1¼ cups heavy cream, whipped
1 9-inch Vanilla Crumb Crust

Heat orange juice and marshmallows in top of a double boiler until smooth. Cool until starting to thicken. Add raspberries. Fold in whipped cream. Pour into shell and refrigerate. Serves 8.

Note: This pie may be garnished with Sour-Sweet Cream* or Sherry Cream*.

Variations

HULA LADY PIE

Substitute ⅔ cup unsweetened pineapple juice for the orange juice and 1 package frozen strawberries for the raspberries. Add:

1 *tablespoon lime juice*

Use a Coconut Pie Shell*.

GOLDEN LADY PIE

Substitute 1½ cups chopped mandarin orange sections for the raspberries. Add:

1 *tablespoon lemon juice*

CHOCOLATE MARSHMALLOW PIE

Omit raspberries. Substitute ⅔ cup light cream for the orange juice. Add to the hot mixture:

2 *squares shaved bitter chocolate*

Garnish with whipped cream and chocolate shavings. Use a Chocolate Crumb Shell* if you prefer.

SHERRY VELVET PIE

This must be refrigerated at least 8 hours before serving . . .

1 *envelope unflavored gelatin*	1 *cup heavy cream, whipped*
¼ *cup cold milk*	2 *egg whites, stiffly beaten*
3 *egg yolks, beaten*	
½ *cup sugar*	1 *10-inch Chocolate Crumb Shell**
1 *cup light cream*	
Dash salt	*Bittersweet chocolate curls for garnish*
½ *teaspoon nutmeg*	
½ *cup dry sherry wine*	

Soften gelatin in the cold milk. Place in the top of a double boiler with the egg yolks, sugar, light cream, salt, and nutmeg. Cook over simmering water until mixture coats a spoon. Remove from heat and add sherry wine very slowly, stirring constantly. Remove from heat and chill. When cold and thick, fold in whipped cream and beaten egg whites. Pile lightly in chilled crust and refrigerate for at least 8 hours. Garnish before serving. Serves 8–10.

Note: Karla's Crunchy Crust* made with pecans may be substituted for the Chocolate Crumb Shell*. The pie may be garnished with chopped pecans instead of chocolate curls.

Variations

EGGNOG RUM PIE

Substitute ¼ cup each bourbon whisky and rum for the sherry.

RUM PIE

Substitute ½ cup light rum for the sherry.

COINTREAU PIE

Substitute ⅓ cup Cointreau or to taste for the sherry.

CREME DE MENTHE PIE

Substitute ⅓ cup green crème de menthe for the sherry.

GRASSHOPPER PIE

Substitute ¼ cup *each* green crème de menthe and white crème de menthe for the sherry.

NESSELRODE PIE

Add to the warm custard mixture:

    ½ cup minced mixed candied fruit

BURIED TREASURE PIE

Use a Graham Cracker Crust*. Cover the bottom with a very thin layer of brandied mincemeat, very well drained, before adding the custard filling.

COFFEE BRANDY PIE

Substitute ⅓ cup brandy for the sherry. Add to the cooking mixture:

2 teaspoons instant coffee

Use a Ladyfinger Crust*. Decorate with chopped walnuts.

FROZEN RASPBERRY PIE

No freezer should be without one of these . . .

1 8-ounce package
softened cream cheese
¼ cup white corn syrup
½ cup powdered sugar
1 teaspoon vanilla
2 10-ounce packages
frozen raspberries,
thawed and drained

1 cup heavy cream,
whipped
1 9-inch Graham Cracker
Crust*

Whip cheese, syrup, powdered sugar, and vanilla until creamy. Combine with raspberries. Fold in whipped cream. Pour into pie shell and freeze. Garnish with whipped cream or Sour-Sweet Cream*. Serves 8.

Note: Pie should be removed from freezer just before serving.

Variations

FROZEN STRAWBERRY PIE

Substitute two 10-ounce packages frozen strawberries for the raspberries.

FROZEN CRANBERRY PIE

Substitute one 1-pound can whole cranberry sauce for the raspberries.

FROZEN PRALINE PIE

Substitute ½ teaspoon maple flavoring for the vanilla. Add:

⅔ cup chopped pecans

FROZEN BANANA PIE

Substitute 2 mashed bananas, whipped into the cheese mixture, for the raspberries. Add:

½ cup chopped walnuts if you wish

FROZEN FUDGE PIE

Omit raspberries. Add to the cheese mixture:

1 6-ounce package chocolate chips which have been melted over hot water

FROZEN PINEAPPLE PECAN PIE

Substitute 1½ cups drained crushed pineapple and ½ cup chopped pecans for the raspberries.

FROZEN CHERRY NUT PIE

Substitute 1 cup chopped maraschino cherries and ½ cup chopped toasted almonds for the raspberries.

SOME ARE A BIT MORE HEARTY . . .

CHERRY PIE ANGELIQUE

Sweet 'n' lovely . . .

⅔ cup cherry juice from
  canned cherries
⅔ cup sugar
2 tablespoons cornstarch
1 tablespoon butter
Red food coloring
  (optional)

1 teaspoon rum extract
2 No. 2 cans pitted sour
  cherries, drained
1 9-inch Coconut Pie
  Shell*
½ cup chopped toasted
  almonds

Blend cherry juice, sugar, and cornstarch. Cook over low heat, stirring constantly, until mixture is thick and clear. Add butter, food coloring, flavoring, and cherries. Chill. Before serving, spoon filling into pie shell and refrigerate at least 2 hours. Sprinkle chopped nuts around the outside edge of the pie as a garnish.

Note: Almond extract to taste may be added to the filling.

Variations

HEAVENLY PINEAPPLE PIE

Reduce sugar to ½ cup. Substitute 2 cups drained crushed pineapple for the cherries, ⅔ cup pineapple juice for the cherry juice, and 1 tablespoon lemon juice for the rum extract.

WALNUT PIE HIBBARD

A rich, unusual, easy do-ahead . . .

3 egg whites
1 cup sugar
½ teaspoon baking powder
12 graham crackers
   crushed to crumbs

1 cup chopped walnuts
1 cup heavy cream,
   whipped

Beat egg whites until stiff. Add sugar gradually and continue beating. Add baking powder; fold in cracker crumbs and walnuts. Pour into well-buttered 9-inch pie plate. Bake at 325 degrees for 40 minutes. Serve cold with whipped cream. Serves 8–10.

Note: This pie may be frozen. Remove from freezer 30 minutes before serving time.

Variations

FUDGIE PIE

Add to mixture:

2 ounces melted chocolate
1 teaspoon vanilla

MACAROON PIE

Add:

2 teaspoons almond extract
¼ cup flaked coconut

SPICE NUT PIE

Add to the pie mixture:

1 *teaspoon allspice*

Dust whipped cream garnish with cinnamon.

CHEESE PIE

Make this elegant pie with your favorite glaze and crust . . .

9 *ounces softened cream*
  cheese
2 *tablespoons softened*
  butter
½ *cup sugar*
2 *eggs*

1 *tablespoon flour*
¼ *teaspoon salt*
¼ *cup milk*
1 *tablespoon lemon juice*
1 *9-inch Graham Cracker*
  Crust*

Mix all ingredients (except pie shell) together in a blender until smooth, *or:* Cream the cheese and butter; add sugar and eggs and beat well. Add flour, salt, milk, and lemon juice. Beat until smooth. Pour into pie shell and bake in a preheated 350-degree oven for 35–40 minutes or until the filling is firm. Chill pie before spooning over your favorite glaze. Serves 8.

Note: An unbaked pastry crust or a crust of your choice may be substituted for the Graham Cracker Crust*. After the glaze has been spooned on the chilled pie, return it to the refrigerator for several hours before serving. The variations given here are in the g'azes.

Variations

These glazes are set with cornstarch . . .

BLUEBERRY GLAZE

1½ cups drained canned   1 tablespoon cornstarch
  blueberries   1 tablespoon lemon juice
1 cup syrup from
  blueberries

Combine all ingredients. Simmer until thick and clear. Cool before spooning over pie.

CHERRY RUM GLAZE

Substitute 1½ cups pitted tart cherries and liquid for the blueberries and syrup. Add to the simmering mixture:

¼ cup sugar or to taste

Add to the cooked mixture:

2 tablespoons rum

Chill.

APPLE SPICE GLAZE

Substitute 2 cups canned applesauce for the blueberries and syrup. Add to the simmering mixture:

1 teaspoon allspice
Vanilla, if you wish

STRAWBERRY GLAZE

Substitute two 10-ounce packages frozen strawberries and syrup for the blueberries and syrup. Add to the cooked mixture:

red food coloring, if you wish

RASPBERRY GLAZE

Substitute two 10-ounce packages frozen raspberries and syrup for the blueberries and syrup. Add:

½ teaspoon almond flavoring, if you wish

BOYSENBERRY GLAZE

Substitute 1½ cups canned boysenberries and syrup for the blueberries and syrup; add boysenberries to the cooked mixture.

BLACKBERRY GLAZE

Substitute two 10-ounce packages frozen blackberries and syrup for the blueberries and syrup; add blackberries to the cooked mixture.

These glazes are set with gelatin . . .

PINEAPPLE GLAZE

1 teaspoon unflavored gelatin
1½ cups drained crushed pineapple

1 cup pineapple syrup
1 tablespoon lemon juice

Sprinkle gelatin over the pineapple, syrup, and lemon juice to soften, then heat slowly until mixture is heated through. Cool until mixture is starting to thicken. Spoon over chilled pie.

GOOSEBERRY GLAZE

Substitute 1½ cups canned gooseberries and 1 cup syrup for the pineapple and syrup. Add:

sugar to taste, if you wish

SWEET CHERRY GLAZE

Substitute 1½ cups dark sweet cherries and 1 cup syrup for the pineapple and syrup.

PEACH GLAZE

Substitute 1½ cups sliced peaches and 1 cup syrup for the pineapple and syrup.

RHUBARB GLAZE

Substitute 2 cups canned or cooked rhubarb for the pineapple and syrup. Add to the cooled mixture:

Vanilla, if you wish

These glazes are set with jelly . . .

PEACHY CURRANT GLAZE

¾ cup red currant jelly
2 teaspoons warm water
1½ cups well drained sliced peaches

Melt jelly and water over hot water until liquid. Cool. Arrange fruit over chilled pie. Spoon cool melted jelly over as a glaze.

APRICOT GLAZE

Substitute ¾ cup crabapple jelly and 1½ cups sliced canned apricots for the currant jelly and peaches.

MINTED PEAR GLAZE

Substitute ¾ cup mint jelly and 1½ cups sliced minted pears for the currant jelly and peaches.

MIXED FRUIT GLAZE

Substitute ¾ cup raspberry jelly for the currant jelly, 2 teaspoons bourbon whisky for the water, and 1½ cups drained fruit cocktail for the peaches.

ORANGE GLAZE

Substitute ¾ cup guava jelly and 1½ cups mandarin orange slices or pieces for the currant jelly and peaches.

COOKING FOR
A CROWD

*. . . We may live without friends; we may
live without books; But civilized man
cannot live without cooks; He may live
without books—what is knowledge but
grieving; He may live without hope—what
is hope but deceiving. He may live without love—what is passion but pining; But
where is the man that can live without
dining?*

OWEN MEREDITH

THERE ARE A FEW TRICKS to serving large groups. The car-
dinal one is to keep the menu simple. Whether it is a
party, a church or club supper, a shindig for the local P.T.A.,
or a gathering of the clan, you are most likely to please the
majority with familiar foods prepared with imagination. Choose

good recipes which can be made well in advance. This will hold last minute preparations to a minimum—a most important consideration.

Before making a firm decision on what you will serve, check all available freezer, refrigerator, and oven space. A cold marinated vegetable can pinch-hit for one which must be heated when the oven already is jammed. A frozen salad may be a must when the refrigerator is loaded—provided the freezer isn't likewise. These are practical considerations, but one must think ahead. For a short period before serving, a large roaster filled with boiling water makes a credible steam table. Placed over heat, it will make do a bit longer.

The recipes given in this section are designed to serve 25 people. Many recipes in other sections can be doubled to serve an approximate number except cake, pastry, or soufflé recipes which must be made in the quantities given. The number of servings given are approximate, so size up your group and guestimate quantities accordingly. Bon appétit!

† Quantity serving chart and cooking directions.

MAIN DISHES . . .

BEEF BRETONNE

Sounds impressive . . . tastes good . . . and makes easy . . .

6 *pounds cubed top sirloin*
2 *cups flour*
1 *teaspoon seasoned salt or to taste*
2 *teaspoons instant coffee*
5 *slices bacon, chopped*
½ *cup butter*
3 *cups chopped onion*
5 *6-ounce cans whole mushrooms including liquid*

¼ *teaspoon liquid pepper or to taste*
3 *tablespoons Worcestershire sauce*
1½ *cups dry red wine*
1½ *cups water*
2 *pints commercial sour cream*
Paprika

Trim any fat from sirloin cubes. Mix flour, salt, and coffee in a large paper sack and shake with beef cubes until each piece is coated. Fry chopped bacon; add butter. Add beef cubes and onion and brown. Add mushrooms, liquid pepper and Worcestershire sauce, wine, and water. Simmer gently for 2 hours or until fork-tender. Refrigerate overnight. Add sour cream and dust with paprika. Heat at 350 degrees for approximately 40 minutes. Serve with rice or noodles. Serves 25.

Note: Beef Bretonne may be baked at 325 degrees for approximately 2 hours or until fork-tender rather than simmered.

Variations

BEEF BURGUNDY

Omit coffee, sour cream, and paprika. Add to the simmering mixture:

> 1 *crushed bay leaf*   1 *clove garlic, pressed*
> ½ *teaspoon thyme*   ¼ *cup cognac*

1 cup carrots sliced thinly and diagonally may be added the last 15 minutes of cooking if desired.

BEEF CALIENTE

Omit coffee and sour cream. Add to the simmering mixture:

> 2 *green peppers, thinly*   3 *cups chopped fresh*
> *sliced*   *tomatoes*
> 1 *clove garlic, pressed*   ½ *cup sliced stuffed green*
> 1 *4-ounce can minced*   *olives*
> *green chilis*

GINGER BEEF

Omit coffee, sour cream, and paprika. Add to the simmering mixture:

> 1 *tablespoon turmeric*
> 2 *tablespoons powdered ginger*
> 3 *cups chopped fresh tomatoes*

GINGER PORK

Substitute 6 pounds lean cubed pork for the beef in Ginger Beef*.

CHINESE PEPPER STEAK

Omit coffee, salt, paprika, and sour cream. Cut meat into thin slices rather than cubes. Add:

¼ cup chopped pimiento
⅓ cup soy sauce
1 clove garlic, pressed
2 cups diagonally sliced
    celery (optional)

1 5-ounce can water
    chestnuts, drained and
    chopped
3 green peppers, coarsely
    chopped

Add vegetables and water chestnuts the last 15 minutes of cooking. Serve either with rice or Chinese noodles.

ARMENIAN LAMB

Omit sour cream. Substitute 6 pounds lean lamb cubes for the beef and ½ cup olive oil for the butter. Add:

1 teaspoon cinnamon
1 cup chopped green
    pepper
2 cups cubed eggplant

3 cups chopped fresh
    tomatoes
1 cup grated Parmesan
    cheese

Add vegetables and cheese the last 15 minutes of cooking time.

TURKEY TENADA

Omit coffee. Reduce simmering time to 10 minutes. Substitute 6 pounds cooked turkey cubes for the beef and 1½ cups dry sherry wine for the red wine. Add:

1 cup toasted slivered almonds
½ cup chopped pimiento
1 cup sliced ripe olives

Combine all ingredients. Refrigerate overnight. Heat in oven as for Beef Bretonne*.

CHICKEN CHOP SUEY

Omit coffee, sour cream, and Worcestershire sauce. Reduce simmering time to 10 minutes. Substitute 6 pounds cooked chicken (or turkey) cubes for the beef and 1½ cups dry white wine for the red wine. Add:

¼ *cup soy sauce or to taste*

3 *cups drained canned bean sprouts*

2 *cups sliced water chestnuts*

1 *cup slivered toasted almonds*

2 *cups thinly sliced celery*

Combine all ingredients. Refrigerate overnight. Heat in oven as for Beef Bretonne*. Serve with rice.

VEGETABLES . . .

SCALLOPED POTATOES

The variations are saucy . . .

10 *cups sliced cooked potatoes*

2 *cups grated onions*

*Triple recipe of thin Basic Cream Sauce**

Butter

Paprika

Layer potatoes, onions, and sauce in large baking pan. Dot with butter and dust with paprika. Bake at 350 degrees for approximately 45 minutes. Serves 25.

Note: Thin the cream sauce with cream, milk, or chicken stock.

Variations

SCALLOPED POTATOES AU GRATIN

Substitute a triple recipe of thin Cream Sauce Cheddar* for the thin Basic Cream Sauce*. Top with 3 cups grated sharp Cheddar cheese.

SCALLOPED POTATOES MORNAY

Substitute a triple recipe of thin Cream Sauce Mornay* for the thin Basic Cream Sauce*. Top with 1 cup grated Parmesan cheese and 2 cups grated Swiss cheese.

EGG SCALLOPED POTATOES

Substitute a triple recipe of thin Egg Cream Sauce* for the thin Basic Cream Sauce*. Layer 2 cups minced hard-cooked eggs with the potatoes if you like.

SALAD SCALLOPED POTATOES

Substitute a triple recipe of thin Elegant Cream Sauce* for the thin Basic Cream Sauce*.

CELERY SCALLOPED POTATOES

Substitute a triple recipe of thin Cream Celery Sauce* for the thin Basic Cream Sauce*.

HERB SCALLOPED POTATOES

Substitute a triple recipe of thin Cream Herb Sauce* for the thin Basic Cream Sauce*.

PIMIENTO SCALLOPED POTATOES

Substitute a triple recipe of thin Pimiento Cream Sauce* for the thin Basic Cream Sauce*. Add:

Chopped pimiento to taste, if you wish

CARROT POTATO SCALLOP

Substitute 5 cups sliced cooked carrots for 5 cups cooked potatoes. Use with a triple recipe of thin Basic Cream Sauce* or your choice of the variant sauce recipes.

PINK POTATO SCALLOP

Substitute a triple recipe of thin Cream Sauce Rosado* for the thin Basic Cream Sauce*. Thin the sauce with tomato juice or sauce, or vegetable juice cocktail. Add:

1 clove garlic, minced, if you wish

SPICY POTATO SCALLOP

Substitute 6 cups Del's Spaghetti Sauce* thinned slightly with beef bouillon for the thin Basic Cream Sauce*.

MUSHROOM SCALLOPED POTATOES

Substitute a triple recipe of Mushroom Cream Sauce* for the thin Basic Cream Sauce*. Add:

Additional chopped mushrooms, if you wish

MEAL-IN-A-DISH POTATO SCALLOP

Add 5 pounds cooked ground sirloin steak (layers) to any of the variant recipes. Add:

Additional sauce, if you wish

COOKED VEGETABLES

Do them singly or in combination . . .

If you are trying for the cook-of-the-year award, these suggestions may help. Allow approximately ½ cup of vegetables for each adult serving. Except for peas or lima beans in the pod, or corn on the cob, 1 pound of vegetables will make about 4 or 5 servings. Cook them just barely. If they are to be reheated or creamed, cook them even less.

CREAMED VEGETABLES

Heat crisp-cooked vegetables in thin or medium Basic Cream Sauce* in these proportions:

Sauce	Vegetable	Approximate Servings
2 cups	4 cups	8
4	8	16
6	12	24
8	16	32
10	20	40
12	24	48

Pan warm or oven heat at 350 degrees until bubbly.

SCALLOPED VEGETABLES

Cover Creamed Vegetables* generously with buttered bread or cracker crumbs. Bake at 350 degrees until crumbs are brown and vegetables are hot.

VEGETABLES AU GRATIN

Add cooked vegetables to Cream Sauce Cheddar*, Garlic Cheese Sauce*, or Bacon Cheese Sauce*. Top with buttered bread crumbs (optional) and grated sharp Cheddar cheese. Bake at 350 degrees until hot and bubbly.

SALADS . . .

HOMINY SALAD

This has several virtues—it is easy, tasty, keeps well, and can be done ahead . . .

1 No. 10 can hominy, rinsed and well drained
1 cup each: diced green pepper, green onions including tops, pimiento, celery, sliced ripe olives
½ cup minced sweet pickle or drained sweet pickle relish

Salt and pepper to taste
Double recipe of Creamy Herb Dressing*, Roquefort Cream Dressing*, Creamy French Dressing*, or Poppy Seed Dressing*

Combine all ingredients and refrigerate overnight. Serves 25.

Note: Ingredient proportions may be altered as you wish. Other dressing variations are equally suitable.

Variations

FAR EAST RICE SALAD

Substitute 12–14 cups cold cooked rice for the hominy. Use Curry Cream Dressing* or Soy Dressing*.

KIDNEY BEAN SALAD

Substitute 1 No. 10 can drained and rinsed kidney beans for the hominy.

BLUE LAKE SALAD

Substitute 1 No. 10 can drained whole green beans for the hominy. Use a dressing of your choice.

FRUIT CREME

Great as a salad or a dessert . . .

2 No. 2 cans chunk pineapple, drained	4 cups miniature marshmallows
4 No. 1 cans mandarin oranges, drained	2 pints commercial sour cream
1 No. 2½ can fruit cocktail, drained	3 cups chopped walnuts
6 bananas sliced diagonally	2 teaspoons vanilla
	2 tablespoons fresh lemon juice

Gently combine all ingredients and refrigerate overnight for marshmallows to soften and flavors to blend. Fold gently before serving on a lettuce leaf as a salad, or garnished with candied citron bits as a dessert. Serves 25.

Note: Be sure fruit is well drained before combining with other ingredients to avoid a watery consistency.

Variations

BRANDY FRUIT CREME

Add to the mixture:

⅓ cup brandy

FRUIT CREME CRUNCH

Substitute 3½ cups chopped crisp tart apples, cored and unpeeled, for the fruit cocktail.

FRUIT CREME DE MENTHE

Add to the mixture:

⅓ cup crème de menthe

Other liqueurs are equally tasty additions.

ANGELA'S DESSERT SALAD

Make it at least 2 days before serving . . .

*1 envelope unflavored
gelatin
¼ cup cold water
2 3-ounce packages lemon
gelatin
2½ cups boiling water
1 8-ounce package
softened cream cheese
1 cup dry sherry wine
1 pound miniature
marshmallows
1 No. 2 can pineapple
tidbits with juice*

*1 1-pound jar preserved
kumquats, drained and
thinly sliced
1 cup halved maraschino
cherries
1½ cups halved seedless
grapes
1½ cups pecan halves
1½ cups commercial sour
cream*

Soften unflavored gelatin in cold water. Dissolve lemon gelatin in boiling water. Combine gelatin mixtures. Add softened cheese, sherry, and marshmallows. When gelatin begins to thicken fold in fruits, pecans, and sour cream. Pour into 2 oiled 9×13-inch pans and refrigerate. Serve in squares. Top with Ginger Cream* or Sherry Cream*. Serves 25–30.

Note: ½ cup mayonnaise may be substituted for ½ cup sour cream.

Variations

FESTIVAL APRICOT MOLD

Substitute orange gelatin for the lemon gelatin and 2 cups quartered canned apricots for the grapes. Add with the sour cream:

2 cups grated sharp Cheddar cheese

GRAPEFRUIT JELLY

Omit sour cream. Substitute 2 cups canned grapefruit sections for the kumquats, and ½ cup each slivered candied grapefruit and candied ginger for the maraschino cherries.

FESTIVE CHICKEN SALAD

Substitute 3 cups cubed cooked chicken for the kumquats and cherries and ¾ cup mayonnaise for ¾ cup sour cream. Add to the slightly thickened mixture:

1 cup diced celery
¼ cup minced pimiento

Increase mayonnaise or sour cream as necessary.

DESSERTS . . .

BLANCMANGE

This pudding has been popular since the sixteenth century . . .

1 cup cornstarch
1½ cups sugar
¾ teaspoon salt or to
taste

3 quarts milk or light
cream
1½ tablespoons vanilla

Blend cornstarch, sugar, and salt with 1½ cups cold milk. Scald remaining milk over boiling water. Stir in cornstarch mixture, stirring constantly. Cook covered for 25 minutes, stirring occasionally. Remove from heat. Add vanilla. Cool quickly, stirring frequently. Chill. Serves 25.

Note: Pour into custard cups or molds before chilling. Serve plain, with whipped cream, heavy cream, or with Sherry Custard Sauce*. Double the sauce recipe if you ladle with a heavy hand.

Variations

CHOCOLATE BLANCMANGE

Add to the warm mixture:

3 *ounces melted unsweetened chocolate*

Serve with Almond Custard Sauce*.

BANANA BLANCMANGE

Add to cooled mixture:

1½ *cups sieved bananas*

COCONUT BLANCMANGE

Add to the cooled mixture:

1–2 *cups flaked coconut*

PINEAPPLE BLANCMANGE

Add to the cooled mixture:

2½ *cups drained dry crushed pineapple*

NUT BLANCMANGE

Add to the cooled mixture:

2 *cups chopped nuts*

TAPIOCA DREAM

Substitute 1⅓ cups quick-cooking tapioca for the cornstarch. Cook all ingredients except vanilla until tapioca is clear. Add vanilla.

KITTY'S CHERRY CHARMAGNE   COQ

A yummy dessert quick-as-a-wink . . .

3 No. 2 cans cherry pie
filling
¼ cup brandy
½ teaspoon almond extract

3 cups chopped almonds
3 boxes yellow cake mix
(loaf size)
1½ cups butter

Combine pie filling, brandy, and almond extract. Spread mixture in two buttered 9×13-inch pans. Sprinkle with chopped almonds. Cover evenly with dry cake mix. Dot with butter. Bake in a preheated oven at 400 degrees for 40 minutes or until golden brown. Serve warm or cold. Serves 25.

Note: A garnish of Brandy Cream* is a nice touch.

Variations

BLUEBERRY FLIP   COQ

Omit almond extract. Substitute 3 No. 2 cans blueberry pie filling for the cherry filling, 3 cups chopped pecans for the almonds, and ¼ cup lemon juice for the brandy.

PINEAPPLE FLIP   COQ

Omit almond extract. Substitute 3 No. 2 cans pineapple pie filling for the cherry filling, 3 cups chopped pecans for the almonds, and ¼ cup rum for the brandy.

APPLE ALICE   COQ

Omit almond extract. Substitute 3 No. 2 cans apple pie filling for the cherry filling, 3 cups chopped walnuts for the almonds, and ¼ cup dry sherry wine for the brandy. Sprinkle with 3 cups raisins before adding dry cake mix.

APRICOT TIZZY   COQ

Omit almond extract. Substitute 3 No. 2 cans apricot pie filling for the cherry filling and ¼ cup bourbon whisky for the brandy. Sprinkle with 2 cups flaked coconut before adding dry cake mix.

STRAWBERRY TILLIE   COQ

Omit almond extract. Substitute 3 No. 2 cans strawberry pie filling for the cherry filling and ¼ cup Cointreau for the brandy.

BEVERAGES . . .

HOT TEA

This allows 1-cup servings . . .

2½ ounces tea
5 quarts boiling water

Tie tea loosely in a cloth bag. Place in an enameled container. Cover with boiling water. Steep 10–15 minutes or until tea reaches desired strength. Serves 25.

Variations

ORANGE TEA

Add to the tea bag:

1 tablespoon grated orange rind

LEMON TEA

Add to the tea bag:

1 tablespoon grated lemon rind

SPICED TEA

Add to the tea bag:

2 *teaspoons ground allspice*

RICH DUTCH COCOA

This allows 1-cup servings . . .

1¼ *cups Dutch cocoa*
1¼ *cups sugar or to taste*
3 *cups boiling water*
4½ *quarts hot milk*

1 *cup hot heavy cream*
2 *teaspoons vanilla*
2 *tablespoons butter*

Mix cocoa and sugar. Add boiling water. Add hot milk and cream to mixture. Heat thoroughly. Add vanilla and butter. Whip before serving. Serves 25.

Note: Condensed milk may be substituted for the heavy cream. One marshmallow may be added to each serving.

Variations

COCOA BRAVO

Add to the cocoa-sugar mixture:

2 *tablespoons cinnamon*

DUTCH COCOA MOCHA

Add to the cocoa-sugar mixture:

⅓ *cup instant coffee*

COFFEE PUNCH

This allows ½-cup servings . . .

2 quarts strong cool coffee
½ cup sugar or to taste
3 cups cold heavy cream

2 teaspoons vanilla
1 quart chocolate ice
cream

Combine coffee and sugar; stir until sugar is dissolved. Add cream and vanilla. Chill. Combine with ice cream.

Note: The coffee-cream mixture may be poured over the broken ice cream in a punch bowl. Vanilla ice cream may be substituted for the chocolate. Punch may be topped with whipped cream before serving. Serves 25.

Variations

AMIGO PUNCH

Add to the sugar before combining with the coffee:

1 tablespoon cinnamon

BETT'S CACAO PUNCH

Substitute ½ cup crème de cacao for the sugar.

RUMMY PUNCH

Substitute ¼ cup dark rum for the vanilla.

BOURBON PUNCH

This allows ½-cup servings . . .

2 6-ounce cans frozen pineapple juice concentrate

1 6-ounce can frozen orange juice concentrate

1 6-ounce can frozen lemonade concentrate

⅓ cup sugar or to taste

2 26-ounce bottles chilled sparkling water

1 fifth chilled bourbon whisky

Combine defrosted fruit juices and sugar. Chill. Before serving combine juice mixture with sparkling water and bourbon. Serve from a punch bowl chilled with Ice Cubes Garni*. Place 1 ice cube in each serving. Serves 25.

ICE CUBES GARNI

Freeze in each ice cube:

¼ lime slice

1 maraschino cherry

1 pineapple tidbit

Mint leaf or a piece of geranium leaf (optional)

Note: In addition to the Ice Cubes Garni, a block of decorative ice can be added to the punch bowl. Fill a metal loaf pan ⅔ full of water and freeze. Decorate with cherries, pineapple, citrus slices, mint or geranium leaves, or whatever you like. Fill pan with water and freeze. Unmold and add to punch, fruit side up.

Variations

GIN DANDY

Substitute 1 fifth gin for the bourbon.

JAMAICA JUICE

Substitute 1 fifth light rum for the bourbon.

WHITE LIGHTNING

Substitute 1 fifth vodka for the bourbon.

COVERINGS AND
ACCOMPANIMENTS

*. . . Sweet courtesy has done its most if
you have made each guest forget that he
himself is not the host.*

THOMAS BAILEY ALDRICH

THIS SECTION is made up of crowning touches—frostings and
fillings, sauces and toppings, dressings, and accompaniments.
These are the wonder workers of cookery. They make swans
out of ducklings. Even plain dishes become distinguished with
a wisely chosen, subtly seasoned sauce or dressing. These recipes
are worth knowing on a first-name basis.

COVERINGS AND ACCOMPANIMENTS

Frostings and Fillings

SOME ARE UNCOOKED . . .

RICH MOCHA FROSTING

Use this with white, chocolate, or yellow cake . . .

⅓ cup soft butter	¾ cup cocoa
3 egg yolks	Salt
1 pound confectioners'	1 teaspoon vanilla
sugar (approximately)	Very strong coffee

Beat butter and egg yolks together. Add sugar, cocoa, salt, and vanilla. Beat until fluffy. Gradually beat in enough coffee for a good spreading consistency. Frosts two 9-inch layers generously.

Note: Egg yolks may be reduced and coffee increased if you wish.

Variations

CHOCOLATE MINT FROSTING

Substitute mint flavoring to taste for the vanilla and evaporated milk for the coffee.

LEMON FROSTING

Smooth and lemony . . .

⅓ cup melted butter
2 tablespoons white corn
    syrup
½ teaspoon grated lemon
    rind

3 cups confectioners' sugar
    (approximately)
Lemon juice

Whip butter, syrup, lemon rind, and sugar until fluffy. Gradually beat in enough lemon juice for a good spreading consistency. Frosts two 9-inch layers.

Note: The melted butter should not be browned.

Variations

ORANGE FROSTING

Substitute orange rind and juice for the lemon rind and juice.

LIME FROSTING

Substitute lime rind and juice for the lemon rind and juice.

BASIC BUTTER ICING

A most versatile icing . . .

¼ pound butter, melted
½ pound confectioners' sugar

Combine and beat until the icing is quite white and thickened. Add more sugar if necessary. Frosts two 9-inch layers.

Note: Do not let the butter brown.

Variations

FLAVORED BUTTER ICING

Add flavoring of your choice, and food color if you wish.

CREAM CHEESE ICING

The cheese is a delicious foil for the sweet . . .

1 3-ounce package softened cream cheese	¼ pound soft butter
1 pound confectioners' sugar	2 teaspoons vanilla Condensed milk

Whip cheese, sugar, butter, and vanilla until fluffy. Add milk as needed for a good spreading consistency. Frosts two 9-inch layers split (4 surfaces).

Note: Cream Cheese Icing is better for cakes which will be used within a reasonably short period.

Variations

CREAM NUT ICING

Add to the whipped mixture:

½ cup diced pecans

SPICY CREAM ICING

Add to the whipping mixture:

1 teaspoon allspice

LIQUEUR CREAM ICING

Substitute 2 teaspoons your favorite liqueur or bourbon whisky or rum for the vanilla.

COFFEE CREAM ICING

Add to the whipping mixture:

Instant coffee to taste

BASIC CREAM CHEESE FILLING

A flavorful base that is only the beginning . . .

1 8-ounce package   *3 tablespoons white corn*
 softened cream cheese   *syrup*
1 teaspoon flavoring   *Cream*

Whip cheese, flavoring, and syrup together until light and fluffy. Add cream to bring to desired spreading consistency. Fills a 9-inch 2-layer cake.

Note: A flavored syrup may be substituted for the clear syrup.

Variations

CHEESE DATE NUT FILLING

Use vanilla, brandy, or rum extract, or bourbon whisky. Add to the whipped mixture:

½ cup each *slivered dates and minced nuts*

STRAWBERRY FILLING

Use strawberry or vanilla extract. Substitute ¼ cup thick strawberry jam for the syrup.

RASPBERRY FILLING

Use lemon or almond extract. Substitute ¼ cup thick raspberry jam for the syrup.

PINEAPPLE CHEESE FILLING

Use fresh lemon juice for flavoring. Substitute ¼ cup thick pineapple jam for the syrup.

ORANGE CHEESE FILLING

Use orange extract. Substitute ¼ cup orange marmalade for the syrup.

GINGER FILLING

Use vanilla extract. Add to the whipped mixture:

3 tablespoons slivered candied ginger

SOME ARE COOKED . . .

MINUTE FUDGE FROSTING HENDRY

This is exceptionally good on yellow cake . . .

1 cup sugar
⅓ cup cocoa
¼ cup milk
¼ cup butter

1 tablespoon clear corn syrup
1 teaspoon vanilla

Combine all ingredients except vanilla. Bring to a rolling boil. Boil exactly 1 minute. Remove from heat, add vanilla, and beat to spreading consistency. Frosts two 9-inch layers.

Note: Watch the boiling time carefully.

Variations

COFFEE FUDGE FROSTING

Add:

Instant coffee to taste

ALMOND FUDGE FROSTING

Substitute 1 teaspoon almond extract for the vanilla. Add to the boiled mixture:

½ cup chopped toasted almonds

ORANGE FUDGE FROSTING

Substitute 1 teaspoon orange extract for the vanilla. Add to the boiled mixture:

1 teaspoon grated orange rind or to taste

SATIN CREAM FILLING

Smooth 'n' sweet . . .

⅓ cup sugar	*1 egg, beaten*
3 tablespoons flour	*1 teaspoon butter*
Salt to taste	*1 teaspoon vanilla*
1 cup light cream	

Combine sugar, flour, and salt in saucepan. Add cream and egg. Cook over low heat, stirring constantly, until mixture thickens. Add butter and vanilla. Chill. Fills a 2-layer 9-inch cake.

Note: When time is short, a package of vanilla pudding (the kind to be cooked) is an excellent substitute. Follow package directions but reduce milk to 1½ cups. Add vanilla to taste.

Variations

CHOCOLATE CREAM FILLING

Increase sugar to taste. Add to the cooking mixture:

1 square shaved cooking chocolate

SHERRY CREAM FILLING

Substitute ¼ cup dry sherry wine for ¼ cup cream. Add the wine slowly at the end of the cooking period.

COFFEE CREAM FILLING

Add to the cooking mixture:

1 teaspoon instant coffee

MAPLE CREAM FILLING

Substitute ⅓ cup brown sugar for the white sugar. Add:

½ teaspoon maple flavoring

BANANA CREAM FILLING

Add to the cooled mixture:

½ cup sieved banana

MINCE SPICE FILLING

Add to the cooking mixture:

⅓ cup prepared mincemeat

RAISIN FILLING

Substitute ⅓ cup brown sugar for the white sugar. Add to the cooking mixture:

⅓ cup chopped raisins

PINEAPPLE CREAM FILLING

Add to the cooked mixture:

½ cup crushed pineapple, drained dry

SWEET FRUIT FILLING

Add to the cooked mixture:

⅓ cup minced glazed mixed fruit

DATE NUT FILLING

Add to the cooked mixture:

¼ cup each minced dates and nuts

If the dates are not the soft type, add them to the cooking mixture.

CHERRY SWEET FILLING

Add to the cooked mixture:

⅓ cup chopped maraschino cherries

COCONUT FILLING

Add to the cooled mixture:

¼ cup flaked coconut

LEMON FILLING

Tangy and terribly good . . .

1 cup sugar	Grated rind 1 lemon
3 tablespoons cornstarch	¾ cup water
Salt to taste	1 tablespoon butter
½ cup fresh lemon juice	

Combine ingredients in order given except butter. Cook over low heat, stirring constantly, until mixture is thick and clear. Add butter. Cool. Fills an 8- or 9-inch 2-layer cake.

Note: For a less tart flavor, reduce lemon juice to taste and increase water to substitute.

Variations

ORANGE FILLING

Substitute ½ cup defrosted frozen orange juice concentrate and orange rind for the lemon juice and rind.

LIME FILLING

Substitute ½ cup lime juice and rind for the lemon juice and rind.

APRICOT FILLING

Reduce lemon juice to 1 tablespoon. Add to the cooking mixture:

½ cup sieved apricot pulp

Lemon rind optional.

PINEAPPLE FILLING

Reduce lemon juice to 1 tablespoon. Substitute ¾ cup pineapple juice for the water. Add to the cooking mixture:

½ cup drained crushed pineapple

Lemon rind optional.

INSTANT FILLING   COQ

Use canned pie filling of your choice to fill cake layers.

Sauces and Toppings

SOME ARE SPICY—SOME ARE NOT . . .

GOLDEN CURRY SAUCE

Excellent with shellfish or fruit . . .

1¼ cups mayonnaise	1 tablespoon curry powder
¼ cup dry white wine	or to taste
1 tablespoon strained	Salt and white pepper to
onion juice	taste

Combine ingredients and refrigerate overnight. Makes 1½ cups.

Note: Add more or less wine for a thinner or thicker sauce.

Variations

DILL SAUCE

Substitute 1 tablespoon crushed dillweed for the curry powder. Use with vegetables, fish, or meat.

MOCK HOLLANDAISE

Omit onion juice, curry powder, and wine. Add:

3 tablespoons lemon juice
Grated lemon rind to taste

Use with artichokes, green vegetables, or fish. This sauce may be warmed slightly by standing it in a pan of warm water.

SHERRY SAUCE

Omit onion juice and curry powder. Substitute ¼ cup dry sherry wine for the white wine. Use with fruit or fruit salads.

HORSERADISH SAUCE

Omit wine and curry powder. Substitute ½ cup commercial sour cream for ½ cup mayonnaise. Add:

3 tablespoons chopped chives
3 tablespoons prepared horseradish or to taste

Use with beef, fish, or vegetables.

MUSTARD SAUCE

Omit curry powder. Add:

⅓ cup salad mustard or to taste

Use with beef, fish, or vegetables.

TARTAR SAUCE

Omit wine and curry powder. Add:

¼ cup minced dill pickle	*¼ cup lemon juice*
1 tablespoon minced parsley	*2 tablespoons minced capers*

Use with fish and shellfish.

BASIC CREAM (OR WHITE) SAUCE

The foundation of countless recipes, and one of the nicest things that can happen to leftovers . . .

¼ cup butter	*White pepper to taste*
¼ cup flour	*2 cups light cream*
½ teaspoon salt or to taste	

Melt butter in saucepan over very low heat. Blend in flour and seasonings. Do not brown. Add cream slowly, stirring constantly until sauce thickens. Cook gently for 3 or 4 minutes. Makes about 2 cups.

Note: This is a medium cream sauce for creamed or scalloped foods. For a thin cream sauce (for soups or creamed vegetables) add additional cream to thin to desired consistency. For a thick cream sauce (for croquettes or soufflés), increase butter and flour to ½ cup each *or* reduce the amount of cream used. For a less rich sauce, substitute milk for the light cream.

Variations

INSTANT CREAM SAUCE   COQ

Use 2 No. 1 cans white or cream sauce. Heat over low heat and add butter as desired for flavoring.

CREAM SAUCE VELOUTE

Substitute 1½ cups chicken broth for 1½ cups cream.

CREAM SAUCE CHEDDAR

Add to the hot cooked mixture:

1 cup shredded sharp Cheddar cheese

CREAM SAUCE PARMESAN

Add to the hot cooked mixture:

1 cup grated Parmesan cheese

CREAM SAUCE CURRY

Add to the hot cooked mixture:

2 teaspoons curry powder or to taste

For an interesting flavor substitute ½ cup canned coconut milk for ½ cup light cream.

CREAM SAUCE MORNAY

Add to the hot cooked mixture:

¼ cup each grated Parmesan cheese and grated Swiss cheese

NEOHOLLANDAISE CREAM SAUCE

Add to the cooked and slightly cooled mixture:

¼ cup mayonnaise
2 tablespoons lemon juice

HORSERADISH CREAM SAUCE

Add to the cooked mixture:

2 tablespoons drained prepared horseradish or to taste

MUSTARD CREAM SAUCE

Add to the cooked mixture:

2 tablespoons prepared mustard or to taste

MUSHROOM CREAM SAUCE

Add to the cooking mixture:

1 cup chopped mushrooms

PIMIENTO CREAM SAUCE

Add to the cooking mixture:

¼ cup minced pimiento

DILL CREAM SAUCE

Add to the cooking mixture:

1 tablespoon minced fresh dill or 1 teaspoon crushed dill-weed
Worcestershire sauce to taste

CREAM SAUCE ROSADO

Substitute one 6-ounce can tomato paste for ½ cup cream. Add to the cooking mixture:

Worcestershire sauce to taste

ONION CREAM SAUCE

Add to the cooking mixture:

2 tablespoons granulated onion

FINES HERBES CREAM SAUCE

Add to the cooking mixture:

2 teaspoons fines herbes or to taste

EGG CREAM SAUCE

Add to the cooked mixture:

3 hard-cooked eggs, sieved
1 teaspoon lemon juice

OLIVE CREAM SAUCE

Add to the cooked mixture:

⅓ cup minced ripe olives

ELEGANT CREAM SAUCE

Add before serving:

½ cup mayonnaise

CAPER CREAM SAUCE

Add to the cooked mixture:

¼ cup minced capers
1 teaspoon lemon juice

GARLIC CHEESE SAUCE

Blend one 5-ounce jar garlic cheese spread into the cooking mixture.

BACON CHEESE SAUCE

Blend one 5-ounce jar bacon cheese spread into the cooking mixture.

OLIVE PIMIENTO SAUCE

Blend one 5-ounce jar olive pimiento spread into the cooking mixture.

PARSLEY SAUCE

Add to the cooking mixture:

3 *tablespoons minced parsley*

WINE CREAM SAUCE

Reduce cream ¼ cup. Blend ¼ cup dry sherry wine *or* extra dry vermouth slowly into the cooked mixture.

CREAM CELERY SAUCE

Add to the cooking mixture:

½ *cup sieved cooked celery*

BECHAMEL SAUCE

Substitute 1 cup chicken stock for 1 cup light cream. Add to the cooking mixture:

1 *piece crushed bay leaf*
1 *tablespoon granulated onion*

Add a dash of nutmeg if you wish.

CREAM CARROT SAUCE

Add to the cooking mixture:

½ cup sieved cooked carrots

CREAM HERB SAUCE

Add to the cooking mixture:

1 tablespoon fresh or 1 teaspoon crushed dried herbs of your choice

GERTRUDE'S FLUFFY LEMON SAUCE

Whip juice 1 lemon into 1 beaten egg yolk. Combine with hot Basic Cream Sauce*. Cool. Fold in stiffly beaten egg white. This is excellent with fish.

DEL'S SPAGHETTI SAUCE

Such a spaghetti sauce . . .

7-bone or chuck roast, any size
Cooking oil or bacon drippings
1 No. 2½ can whole tomatoes with juice
3 6-ounce cans tomato paste
7 cups water

2 large onions, chopped
2 cloves garlic, pressed or minced
Scant teaspoon each oregano and sweet basil
½ teaspoon each rosemary and anise
Salt and pepper to taste

Brown roast in oil. Combine remaining ingredients and pour over roast. Simmer slowly for several hours, stirring as necessary, until roast is tender and sauce has thickened to desired consistency. Remove roast and serve it thinly sliced as an accompaniment with the sauced dish, or use it for another meal or for sandwiches. Makes approximately 6–8 cups of sauce. Serve this with spaghetti, ravioli, lasagna, or as a meat or vegetable sauce.

Note: This sauce also can be used with rice or noodles. It is excellent with lima beans, Italian green beans, or zucchini squash. It freezes well, and is the basis for an outstanding quick meal. A small amount of it will make canned rice or pastas taste homemade.

Variations

SPAGHETTI SAUCE MARISSA

Substitute 3 cups dry red wine for 3 cups water. Add:

1 cup each *sliced mushrooms and sliced ripe olives*
½ cup *grated Parmesan cheese (for topping)*

SPAGHETTI SAUCE PEPPERONI

Add:

1 cup *finely chopped pepperoni*	2 tablespoons *parsley flakes*
1 teaspoon *chili powder*	1 cup *sliced mushrooms*

SPAGHETTI MEAT SAUCE

Substitute for the roast ¾ pound ground sirloin steak and ¾ pound ground lean pork.
Substitute 3 cups red table wine for 3 cups water.
Add:

1 cup *sliced mushrooms*	*Liquid pepper to taste*
¼ teaspoon each *thyme and marjoram*	¼ cup *minced fresh parsley*

WAYNE'S SALSA

Serve it hot or cold—or uncooked . . .

*1 4-ounce can green
chilis, chopped and
seeded
3 cloves garlic, pressed
2 1-pound cans solid pack
tomatoes, chopped*

*1 teaspoon salt or to taste
1 teaspoon oregano
1 medium onion, chopped*

Combine all ingredients and simmer for 15 minutes. Makes 2½ or 3 cups. Serve with meat, eggs, steak, or vegetables which are complemented by a peppery sauce.

Note: This sauce can be served uncooked if it is refrigerated for 24 hours for flavors to blend. Drain excess juice off before serving uncooked.

Variations

SPICED SALSA

Add:

½ teaspoon each coriander and chili powder

SPANISH SAUCE

Substitute ½ cup chopped green pepper for the green chilis.

SOME ARE SWEET . . .

HARD SAUCE

Wonderful with puddings—and other things . . .

½ cup soft butter
1¼ cups sifted confectioners' sugar
½ teaspoon vanilla

Whip butter and sugar together until light and fluffy. Beat in vanilla. Serves 10.

Note: Any extract of your choice may be substituted for the vanilla.

Variations

FLUFFY HARD SAUCE

Fold ⅓ cup whipped cream into the Hard Sauce*.

ORANGE HARD SAUCE

Substitute orange extract for the vanilla, and add to the mixture:

1 teaspoon grated orange rind

LEMON HARD SAUCE

Substitute lemon extract for the vanilla, and add to the mixture:

1 teaspoon grated lemon rind

MOCHA HARD SAUCE

Add to the mixture:

1 teaspoon each dry cocoa and instant coffee

BRANDY HARD SAUCE

Substitute 1 cup granulated sugar for the confectioners' sugar and 2 tablespoons brandy for the vanilla.

SAUCE STERLING

Substitute 1 cup brown sugar for the confectioners' sugar and 1 tablespoon condensed milk for the vanilla. Add:

3 tablespoons brandy or *dry sherry wine*

Add the milk to the beaten butter-sugar mixture very slowly; then, add the brandy or sherry very slowly.

CUSTARD SAUCE

Serve it hot or cold—with ice cream, fruit, or puddings . . .

⅓ cup sugar
1 egg, slightly beaten
2 egg yolks, slightly beaten

2 cups scalded milk
Salt to taste
1 teaspoon vanilla

Blend sugar with eggs. Add hot milk very slowly. Add salt. Place in top of a double boiler and cook over hot (not boiling) water until mixture coats a spoon, about 8–10 minutes. Remove from heat, cool. Add vanilla. Chill. Makes about 2¼ cups.

Note: If the water boils, or the custard is over-cooked, it may curdle. If this happens, place the custard in a pan of cold water and beat it vigorously. It will be thinner—but smooth. This sauce thickens as it cools.

Variations

SHERRY CUSTARD SAUCE

Substitute dry sherry wine to taste for the vanilla.

EGGNOG SAUCE

Substitute 2 tablespoons rum or bourbon whisky for the vanilla. Add to the cooking mixture:

Nutmeg or *mace to taste*

Fold in ½ cup whipped cream.

LEMON CUSTARD SAUCE

Substitute lemon extract for the vanilla. Add to the cold mixture:

Grated lemon rind, if you wish

ALMOND CUSTARD SAUCE

Substitute almond extract for the vanilla.

BRANDY CUSTARD SAUCE

Substitute brandy to taste for the vanilla.

VANILLA SAUCE

This covers no end of lovely things . . .

¾ cup sugar	Salt
1 tablespoon cornstarch	2 tablespoons butter
½ cup heavy cream	1 teaspoon vanilla
2 eggs, beaten	

Combine sugar and cornstarch. Add cream, eggs, and salt. Cook over very low heat, stirring constantly, until mixture is thick. Add butter and vanilla. Chill. Makes 2 cups of sauce.

Note: This may be served hot or cold. It is fine for steamed puddings or fruit.

Variations

CHOCOLATE SAUCE

Add to the cooking mixture:

2 *ounces shaved unsweetened chocolate or to taste*

SCOTCH SAUCE

Substitute ¾ cup packed brown sugar for the white sugar. Increase butter to ¼ cup.

NUTMEG SAUCE

Add to the cooking mixture:

2 *teaspoons nutmeg*

Use either rum or brandy extract if you prefer.

NUT SAUCE

Add to any of the variations:

½ *cup minced nuts of your choice*

SAUCE LAURI

Add to the hot cooked mixture:

½ *cup mixed candied fruits*

LEMON SAUCE

Omit vanilla. Substitute ¼ cup each water and lemon juice for the heavy cream. Correct sugar to taste.

DRINKIN' COUSIN SAUCE

Substitute brandy, rum, or whisky to taste for the vanilla.

SOUR-SWEET CREAM

A touch of elegance for fruits, pies, cakes, or puddings . . .

1 *pint commercial sour cream*
2 *tablespoons sugar*
1 *teaspoon vanilla or variant flavoring*

Combine ingredients and chill until serving time. Makes 2 cups of cream.

Note: This is a basic recipe and the flavorings change in the variant recipes.

Variations

MAPLE CREAM

Use brown sugar to taste and maple flavoring.

SHERRY CREAM

Substitute dry sherry wine to taste for the vanilla.

BRANDY CREAM

Substitute brandy extract or brandy to taste for the vanilla.

RUM CREAM

Substitute rum extract or rum to taste for the vanilla.

ORANGE CREAM

Substitute orange extract or your favorite orange-flavored liqueur to taste for the vanilla.

PINEAPPLE CREAM

Substitute ½ teaspoon lemon extract for the vanilla. Add:

½ cup pineapple jam

BERRY CREAM

Add:

½ cup berry jam of your choice

NUT CRUNCH CREAM

Use white or brown sugar to taste. Add:

½ cup minced nuts

APPLE FLUFF

Use brown sugar to taste. Add:

½ cup canned applesauce
Additional spices to taste

GINGER CREAM

Add:

2 tablespoons grated candied ginger

MINT CREAM

Omit sugar and vanilla. Beat ¾ cup mint jelly or jelly of your choice until smooth and combine with the sour cream.

Dressings

SOME HAVE A CREAMY BASE . . .

BASIC CREAM DRESSING

This is an omnibus salad dressing recipe with a cream base . . .

1 cup commercial sour cream	1 tablespoon Worcestershire sauce or to taste
1 cup mayonnaise	
2 tablespoons lemon juice	Salt and pepper to taste

Combine all ingredients and refrigerate at least overnight before serving. Makes 2¼ cups.

Note: This dressing will keep well for several days. Suggestions for compatible salads are made with each variant recipe.

Variations

CREAMY HERB DRESSING

Add:

½ teaspoon each *sweet basil, oregano, marjoram, and chervil*

Use with green, egg, or seafood salads.

ROQUEFORT CREAM DRESSING

Add:

4 ounces soft Roquefort cheese	1 clove garlic, pressed
1 tablespoon grated Parmesan cheese	¼ cup beer

Make a paste of the cheeses, garlic, and lemon juice. Blend thoroughly with other ingredients. Use with green, vegetable, or fruit salads.

CHUTNEY CREAM DRESSING

Add:

> 1 clove garlic, pressed
> ¼ cup drained chopped chutney

Use with fruit or meat salads.

RUSSIAN CREAM DRESSING

Add:

> ½ cup drained chili sauce
> 3 tablespoons minced green pepper
> 2 tablespoons minced pimiento

Use with lettuce wedges or green salads.

HORSERADISH CREAM DRESSING

Add:

> 2 tablespoons prepared horseradish or to taste

Use with molded fruit, fruit, vegetable, meat, or seafood salads.

CURRY CREAM DRESSING

Omit Worcestershire sauce. Add:

> 2 tablespoons curry powder or to taste
> ¼ cup dry sherry wine

Use with fruit, vegetable, or seafood salads.

HONEY-LEMON CREAM DRESSING

Omit Worcestershire sauce. Add:

> ½ cup light honey
> ¼ teaspoon celery salt
> ¼ teaspoon prepared mustard
> ¼ teaspoon prepared horseradish

Use with fruit salads or sweet slaws.

GREEN GODDESS DRESSING

Add:

¼ cup minced parsley
2 tablespoons minced
chives

3 anchovy fillets, minced
½ teaspoon garlic powder

Use with green or seafood salads.

FRUIT DRESSING

Omit Worcestershire sauce. Add:

½ cup light corn syrup
½ teaspoon each ginger and nutmeg

Particularly good with fresh fruit or fruit salads.

GUACAMOLE DRESSING

Add:

3 ripe avocados, mashed
1 clove garlic, pressed
Chili powder to taste

Use with green or vegetable salads; omit garlic and chili powder and use with fruit salads.

HONEY-ORANGE CREAM DRESSING

Omit Worcestershire sauce and commercial sour cream. Add:

1 cup mayonnaise (a total
of 2 cups)
2 tablespoons frozen
orange juice concentrate

2 tablespoons honey
1 teaspoon dry mustard
½ teaspoon paprika

Mix well. Excellent with fresh fruit or fruit salads.

DILL CREAM DRESSING

Add:

¼ cup fresh minced dill or *2 tablespoons dillweed*

Use with green, meat, fish, or vegetable salads, or with slaw.

PEANUT CREAM DRESSING

Add:

¼ cup smooth peanut butter
¼ cup grated onion

Use with green, vegetable, fish, or fruit salads.

SOME HAVE A VINAIGRETTE BASE . . .

BASIC FRENCH DRESSING

This is an omnibus salad dressing recipe with an oil and vinegar
base . . .

1½ cups salad oil
½ cup salad vinegar or
lemon juice
1 teaspoon salt or to
taste

¼ teaspoon pepper or to
taste
1 clove garlic, cut in half

Combine all ingredients. Add a trace of sugar if you wish.
Refrigerate for at least 24 hours before using. Remove garlic
pieces and shake well before serving. Makes 2 cups.

Note: This dressing will keep well for long periods of time.
Suggestions for compatible salads are made with each variant
recipe.

Variations

TANGY FRENCH DRESSING

Add:

> 1 teaspoon each dry mustard, celery seed, and paprika
> 1 tablespoon prepared horseradish
> 2 tablespoons tomato paste

Use with green, vegetable, or seafood salads.

FRENCH PARMESAN DRESSING

Add:

> ½ cup grated Parmesan cheese
> 1 tablespoon Worcestershire sauce

Use with green or fruit salads.

FRENCH CURRY DRESSING

Add:

> 1 tablespoon curry powder or to taste

Use with meat, seafood, or fruit salads.

ROQUEFORT FRENCH DRESSING

Add:

> 4 ounces Roquefort cheese, crumbled
> 1 teaspoon each dry mustard and paprika

Use with green or fruit salads.

COINTREAU DRESSING

Omit garlic. Add:

> 2 tablespoons Cointreau or to taste

Use with fruit or mixed green salads.

CREAMY FRENCH DRESSING

Add:

3 tablespoons commercial sour cream
1 10½-ounce can tomato soup
1 tablespoon sugar or to taste

Makes 3½ cups. Serve with green or vegetable salads.

FRENCH CHUTNEY DRESSING

Use lemon juice in the basic dressing. Add:

¼ cup finely chopped chutney
1 teaspoon allspice
1 teaspoon grated lemon rind

Use with fruit or meat salads.

ANCHOVY FRENCH DRESSING

Use lemon juice in the basic dressing. Add:

4 anchovy fillets, drained and mashed
1 teaspoon each minced fresh tarragon and parsley

Substitute ¼ teaspoon dry tarragon for the fresh if you must. Use with green or seafood salads.

POPPY SEED DRESSING

Add:

¼ cup sugar or to taste   2 tablespoons onion juice
1 teaspoon dry mustard   3 tablespoons poppy seed

Use with fruit or cabbage salads.

FRENCH HERB DRESSING

Use lemon juice in the basic dressing. Add:

1 teaspoon each oregano, sweet basil, and tarragon
½ teaspoon each sugar and dry mustard

FRENCH DRESSING PAREE

Reduce lemon juice in the basic dressing to ¼ cup. Add:

⅓ cup sugar or to taste　　　*1 tablespoon onion juice*
⅓ cup catsup　　　　　　　　*1 teaspoon paprika*
2 tablespoons brandy

Use with green salads.

SOY DRESSING

Omit salt. Add:

¼ cup soy sauce
1 teaspoon sugar or to taste

Use with green, seafood, or fruit salads.

Accompaniments

SOME ARE SPICY . . .

FRUIT CHUTNEY

Chutneys are a must with curry dishes . . .

7 large tart apples, peeled　　*1 cup very firmly packed*
*　and cored*　　　　　　　　　*　dark brown sugar*
7 very firm tomatoes　　　　　*2 teaspoons salt or to*
2 green peppers　　　　　　　*　taste*
4 medium onions　　　　　　　*½ teaspoon each dry*
1½ cups seedless raisins　　　*　mustard, ground cloves,*
2 cloves garlic　　　　　　　　*　and nutmeg*
⅔ cup candied ginger　　　　　*¼ teaspoon cayenne*
1½ cups cider vinegar　　　　　*　pepper*

Coarsely grind the apples, tomatoes, green peppers, onions, raisins, garlic, and ginger. Combine the vinegar, sugar, salt, mustard, cloves, nutmeg and pepper, and bring to a boil. Add the fruit-vegetable mixture. Simmer until thick and dark, about 1½ hours, stirring as necessary. Pour to the top of sterilized pint jars and seal. Makes 4 pints.

Note: A teaspoon of ground ginger may be substituted for the candied ginger. Proportions may be altered to suit individual tastes.

Variations

PEACH CHUTNEY

Substitute 2 No. 2½ cans drained cling peaches for the apples and tomatoes. Add to the fruit-vegetable mixture:

½ cup currants
1 teaspoon chili powder

CRANBERRY CHUTNEY

Substitute 1½ pounds fresh cranberries for the apples and tomatoes. Increase sugar to 2 cups or to taste.

GOOSEBERRY CHUTNEY

Substitute 1½ pounds gooseberries for the apples and tomatoes. Increase sugar to 2 cups or to taste. Add to the fruit-vegetable mixture:

1 tablespoon curry powder

PINEAPPLE CHUTNEY

Substitute 2 No. 2½ cans drained crushed pineapple for the apples and tomatoes. Correct sugar to taste. Add to the fruit-vegetable mixture:

1 cup ground almonds

INDIAN CHUTNEY

Omit tomatoes and green peppers. Increase:

Onions to ¾ pound	Raisins to 2 cups
Cayenne to ½ teaspoon	Brown sugar to 2 cups or
Apples to 8	to taste
Garlic to 4 cloves	

Add to the fruit-vegetable mixture:

1 tablespoon curry powder

ONION RELISH

This is hot, good, and you don't have to cook it . . .

1 large onion	½ teaspoon dry mustard
1 green pepper	1 teaspoon lemon juice
2 green tomatoes	½ teaspoon grated lemon
1 teaspoon salt or to taste	rind
¼ teaspoon liquid pepper	1 tablespoon wine vinegar
or to taste	

Grind with a fine blade the onion, pepper, and tomatoes. Add remaining ingredients. Mix well. Refrigerate overnight. Makes 4 cups.

Note: This is an excellent accompaniment for meat, barbecued chicken, or Mexican food. It keeps well.

Variations

HOT RELISH

Omit dry mustard. Increase vinegar to ⅓ cup. Add:

5 small yellow chili peppers, finely minced
2 green chilis, seeded and minced
2 teaspoons sugar or to taste

KRAUT RELISH

Omit tomatoes, dry mustard, lemon juice, and rind. Add:

1 *cup sugar*	2 *ounces minced pimiento*
1 *cup minced celery*	1 *No. 2½ can sauerkraut,*
1 *tablespoon celery seed*	*drained and chopped*

Makes 7 cups.

SAUTERNE CELERY RELISH

Omit green pepper, tomatoes, and mustard. Increase vinegar to ¼ cup. Add:

¼ *cup sauterne wine*	1 *tablespoon minced*
½ *teaspoon each seasoned*	*parsley*
salt, seasoned pepper,	4 *cups thinly sliced*
and sweet basil	*celery*

Makes about 4 cups.

QUICK CORN RELISH   COQ

Substitute 1 No. 1 can Mexicorn niblets, well drained, for the tomatoes, onion, and green pepper. Add:

1 *teaspoon each celery seed, turmeric, sugar, green pepper flakes, dehydrated onion, and ¼ cup sweet pickle relish*

RAW CRANBERRY RELISH

Crisp, crunchy, and good at any meal . . .

1 *pound raw cranberries*	1 *cup walnuts*
1 *large orange, unpeeled*	2 *cups sugar or to taste*
2 *red apples, cored and*	
unpeeled	

Grind with a coarse blade the cranberries, orange, apples, and walnuts. Add sugar and mix thoroughly. Refrigerate at least 24 hours before serving. Makes 4 cups.

Note: Serve with pork or poultry.

Variations

CRANBERRY GARDEN RELISH

Omit apples. Reduce sugar to 1 cup or to taste. Add:

> ½ *large onion*
> 1 *green pepper*
> 1 *cup celery pieces*

Do not grind the onion, pepper, and celery, but mince fine before adding to the cranberry mixture.

QUICK CRANBERRY RELISH   COQ

These are ready immediately . . .

> 1 *1-pound can whole*   1 *teaspoon lemon juice*
> *cranberry sauce*   ¼ *cup diced walnuts*
> 3 *tablespoons frozen*
> *orange juice concentrate*

Combine and refrigerate. Makes about 2 cups.

Note: This relish is better if it stands several hours before serving.

Variations

ZIPPY CRANBERRY RELISH   COQ

Omit lemon juice. Substitute diced almonds for the walnuts. Add:

> 2 *tablespoons sweet pickle relish*

Add:

¼ *cup canned applesauce*
½ *teaspoon* each *ground ginger, nutmeg, cinnamon, and granulated onion*
¼ *teaspoon celery seed* or 2 *tablespoons minced celery*

SOME ARE SWEET . . .

WATERMELON CONSERVE

Very good—and very easy . . .

2 *cups peeled ground*   2 *cups sugar*
  watermelon rind   2 *tablespoons lemon juice*
1 *cup crushed pineapple*   1 *cup chopped almonds*

Combine all ingredients except almonds. Simmer until clear and starting to thicken. Stir occasionally to prevent sticking. Add almonds. Pour into sterilized jars and seal. Makes about 4 pints.

Note: Walnuts may be substituted for the almonds. For smaller units, seal in 8 half-pint jars.

Variations

GINGER WATERMELON CONSERVE

Add to the simmering mixture:

2 *tablespoons grated candied ginger*

HAWAIIAN WATERMELON CONSERVE

Substitute 1 cup chopped shredded coconut for the almonds.

CHERRY WATERMELON CONSERVE

Substitute 1 cup chopped maraschino cherries for the pineapple. Add to the simmering mixture:

½ teaspoon each *cloves, cinnamon, and allspice*
3 drops red food coloring (optional)

CRANBERRY CONSERVE

Substitute 2 cups minced raw cranberries for the watermelon rind. Add:

Additional sugar to taste

CARROT CONSERVE

Substitute 2 cups shredded carrots for the watermelon rind.

NANA'S ROSE PETAL JELLY

The likes of which cannot be found . . .

Petals 3 dozen fresh roses   *¼ cup lemon juice*
1 quart boiling water   *strained through a cloth*
2 pounds extra-fine
granulated sugar

Steep rose petals in boiling water for 30 minutes. Strain liquid. Add sugar and strained lemon juice. Bring to a full boil and cook for about 20 minutes or until a drop of the liquid "sets" on a cold plate. Pour into hot sterilized glasses—it will take 4 or 5. Cool. Cover with melted paraffin. Tilt the glass slightly and turn so the liquid wax will make a tight seal.

Note: This is sheer ambrosia, and a traditional delicacy. It makes a very special occasion whenever it is served.

Variations

ROSE-GERANIUM JELLY

Suspend 1 rose geranium leaf near the center of each glass of jelly.

POMEGRANATE JELLY

Substitute 1 quart strained pomegranate juice for the rose water. Nana sometimes suspended a rose geranium leaf in each pomegranate glass, too. It's wonderful either way.

HOW MUCH?

IN THESE STANDARD EQUIVALENTS, the measurements are level . . .

MEASUREMENTS AND EQUIVALENTS

1 teaspoon		60 drops
3 teaspoons	½ fluid ounce	1 teaspoon
2 tablespoons	1 fluid ounce	⅛ cup
4 tablespoons	2 ounces	¼ cup
8 tablespoons	4 ounces	½ cup
16 tablespoons	8 ounces	1 cup
2 cups	16 ounces	1 pint
4 cups	2 pints	1 quart
½ cup butter	¼ pound	1 stick
cups granulated sugar		1 pound

4 cups flour		1 pound
1 square chocolate		1 ounce
1 cup raw rice	cooked, about	3½ cups
1 cup spaghetti or macaroni	cooked, about	2 cups
1 cup noodles	cooked, about	1¼ cups
1 cup shelled walnuts	chopped, about	¼ pound
1 tablespoon fresh herbs		1 tablespoon dry herbs
1 cup whipping cream	½ pint about	2 cups whipped

ABOUT CAN SIZES AND CONTENTS

The weights and contents are approximate . . .

Buffet	8 ounces	1 cup
No. 1 (Picnic)	11 ounces	1⅓ cups
No. 1½ (303 can)	1 pound	1¾ cups
No. 2	1 pound 4 ounces	2½ cups
No. 2½	1 pound 12 ounces	3½ cups
No. 3	2 pounds	4 cups
No. 5	3½ pounds	7 cups
No. 10	6½ pounds	13 cups

INDEX